To Carl, my King Under the Mountain, and to Dale—you were right!

CONTENTS

PRELUDE

How can anyone really know a place like Maine?

Maine is something you feel more in your heart than know in your head. It's a geographically specific place, a recognizable shape on the map, but it is a feeling as well—amorphous yet readily identifiable, undeniable but ephemeral, like the subtle, yet unmistakable scent of balsam drifting by on the morning fog.

Defining Maine is a classic conundrum, the answer to which is no less complicated than the response to asking how well anyone really knows another human being.

How well do you know Maine? How well do any of us really know ourselves?

To craft an answer, there's no definitive checklist of must-sees, though not for lack of nomination. There is no mandatory minimum number of experiences, no predictable "eureka" moment when clarity emerges from confusion.

It is akin to what the late astronomer Carl Sagan liked to say about the evolution of life and the miracle of sentience. "We," he said, "are a way for the Cosmos to know itself." In a way, his observation is another take on the classic T.S. Eliot quote "We shall not cease from exploration, and the end of all our exploring will be to arrive where we started and know the place for the first time."

Really knowing Maine requires the soul of an explorer—a desire to run its rivers, fish its lakes, climb its mountains, drink deep of the cool damp quiet of the great northern forest. At the same time, the story of that spectacular landscape, that unrivaled fresco of nature, is, by itself, a hollow tale devoid of context and flavor without recognition of the brushstrokes of human history—rusting remnants of industrious natures, echoes of heartfelt endeavor.

There, the answers lie in forlorn graves along wild rivers, in the scribbled journals of woodcutters and hardscrabble farmers, in abandoned cellar holes along forgotten roads, and in the ghosts that tarry in the clouds atop barren, unfinished mountaintops at dawn.

These essays, then, only begin to scratch the surface of a state where the scope of human perseverance stretches from a steely gaze at the helm of a lobster boat along the rugged coast to weathered hands in Aroostook County plucking the abundant fruit of autumn from the rich, fertile earth.

The scale of time for the land here is glacial. For its most recent inhabitants, it spans sixteen generations. Either range transcends what can be fathomed in a single lifetime. To the first is ascribed a single virtue—patience. The second is defined by a single word—permanence.

Writing this book has been, after a fashion, an entirely selfish venture. In an attempt to delineate and share the character, the color, the truth of Maine, I hope to better comprehend the entirety of it myself.

Along with decades spent afoot and afloat in the wild, the journey has included a celebration of the spiritual gifts of those adventures—unbreakable bonds of friendship, the undying love of family, rare quiet moments to contemplate a raw, inescapable sense of place. Only one fact is sure. To really grasp the totality of the power of these places, these great forces, these great spirits, one must embrace, one must savor them all.

Few among us will be lucky enough to be the ones to whom the universe surrenders her secrets. Yet all who have heard the siren song of the places in these pages, or are inspired to begin a quest of their own, are well on the way to knowing the heart and soul of a truly extraordinary place—Maine.

—Earl Brechlin

RETURN TO MOOSE RIVER

"Everyone must believe in something. I believe I'll go canoeing."
—HENRY DAVID THOREAU

THE RIVER AND FOREST ARE MORE BEAUTIFUL THAN I REMEMBER. Granted, it has been eleven years since I last paddled the Moose River. But the scenery this time seems softer, the water more peaceful, the wildness of the remote swampy terrain no less formidable, yet somehow less intimidating.

I strain to spot landmarks on riverbanks scarred and reworked by relentless cycles of ice and flood. Even the official campsites sprinkled here and there along the way do not look familiar. It is like driving through your old neighborhood and trying to remember the way it was when you were little in the hopes that something there might magically return you to that time of innocence.

In spring, ice-out releases a torrent of water that breaks up several feet of ice and hurls it headlong downstream. Great waves of dirty, groaning icebergs pluck unlucky trees and rocks from the banks as they go. Where this wintry lava floe deposits its detritus is entirely dependent on chance. Usually, the outsides of bends in the river are scoured bare. Low-angled trees that last summer provided a shady spot for trout to linger are often among the first victims.

Places where the river makes a hard turn end up buried under a pile of twisted trees and limbs stripped bare of every shred of bark. In summer, these smooth skeletons bleach bright white in the sun. By fall, left high and dry on a sandbar or bank, this dry-ki, as it is called, makes excellent firewood for intrepid campers hoping to ward off the evening's deepening chill.

After a while, I resign myself to enjoying the unfamiliar familiarity: wide, generic alder-choked banks, mudflats unbroken save for the occasional black bear or raccoon track, sporadic moose sightings, and riverside maples turned a vivid crimson by the first hint of frost.

The Moose River rises from hardscrabble streams that flow down the mountains that line the border with Canada just west of Jackman, Maine. There are no towns here, just townships and places marked on the map that used to be somewhere and home to somebody. Now they are little more than clusters of tumbledown cellar holes. In a place that measures time on a geologic scale, nearly two centuries of logging and erstwhile settlement have come and gone with barely a nod from the river.

There are some dozen and a half tributaries that contribute to the upper reaches of the Moose. As is convention in Maine, the repetitiveness of their names betrays a commonsense approach to bestowing cartographical individuality on watercourses that in most cases are indistinguishable.

To set the record straight, there is no hierarchy or protocol on how such places are named. Some are brooks, some are streams, and some are called rivers without any apparent correlation to size or reliability of flow. Tourists along the coast often mistakenly ask how long it takes for a smallish crab to grow into a lobster. Of course, they are totally separate beasts.

Likewise, a stream is not a brook that has suddenly reached puberty.

At some point, a person can easily cross any brook, stream, or river with just a single extended step. Conversely, at other points along their length, a bridge, boat, or canoe is the only way to get across safely.

A quick look at that indispensable bible of the outdoors in Maine, DeLorme's *Maine Atlas and Gazetteer,* shows the East Branch of Gulf Stream, the West Branch of Gulf Stream, and Little Gulf Stream that eventually form, naturally, just plain Gulf Stream. The Moose itself has both an East Branch and a West Branch that join to form the South Branch where the water actually flows north.

There is no North Branch.

Other named brooks include Hogan, Bog, Boundary, Smart, and Smith. Another is simply called Number One Brook, which is not to be confused with nearby Number Six Brook. Why some harried mapmaker decided to do away with brooks two through five, which are nowhere to be found, is not entirely clear.

The discounting of size when naming things manifests itself again when it comes to deciding whether a large standing body of water is either a pond or a lake. Most folks operate under the assumption that something you can skip a rock across is a pond. Anything larger is viewed as a lake.

Not so in Maine.

The only way to tell the size is by looking on a map. Duck Lake may be a hundred feet across while Duck Pond may be one mile long. The only agreement seems to be when calling something a flowage, although this term for a wide, slow-moving part of a river also ignores size as criteria. It has been applied with equal regularity to wide, swampy places along a stream and to artificial lakes impounding thousands of acres of water. Of course, a flowage that now looks like a lake may have been just a winding stream before the dam was built. Much like the way some Mainers like to give directions, it all depends deeply on your knowledge of what used to be there years ago. Naturally, no trace remains today. It matters not if you've lived there all your life or just rolled into town yesterday. If you don't know how far to go past something that used to be there, be it house, farm, store, or old oak tree, you are out of luck.

Repetitiveness in place-names runs rampant in a state that is nearly as big as the rest of New England combined.

The Moose River watershed is quintessential in Maine in that it includes at least one Mud Pond, one Clear Pond, and one Trout Pond. All of Maine's major river systems, including the mighty St. John, Allagash, St. Croix, Penobscot, Androscoggin, and Kennebec (into which the Moose flows after a detour through Moosehead Lake and a couple of hydroelectric dams), have at least one of each.

In total, Maine has sixty-five Mud Ponds, forty-six Long Ponds, thirty-seven Bog Brooks, and thirty-two Round Ponds. Terrestrial landmarks don't escape this onslaught of geographic redundancy. There are twenty-two Ram Islands, nineteen Bald Mountains, and half a dozen or so places called Black Point. There are eighteen Moose Ponds, eight Moose Brooks, and seven Moose Islands (curiously, just as many as there are Mouse Islands).

But there is only one Moose River.

~

Depending on water levels, the canoeable portion of the Moose begins at the state boat landing on the north shore of Holeb Pond. Some people start where the trip also ends in nearby Attean Pond, although that version of the infamous "Bow" trip requires a one-mile, uphill portage between those big lakes.

When it comes to the art of portage, only a masochist will tell you it's fun. One of the true joys of canoe camping is that you can bring lots of stuff. Stuff like inflatable mattresses, cushy collapsible camp chairs, and coolers with that indispensable staple of civilization—ice.

Don't get me wrong, I love backpacking for exactly the opposite reason. There, you have to winnow everything down to the barest of essentials to pare as much weight as possible from your pack, or your body will pay the consequences. To do so takes much more skill and is inherently more earnest than just tossing in everything out of the camping gear closet that will fit between the gunwales.

However, when you have to portage, in effect you are turning part of your canoe trip into a backpacking excursion. Needless to say, if you don't factor into account how far you'll be lugging everything, outdoor worlds will collide with the likelihood you'll be coming home with less gear than you left with. The difference ends up being sacrificed to the fire gods or left behind in the remote hopes the next party through might be able to use it.

The major benefit of enduring the lake portage on the Moose River Bow Trip is that it does not require anyone to shuttle vehicles or gear from one end to the other—a costly and time-consuming proposition. On the map, it looks like only a forty-five-mile drive—one way. But don't forget, on some dirt roads, you'll be lucky to average fifteen miles per hour. That means when you drag the canoes ashore at the take-out at five o'clock in the afternoon, your companions will be waiting until eleven at the earliest before you're back with the vehicles. That's provided no one gets lost en route, all the trucks are gassed up, and no one suffers a flat tire.

Some paddlers start in what was once the village of Holeb, a wide, flat place along the Canadian Pacific Railroad line where trains used to stop so passengers could clear U.S. Customs. Today it's home to a handful of private seasonal camps. A few old buildings remain, some unused and surrendering to the forest, although to call the place a ghost town would seem an oddly Western affectation.

Running due west to east, the CP line bisects many of the great adventure corridors in the state of Maine, including the Appalachian Trail. You know for sure you're in northern Maine when you cross the CP line, although where the official boundary of Maine's Great North Woods begins and ends is subject to considerable disagreement.

As the Moose River heads toward Moosehead Lake to the east, it passes through thousands of acres of peat bogs along its low and meandering course. Rain leaches tannins from the decaying vegetation along the way, staining the water a rich amber, the distinctive color of a strong cup of tea. It isn't murky, nor is it cloudy with sediment. In fact, it tastes fine. However, when taking a paddle stroke, the end of your blade often disappears from sight, even though it is only a few feet below the surface. Not being able to discern the depth of the water by merely looking at it can be disconcerting. It seems as though at any moment the paddle could slip from your hands and continue down unabated to the unfathomed bottom of some great abyss. At other times, the tip hits bottom with an annoying and shoulder-jarring *clunk* when you are only halfway through a stroke.

That first year, our waterproof gear consisted of little more than cheap department store backpacks covered with flimsy trash bags. In retrospect, it is doubtful they would have kept things dry during a modest rain shower, much less an unexpected flip in serious rapids.

Having little to no experience running truly wild rivers, we feared the short stretches of white water at places like Mosquito Rips, Spencer Rips, and Attean Falls. Here again, names give no clue to the difficulties that lie ahead. Rips can be more like a rapid, and something called a falls is not always a perpendicular drop— sometimes it's just a long rapid. Sometimes falls or a long drop is just called a pitch—not to get confused with the stuff that gets stuck to your hands if you grab a hold of an overly philanthropic fir tree. Riffles on the river are not something you shoot with but rather anemic rapids.

Anything, of course, can be dangerous or unrunnable depending on the water level. A favorite joke on the drive to a put-in is to check out drainage ditches along the way and, finding one swollen with runoff, announce that it "looks runnable."

Most rapids on the Moose are not considered too difficult or overly technical, with a few notable exceptions. The most dangerous is Holeb Falls, where there is a mandatory portage around an unrunnable waterfall featuring a fifteen-foot drop. Guidebooks advise that there are signs to help you avoid becoming a headline about heroic game warden rescuers in the *Bangor Daily News*.

Maps show an obvious left turn—needed to avoid a long, complicated, and dangerous set of unrunnable rapids—followed by a quick right. Then, you need to take your "second left at the portage trail sign." No one I've spoken to who has done the river has ever seen any kind of obvious sign. To make matters worse, there are about four places that arguably could be candidates for the second left. Fortunately, fallen trees and debris now clog the waterfall channel, making an accidental trip over the brink unlikely.

Ears strained that first year to pick up the unmistakable rush of water over rocks in the distance. We quickly learned that anytime you saw what amounted to a clear line running from river left to river right, it meant a drastic change in water level. To be safe, we portaged, carried, or dragged around anything remotely resembling a rapid. Considering the high temperature that Columbus Day, around 28 degrees, it was probably just as well we were cautious. When the air and water temperature combined don't total more than 100, life-threatening hypothermia is your constant companion.

But now, more than a decade later, on a comparatively warm, mid-September day, we welcome the distinctive sound of the Moose's dark water coursing over ledges as a pleasant break from miles of mind-numbing flat water. With eleven years of experience and numerous runs on more difficult rivers under our belts, and with updated dry gear, we run the rapids with little more than a cursory glance from upstream.

We've learned, of course, that the river always shows you the way. Like a good book, it's all laid out for those who know its alphabet. Head for the center of the wide part of the "V" and adjust for current coming from the left or the right to keep the boat straight. Watch out for upwellings that betray the presence of rocks lurking just under the surface as you proceed, and if the run out at the bottom looks a little boney, paddle hard and give it "ramming speed" to help the boat skid over the last few semi-submerged obstructions. When all else fails, get out and drag it the last few feet to deeper water.

———❦———

On this second trip, rather than being a source of intimidation, the rock-strewn turbulent froth became instead a place of inspiration, a chance to playfully test the river's stuff and our own as well.

Since that first trip in 1986, the same group of guys—family members and close friends who grew up together—have paddled a different river each fall. Through trials and tribulations, in good times and in bad, the annual expedition long ago dubbed simply "the Moose trip," regardless of destination, has become an anchor for each of us. Over the years, we have shared more than tall stories, smoky campfires, battered canoes, and liberal applications of Canadian Club. Just as our bodies have endured long days of paddling, muddy portages, cold rains, and devilish headwinds, our spirits have weathered the climatic changes of life: the deaths of fathers, loves lost or won, careers come and gone, and the satisfaction of those with beards ever so slightly tinged with gray at seeing their sons now take up the paddle.

Steady rain falls as we endure twelve miles on the second day. Years ago on such trips, I hated the rain, cursing at whatever deity we must have offended. On this trip, however, I simply cinch up my hood, greeting the rain as companion. If you don't go camping in Maine when there is rain in the forecast, there's a good chance you'll never go.

I learned long ago the folly and waste of railing against that which does no lasting harm and which we have no power to change. Prepare. Adapt. Live with it.

While others obsess over the long-range forecast before a trip, for me it is immaterial. You bring good rain gear. You pack plenty of tarps. And if the skies open up, you deal with it—blizzards, hurricanes, and the unexpected loss of a major portion of our whiskey and cigars, of suspicious pedigree of course, only excepted.

More than once, "Bartertown" has sprouted on some riverbank, as a maze of tarps, ropes, poles, and upright paddles sprang up to fight off the wet. It may not be as luxurious as sitting in an easy chair, cable remote in hand, but it's eminently more satisfying. Thoreau once said that he went to the woods to confront the essentials of life. In a sense, that's what people still do when they venture out and go wilderness camping. You learn to live with nature, for however brief an interval, on her terms, although taking a few hallmarks of civilization along on the river is part of the fun.

People often remark that you can't call a trip an adventure if everything goes according to plan. By that measure, the Moose River Camping Club (MRCC), as the group came to be known, has enjoyed some great adventures over the years. That which we once avoided, resisted, and fretted over has now become the best part of the telling.

Over the years, too, I have refined my thoughts on river trip as metaphor. While hardly an original notion, the similarity to the arc of our mortality holds true from start to finish.

In both, there is a specific time and place to put in. You paddle as best you can, and pray you have the skills to make it through the occasional rapids, keeping the boat upright and the gear dry. If you pay attention and keep your eyes open, you may even get a little better at it as you go along.

For most of the trip on a river you've never paddled before, you have few clues to what awaits around the next bend. Maps and GPS units may give you an idea of where you are but stop far short of providing precise tactical details. Sometimes you just have to wing it.

On the river, there are good trip mates and bad, sweet campsites and horrid ones, and the occasional stop for repairs, to resupply, or to regroup. If the sun is shining and you're fortunate enough to take time out on that perfect sandbar for lunch, life is oh so good. On both voyages, the fortunate and observant can relish an unspoken bond that develops between those who share—for what inevitably becomes too short a time—the burdens, sacrifices, and joys of the universe's grandest one-way journey.

At the end, of course, awaits the final take-out point. It's finite, fixed, and yet fluid, always, it seems, still uncountable paddle strokes away, yet drawing inexorably closer every day.

~

My favorite photograph from that first trip is one of my little nephew Ryan, just nine years old, down by the stream brushing his teeth, a red knit cap much too big for him covering most of his head. Overnight, the temperature dipped to around 18 degrees, and the long, low rays of the rising sun had yet to nudge the mercury in the thermometer from its slumber. The water left in an old enameled coffeepot after washing the dinner dishes is now one solid chunk of ice.

Behind Ryan, the waters of the tumbling run-out from Attean Falls put up a roiling cloud of mist as the river tries to fend off winter's frosty advances. And just out of sight, watching closely but not hovering, stands his dad, my identical twin brother, Carl.

As most people suspect, there's a special closeness that comes from being a twin. When you've known someone literally since before you were born, when you have the exact same DNA, when you share the same childhood experiences from the standpoint of both nature and nurture, the bond that forms is extraordinary.

You find in each other unique strengths, and you automatically recognize and abide familiar weaknesses. You always have a place to go where you can say anything out loud, and it never goes any further. Even the rants are automatically afforded the same discretion as if they were voiced only in the sanctuary of your own mind.

Not long after high school, our lives, not unpredictably, began to head in different directions. Looking back at that time reminds me of the iconic Robert Frost poem, "The Road Not Taken." Two lives, once lived shoulder to shoulder, took diverging paths.

Carl stayed in Connecticut, got married, had four kids, and worked his way up through the business world, eventually becoming chief financial officer of several large companies. Tired of the corporate grind, he went on to found his own auction firm. I, on the other hand, moved to Maine, studied forestry, got into the newspaper business, and earned a Maine Guide license. I did not marry until many years later and never had children of my own.

I went to the University of Maine. He took community college courses.

Despite being separated by hundreds of miles, we always remained close, seeing each other as often as possible, speaking every day on the phone. He became chief organizer of Moose River Camping Club expeditions—a backpacking trip every spring and a canoe trip every fall. We both owned Old Town Tripper canoes. I dubbed mine Sneak Route, in homage to the term for taking the easiest, though not always obvious, route through difficult rapids. He named his City Slicker.

As we followed different roads, we each got to share vicariously in the life of the other. Our disparate paths allowed us, in effect, to experience two lifetimes at once.

On that very first Moose trip, we discovered how special it was to spend time with each other away from the artificial pressures that inexorably expand to preoccupy modern life. It was also most comfortable to paddle side by side in the wilds, far from the inevitable stares and whispers that naturally follow from people surprised at seeing two big men with beards who look exactly alike.

The trip quickly became our common denominator, a shared plane of existence, a safe and welcoming base camp upon which to return after ranging farther afield solo during the rest of the year.

Carl especially loved the Moose River. It was here, he said, he felt most alive.

How many of these trips does one get in a lifetime, I wondered out loud one night while sitting around the campfire. The number is obviously finite. Will there be twenty Moose trips? Will there be forty? That, of course, like any aspect of life, is not for any of us to know. But the acknowledgment of it being finite makes the ephemeral nature of the experience all the more poignant and precious.

———

As a guide, I see it as a point of honor—and a responsibility—to put the most inexperienced greenhorn in the bow of my boat. On the first Moose trip, little Ryan's paddle barely reached all the way to the water. So, he paddled with me, although when we were hit by some serious headwinds on long flat stretches and fell behind the others, I quickly began to doubt the wisdom of that philosophy.

Now, on this return trip, as an adult, he is in the stern of his own canoe, paddling fearlessly with great slashing strokes through three-foot whitecaps on windswept Attean Lake. His father and uncles paddle close by, all equally skilled voyagers in the eyes of the Moose.

Preoccupied with timing the swells and fighting to keep the canoe from getting swung around broadside in the gusty northwest wind, I'm surprised at how much time I still have to think. Looking at Ryan, now clearly an experienced river runner in his own right, I realize how few opportunities there are to step back and acknowledge the subtle yet sweeping changes that define our lives. I smile, recognizing in the brief moments between efforts to keep the canoe upright that I've stopped being distracted by the petty, yapping diversions of life long enough to see the graceful curve of the entire arc.

In that moment, I understand it isn't just the river or the forest that is different after more than decade, but each of us that has changed in ways both obvious and subtle. Nothing, of course, can ever be exactly the same in life—nor should it be. As novelist Thomas Wolfe wrote, "You can't go home again." Yet there is an innate need in each of us for a touchstone in life, even one in which impermanence is the only foundation. No matter where I am, no matter what I'm doing, no matter what happens, I will always take comfort in knowing that around each sandy bend along the Moose River awaits the passing of seasons, the graying of beards, unbreakable bonds of companionship, and echoes of timeless mysteries written in the flow of dark, ancient, untamed waters.

ABOUT THREE BEERS

Rising from a series of headwater lakes on the border between Maine and New Brunswick, the storied St. Croix River begins in earnest in the foam and froth at the foot of the dam in the tiny village of Vanceboro.

Little more than two stores and a couple of houses on a sharp curve in the road, the town achieved a modest level of notoriety in 1915 when a German saboteur attempted to destroy the railroad bridge over the river there during World War I. It held great strategic import as the tracks connected the industrial might of the United States to the port of Halifax in Nova Scotia, where ships were filled with war supplies and material bound for the Western Front in the "War to End All Wars."

The explosion caused only minor damage to the steel, although it did manage to blow out numerous windows in Vanceboro and in St. Croix, the village on the Canadian side where the border crossing station is today. The saboteur, Werner Horn, suffered frostbite to his hands from repeated attempts to reposition the bomb in the wee hours of February 2. The temperature that morning was a balmy 30 degrees below zero.

Horn wore his German army uniform while he did the deed on the theory that if he were captured, he might avoid the death penalty for being a spy. It didn't take long for him to be taken into custody, as there were few people walking gloveless around Vanceboro after the blast, mumbling about the Fatherland and unable to tie their shoes.

There is no record of whether he topped off his outfit with one of those distinctive spiked helmets.

Six years later, in 1921, Horn was declared insane and deported, although an argument could be made that anyone who thinks it's a good idea to sneak around a tiny outpost in Maine in February with a Louis Vuitton suitcase full of dynamite had long ago crossed that bridge.

From the dam, the St. Croix trends due south, its hypothetical centerline forming part of what most guidebooks refer to as "the world's longest undefended border," which is probably one of the reasons Horn thought he had a shot. There's no question, however, that when you paddle the St. Croix, you're definitely in what amounts to a geographical no-man's-land.

River left is Canada. River right is the United States. River left is home to a population of extraordinarily polite people. River right has given the world Kim Kardashian and Rush Limbaugh.

Temperatures on the river left are reported in Celsius, while on river right, it's done in Fahrenheit. When it's zero in St. Croix, there's still time to get the last of the squash picked in Vanceboro.

Computer keyboards on river left require frequent replacement of the "u" because of the Canadian predilection for inserting that letter into every word that ends in "or." On river right, keyboards seldom wear out because no one bothers to use capital letters or punctuation marks in written communications anymore.

How do you set your watch when on river left it's nine o'clock in the morning but on river right it's only eight o'clock? Einstein's theory of relativity aside, it's one of the few places in North

America where you can throw a stone across a body of water and have it hit the opposite shore an hour before it left.

The thirty-three-mile stretch of the St. Croix from Vanceboro to the high concrete dam and powerhouse at Kellyland is one of the best river trips in eastern North America. Thanks to those headwater lakes that store water for generating electrical power, it often has a dependable flow in late summer when other rivers and streams have become shadows of their former selves.

There are nearly two dozen rapids in the first twenty miles down to a wide spot in the river known as Loon Bay where a single power line spans what amounts to a long, narrow lake providing a permanent high-tension handshake between two North American powerhouses.

Most of the rapids in the upper river are easy Class I and II with obvious and wide passages between the rocks. The sole exception is at Little Falls, where a respectable seven-foot change in elevation has created a short yet challenging drop that can be considered Class III at higher water flows. The most obvious passage hugs the Canadian side, although the location on the outside of a bend requires paddlers to expend considerable energy and expertise to keep from being smashed into the unyielding rock. There's a sneak route hard on river right that always gets my vote.

Many parties simply decide to portage. There are trails on both sides so you can decide if you'd rather get your exercise in kilometers or miles.

Below Loon Bay, the number of rapids diminishes, although a river-wide ledge drop at Canoose Rips can run Class III to a heart-pounding IV depending on flow.

The majority of the St. Croix's rapids are also long, often requiring paddlers to navigate through a series of curves instead of just the short, straight shots often found elsewhere. Mostly it means it's a heck of a lot of fun and a great river upon which to hone your paddling skills with a minimal amount of risk. One need look no farther than the frequent patches of colored pigment on rocks from canoes that have banged and scraped their ways downstream, otherwise relatively unscathed, to know that this is a forgiving place to paddle.

On the Moose River Camping Club's first expedition on the St. Croix, we elect to stay in a sporting camp in Princeton, Long Lake Camps, on—you guessed it—Long Lake, the night before getting on the river. Because of time constraints, we contract with the operators of the camp to shuttle our trucks so we can avoid having to spend several hours on the last day retrieving vehicles left at the start.

One of the erstwhile shuttle drivers is the eighty-year-old woman who is also the camp's chief cook. Short and lean, with an air of authority that comes from decades of bossing around customers and coworkers alike, she radiates energy that leaves no doubt she is a force to be reckoned with.

That evening, she emerges from her fluorescent-lit domain behind the dining room's massive stone fireplace to chat with those of us enjoying a sip of whiskey and post-dinner Cohiba on the main lodge's front porch overlooking the flat, calm waters of the lake.

With a pair of loons providing a soundtrack right out of the movie *On Golden Pond*, I invite her to join us, sliding a fifth of Canadian Club her way. Without hesitation, she picks it up, and upon removing the unfiltered Chesterfield cigarette she is smoking from her thin, furrowed lips, tips it up to take a swig, the muscles in her wrinkled neck betraying a series of three long gulps. "Sweeeet," she says in a husky exhale as the bottle returns to the table and the damp end of the Chesterfield to her mouth.

While making small talk about the plan for the next morning, I casually ask, having never been there before, exactly how far it is from the camp to Vanceboro. Without pause, she responds in a thick Maine accent, "Oh, 'bout three beers."

With my mind suddenly jolted from listening to loons to worrying about insurance deductibles, I ponder how my own aging Ford Ranger might weather being operated by such an experienced hand. I mention that one of our guys, Pauley, who has already retired for the evening, has a new GMC pickup on this trip. "You might enjoy driving that one," I say. "It's an automatic."

The measurement of distance by a unit other than miles is only natural in a state as large as Maine, where on many roads endlessly lined with trees, distinctive landmarks are few and far between. Ask just about anyone how far it is between two points, and you almost always will get a response in time rather than miles.

How far is it between Bar Harbor and Bangor? Oh, about an hour and a half. Bar Harbor to Boston? A good five hours.

Looking at it that way acknowledges there are several factors in addition to distance that need to be taken into account when hitting the highway in Maine. Chief among them are the weather, time of day, traffic, condition and type of the roads themselves, and the availability of fuel and restroom facilities along the chosen route. Pilots flying DC-3s over the Himalayas from Burma to China during World War II had a shorter preflight checklist than someone setting out from Kennebunkport hoping to make it to Madawaska before dark.

Maine has more than twenty-three thousand miles of paved roads and probably that number again composed of dirt, mostly private roads owned by paper companies. Depending on where you want to be, a dirt road may be your best bet. And in some cases, a well-cared-for dirt road is preferable to a teeth-rattling ride over poorly maintained pavement full of potholes and cracked asphalt.

Some dirt roads in Maine are major arteries for hauling pulpwood, chips, and sawlogs out of the forest. Of course, a good way out is also a good way in, and hunters, fishermen, campers, and other recreationalists flock to those same roads. Legendary among them are the Golden Road that runs from Millinocket to the Quebec border at St. Zacharie and the Stud Mill Road in Eastern Maine that runs from the sawmills on the banks of the Penobscot River in Costigan due east to Princeton where Long Lake Camps is located.

Signs on many of these roads warn that logging trucks have the right-of-way.

Believe it.

It is not unusual for double-trailer rigs to weigh as much as two hundred thousand pounds, and a hundred tons of anything doesn't stop on a dime. On many of these roads, especially on curves, the dirt can get pushed up into a washboard pattern. The physics are interesting here as the dirt actually behaves as a waveform—the spacing between peaks and valleys is a function of the average speed. Drive the average speed, and your wheels and suspension will be perfectly in tune with the "periodicity" of the road and you'll shake and feel every bump. Driving slower or faster, however, avoids establishment of any harmonic resonance, resulting in a smoother ride.

Energetic French-Canadian logging truck drivers are perpetually in search of a smoother ride. And, being paid by the load, not the hour, it never occurs to them to slow down. The first time you spot one of these trains without tracks skidding around a curve in your lane with a tsunami of dust behind it, you'll have no doubt what sits atop the food chain on these roads.

Providing you've managed to avoid becoming a hood ornament on a big Peterbilt or Kentworth, the only other thing you have to worry about besides the odd collapsed culvert, obstructionist moose, or rock in the suspension is the dirt surface itself. A thin layer of dust is as slippery as rain-soaked pavement. When it does actually rain on hard-packed dirt, the thin layer of mud that forms causes vehicles to behave like they're on black ice.

Before you know it, you're out of control and about to learn what it means when an old-timer talks about going "ass over tea-kettle into the rhubarb."

It's enough to drive even a teetotaler to drink, which is probably why Miss Chesterfield 1933 knew exactly how many beers it is from Princeton to Vanceboro.

In winter, all bets are off on calculating travel time, as conditions can literally change from mile to mile varying with altitude, proximity to the coast, and whether the local department of transportation foreman has had his second cup of coffee yet. Springtime, of course, is the worst, thanks to frost heaves that form when water gets under the asphalt and freezes, forming impressive mounds and dips that no doubt inspired the theory of plate tectonics and continental drift.

Traffic also plays a role. Vehicles with license plates from Canadian provinces often travel well below the speed limit, but at least they have a legitimate excuse. It can sometimes take them a day or two to realize speed limit signs here are in miles per hour, not kilometers per hour. The signs say 55, but in kilometers, that's only 35 miles per hour.

Signs after you cross into Canada remind Americans that speed limits are in kilometers per hour, which no doubt helps cut down on the number of cars going eighty on two-lane highways. I once asked the commissioner of the Maine Department of Transportation why we don't return the favor, and he said it would be condescending.

Back in Maine, giant recreational vehicles moving at glacial speeds, especially when they raft up, create rolling roadblocks. Perhaps they are worried that driving at anything resembling the speed limit will cause the paint on their rig to spontaneously combust from friction with the atmosphere. Regardless of the reasons, most are blissfully unaware of the inconvenience. They assume local residents automatically take the back way to avoid traffic. Wrong.

For the most part in Maine, there is only one way to get to any place, and potential shortcuts usually involve a need to "put 'er in four-wheel drive low" and have a chainsaw handy for the inevitable trees across the road.

Of course, no self-respecting Mainer will direct you the back way, because, while it may be half the distance, it would take twice as much time.

No one who knows any better goes anywhere in Maine without a copy of that indispensable bible of rural navigation, *The Maine Atlas and Gazetteer*. It's published by DeLorme, an outfit with a giant globe named Eartha in its lobby, just down the road from L.L. Bean in Freeport. In the atlas, the entire state is broken down in a series of maps taking up some seventy pages that provide a level of detail unavailable anywhere else. You know you're in the boondocks when you need map number sixty-nine.

The *Gazetteer* is an incredible inspiration for outdoor adventure. Who can help but look at places on the map like Misery Gore, Moxie Falls, or Bailey's Mistake and not want to go there?

Getting the latest edition is a standing item on most Mainers' Christmas lists. It is updated annually and is indispensable when trying to figure out which dirt road you're actually on in the middle of nowhere. If there is a tiny circle on a dirt road over a brook in the *Gazetteer*, you can be assured the bridge there is actually out. The closed gate symbol, however, means you might have a chance of getting through because sometimes the guy with the key forgets to lock up.

The only flaw in the *Gazetteer's* design is noticed when you want to go someplace where four maps intersect. That makes for a lot of fumbling between pages. When that happens, the best strategy is to drive straight ahead as fast as you can until you're in the middle of another page and can figure out where you are.

My copy is ensconced right behind the seat in my truck, protected in its own special nylon and plastic atlas and gazetteer cozy, which, the company notes, is "durable and stylish."

When a new atlas appears under the Christmas tree, it goes straight into the truck. The older version is retired to the bookshelf behind my desk. The one that was there is then downgraded to being cut up and photocopied as needed for various expeditions and misadventures in the field.

Unfortunately, when paddling the St. Croix, the *Gazetteer* leaves most of the detail on the Canadian side blank. Perhaps that's to encourage the purchase of the *New Brunswick Atlas and Gazetteer*, but alas, DeLorme only makes them for the fifty U.S. states.

<hr>

The trip up to Vanceboro is relatively uneventful, although the actual shuttle of vehicles down to Loon Bay on the area's system of unmarked dirt roads won't be finished until much later.

We busy ourselves with loading the gear into the canoes, and only now can I clearly see that everyone has brought way too much stuff. Ideally you don't want the dunnage to extend above the gunwales, as it can create too high a profile, which makes it more difficult to paddle in the wind. And, everything needs to be secured so that in the event of a flip, others don't have to round up bobbing gear as well as gasping paddlers from the river.

Like me, my boat, Sneak Route, is a faded and weather-beaten veteran. The baby blue Old Town Tripper doesn't look too bad for its age. Only a single tent in a river bag and the handles of extra paddles are sticking up.

Glancing over at Pauley's Tripper, Buck and Rudy, however, provides a startling contrast.

Pauley is a quality control engineer for a jet engine manufacturer in Connecticut. Precision is his watchword. Fastidiousness is his middle name. His enthusiasm, good humor, and zest for life make him the perfect companion on a wilderness expedition.

While far from being a doomsday prepper or black-helicopter-fearing gun nut, he is among the many of my friends and acquaintances who rushed out to buy an AR15 semiautomatic rifle (or two) when it looked like the government was going to put restrictions on them. In the end, he was far more afraid about what his lovely wife, Karen, might say about that impulse than he was paranoid about the government knowing he had one.

Rather than march it through the front door and face that music, he managed to secrete it into the house and stash it in the back of a seldom-visited closet. That way, when it's eventually discovered, perhaps during an unscheduled inventory of bath towels and fragrant guest soaps, he'll be able to use the classic "Honey, I've always had that" defense.

I'm always amazed how a guy who spends all day quibbling about tolerances of tens of thousandths of an inch might as well have the vanity license plate "CLOSE ENOUGH" on his truck when it comes to loading his canoe. Included in the mound awaiting placement on this trip are two cast-iron Dutch ovens, a pair of "Barcolounger" collapsible chairs (with adjustable footrests), a

Coleman lantern so powerful it can be spotted from the International Space Station, and a cooler large enough to conceal half a dozen illegal immigrants with room left over for a vintage Louis Vuitton suitcase full of dynamite.

His undiagnosed obsessive-compulsive disorder, however, manifests itself primarily in his overall level of preparedness. He brings a repair kit for everything and always packs two spatulas in case everyone else forgets theirs.

The ritualistic manner in which he suits up prior to getting into the boat is not entirely dissimilar from the way technicians prepare to enter the rubble of the containment structure in the aftermath of an accident at a nuclear power station.

First comes the high-tech underwear followed by that year's commemorative MRCC T-shirt. The next layer requires struggling to get into a full wet suit and booties. By then, the only remaining exposed skin is on his bearded and somewhat chubby-cheeked face.

Next come the waterproof paddling parka, wind pants, and a colorful life vest sized appropriately for his corpulent constitution. It, of course, sports numerous pockets and flaps for all his fly-fishing gear. Whatever you do, don't ask to borrow the fingernail clippers, which he uses to trim fly knots. It hangs on a little chain attached to his life vest's zipper pull and never leaves his side.

Topping it off is a safari hat with wide brim to reduce the risk of cancer-causing sunburn, no-glare sunglasses with color-coordinated nerd strap, and a pair of fingerless paddling gloves from Northwest River Supply.

Just about the time he pulls on the second glove is when he realizes he really should not have had that third cup of coffee.

Getting fourteen people and all their gear into some kind of logical order and onto the river is nothing short of organized chaos. Gear is strewn all over the launch area, a privately owned put-in called Russell's Landing. The ground looks like a median strip on the interstate after a rollover accident involving the semitrailer carrying all the merchandise for an L.L. Bean catalog photo shoot. Piece by piece, everything finds a home in a canoe. People are pretty good about taking their share of the communal gear; however, on each and every trip, one item inevitably remains sitting in the dew-covered grass—the metal broiler basket with long handle used to cook river dogs over a campfire at lunch. Although it is wrapped in the remnants of a white plastic kitchen trash bag, it's always greasy and an awkward item to stow. On top of that, it's only going to get less appetizing as the trip progresses. "Anyone want to take that?" I ask as the group suddenly goes silent.

That's settled then—into my boat it goes.

Pauley manages to get everything into the bulging blue hull of Buck and Rudy, although the pile is so high it will provide effective cover should a German sniper begin taking potshots at us from the Canadian side.

Once launched, however, a slight problem reveals itself in the Buck and Rudy's ten-degree list to starboard. Apparently, in the haste to get going, both Dutch ovens were stacked well right of the centerline. Both Pauley and his bow paddler, Keith, will have to shift their weight far to the left in their seats to keep from going around in circles all day.

Once all boats are free of the shore with bows pointed downstream, it's time for the trip's first long exhale. The air is cool, the sky blue, and the new day still holds all its promise.

The noise and hustle of the shore surrenders to the rhythm of paddle strokes and the hum of the forest. Spirits take their first halting steps toward casting aside the outer layers of urban living.

The St. Croix has good current for much of its run. It's not difficult to keep up a pace of two to three miles per hour.

While in Maine, distance by road may be expressed in hours, on a river such as the St. Croix, progress is measured in days. Our goal at the end of the first day is Little Falls, where we'll camp for two nights. Then it's another half day to the take-out at Loon Bay.

It doesn't take long for the speedsters on pointe to resume an annoying habit that seems inherent in every greenhorn. "Rock!" they shout while wildly pointing in one direction or another.

As usual, on a trip, I remind myself that folks are only trying to help, and I ignore it. "Rock!" I hear again. Then "Rock!" "Rock!" "Rock!"

Granted, driving a canoe up hard on a boulder just an inch or two below the surface is disconcerting and embarrassing. In swift water, you can keep an eye out for the telltale swirl on the surface that betrays the fact that a large rock lurks a foot or two upstream. But even that is not always possible to see in time to take evasive action, especially when the sun is at a low angle.

Scraping along a large rock or even hitting one bow on, however, happens to the best of paddlers, sometimes multiple times a day. It isn't the preferred alternative, but it's not a question of if but rather when. It's too bad the river isn't a court of law so all the greenhorn "lawyers" with their objections could just stipulate that there are rocks everywhere you look and move on to the next line of questioning.

~

We make Little Falls by late afternoon, all boats having managed to remain upright and intact despite descending rapids with names such as Kill Me Quick and Tunnel Rips. We make excellent headway even though the backwater stretch above English Cove is a bit of a slog, thanks to an irksome headwind.

In such situations, paddling a canoe with another person is like pedaling a tandem bicycle. At some point when progress slows you invariably suspect they are not working as hard as you are. Working together, of course, is the key to efficiency.

Someone, however, needs to pick the route, be responsible for keeping things on course. Because of the mechanical advantage afforded to the paddler in the stern, the person in charge is usually in the back. It's also the perfect vantage from which to keep an eye on how hard the person in the bow is paddling.

At Little Falls, the decision is made to stay on the American side, as the choice campsite at the top of the drop is available. Like all sites on the St. Croix, its care and maintenance are entrusted to an international commission that oversees everything on both sides of the river.

There are plenty of places to pitch tents where the rush of the falls serenades you to sleep at night. The waters of two nations, indistinguishable, rush over and around the ledges, composing an aqueous sonata on the fly. No two ripples contribute the same note or repeat the same measure, yet the result is a timeless symphony that never changes.

It has the added benefit of masking the incessant snoring frequently emanating from other tents, especially after a long day of paddling topped off with a hearty meal and a generous cocktail.

The site's popularity requires that you range farther afield to find firewood, but the outhouse is handy, its floor is relatively level, and the roof is free of leaks.

The portage trail to the wide and convenient landing at the foot of the falls, where the canoes will return to the river, is relatively straight and entirely downhill. The vantage is perfect for taking a lay day in camp so members of the company can fish, photograph, and take multiple practice runs down the falls in various combinations. Best of all, it holds the prospect of having a day to do nothing at all, a pastime with which few members of our company are intimately acquainted.

That evening, while sitting beside the crackling campfire, talk turns to which river we'll tackle next. In more than a decade of annual trips, we realize we've barely begun to scratch the surface when it comes to potential. While a relative pip-squeak compared to the giant states out west such as Texas, Maine is still a pretty big place. There is no end of places to explore.

Maine, in addition to being the only state in the lower forty-eight that touches just one other state (it's also the only one with a one-syllable name), is the biggest New England state. It comes very close to being larger than the other five combined.

In order from largest to smallest, New England includes Maine, Vermont (bet that one surprised you, but look at a map), and New Hampshire (if you count the tollbooths and liquor stores on the turnpike twice), followed by Massachusetts, Connecticut, and then, last but not least, Rhode Island.

Maine, in fact, has all kinds of places and areas that are "approximately the size of Rhode Island."

Maine's geographic superlatives appear to have no bounds. Lubec and Eastport are the easternmost cities in the country. Moosehead Lake is the largest lake in New England contained within a single state.

Katahdin in Baxter State Park is the northern terminus of the storied Appalachian Trail, which stretches more than 2,100 miles from Georgia. The park being 220,000 acres in size, you would only need three Baxter State Parks to equal Rhode Island, making it one of the few major features in Maine actually smaller than that state.

In all, Maine has some 35,385 square miles, making it approximately thirty times the size of you-know-where. Aroostook County alone is approximately five and a half times bigger. Even if Rhode Island annexes Connecticut, Aroostook will still be bigger.

For paddlers, there are five thousand rivers and streams with a total length of approximately thirty-seven thousand miles. There are more than six thousand lakes and ponds.

Maine has more than thirty-five hundred miles of coastline, which all travel writers are required by constitutional amendment to describe as "rugged and rocky." That alone could easily qualify Maine to be called the Ocean State. Of course, that motto is already taken by—wait for it—Rhode Island. Rhode Islanders have 384 miles of much less rugged shores. Good for them.

In the cosmic scheme of things, Maine ranks just thirty-ninth on a list of the largest states, which coincides with where it always seems to fall in social demographics such as personal income levels, places that root for the Yankees, and wine refrigerator ownership.

While people in Maine may take comfort in the fact that geographically their state is the big dog of New England, they have developed various coping mechanisms for dealing with feelings of inferiority over how it compares to the dozens of other states that score higher in most other metrics.

The late humorist Marshall Dodge told a story about how a Maine farmer would respond to one from Texas bragging about the massive size of his spread. "My ranch in Texas is so big, it takes me four days to drive around it in my car," the rancher would say. According to Dodge, the farmer from Maine would pause, put his thumbs behind the shoulder straps of his overalls and respond "Ayuh, back on my farm in Maine, we've got a car just like that."

In some respects, Maine is the Texas of New England, no better evidenced than when listening to some Mainer talking about how long it takes, for example, to drive from Kennebunkport to Madawaska.

I can see some old blue blood down in Rhode Island now shaking his white-haired head in acknowledgment. "Yeeeessss," he'd say through tightly clenched teeth, lower jaw extended. "Back at my mansion in Newport we've got a yacht just like that."

Because of its size, Maine boasts the fewest people per square mile east of the Mississippi. The unorganized territories have a population density of just one person for every 267 square miles or so. For Rhode Island to make that claim, its entire population would have to be four.

Granted, in Maine there are lots of folks passing through: hunters, fishermen, loggers, and a handful of career criminals on the run from the federal grand jury in Providence. That, in total, probably gets the population up to something around one person in every 250 square miles, which no doubt has some of the natives contemplating a move due to overcrowding.

The highest recorded temperature in Maine was 105 degrees Fahrenheit (equivalent to a balmy 40.5 Celsius if you were on the Canadian side of the St. Croix) in July 1911, in Bridgeton.

The lowest temperature ever recorded was along the Big Black River in far northern Maine in January 2009. The mercury dropped to 50 degrees below zero.

Back in frontier days, that area was known as the Republic of Madawaska. Eventually, a treaty no history class has ever discussed was signed in someplace with a name no one can pronounce, after the undeclared Aroostook War in which no one was hurt because not a single shot was fired. The treaty formally made the republic, including land along the Big Black River, part of the United States. Apparently, the Republic's greatest contribution now is ruining the high–low temperature curve for the entire state of Maine thanks to frigid, undocumented Canadian air sneaking down over the world's longest undefended border under cover of darkness.

The MRCC has done plenty of cold weather and winter camp-ing, but nothing harsher than ten below or so. Climbing out of a sleeping bag when it's anything below zero is not anyone's idea of a picnic. On crazy cold mornings, my brother Carl likes to say that there are two kinds of cold. It's akin to the expression that it's not the heat; it's the moron who reminds you it's the humidity.

"There's cold," he'll say, "and there's F'ing cold."

He's right. There are two kinds of everything in life. There's yahoo and ya-F'ing-hoo. Some things are great, and then some are F'ing great. Sometimes things are bad, and sometimes they are F'ing bad. It's hot out, and then it can be F'ing hot out, or at least it was once in Bridgton in 1911. You get the picture.

Minus 50 is definitely what Carl refers to in polite company as "the second kind of cold."

Maine became a state in 1820 when it got tired of being part of Massachusetts. Records show there was plenty of talk about self-determination and independence, but my theory is that the state's founders wanted to spare future generations the embarrass-ment of owning cars with license plates identifying them as New England's worst drivers.

Every state has another state whose drivers they hate the most. In Connecticut, it's New Jersey. In Massachusetts, it's New York. No one hates Maine, although vehicles with Maine plates are often singled out for harassment just for sport. Drive along Interstate 495 outside Haverhill with a Maine plate on your vehicle and I guarantee you'll have some Masshole in a BMW humping your bumper the entire way.

Vermont drivers don't seem to piss off anyone. New Hampshire drivers aren't too bad either, although every time folks elsewhere in New England see a Granite State license plate, we shake our heads because they still feature an image of the Old Man in the

Mountain even though it tumbled off the cliff in the middle of the night years ago.

On top of that, the rest of us are jealous they get out of paying state sales tax.

Rhode Island drivers are the third worst in the country, according to an insurance industry study.

Well, it's nice to know they have Maine beat on at least one list.

———

On the third day, we break camp early. Ahead lies Pork Rips, purportedly named after a vital barrel of salt pork that was lost when a freight canoe overturned there more than a hundred years ago.

After that, we take on rapids at Duck Point, as well as at Cedar Island. Just downstream from the island is the grave of a baby girl discovered by loggers along the river in the late 1899s. It is believed she was born aboard a train and thrown into the river as it crossed the bridge in Vanceboro. Area woodsmen erected a stone and have cared for the plot ever since.

Next up are Tyler, Courant, Rocky, Split Rock, Meetinghouse, and Haycock Rips, the last marking the official beginning of Loon Bay.

While paddling between several low grassy islands just before noon, I spot a telltale sign the take-out is close. A single high-tension line hangs high above the river just ahead.

I yell to everyone to stick to river right. I back paddle hard to swing the nose toward shore. Canoes take turns returning to terra firma with the usual welcoming crunch. It's just a short ways up a steep and rutted road to the parking area.

As agreed upon, the trucks are all there, keys hidden in the appointed spots. Sure, they're a little dusty, but none of the tires are flat; windows and taillights remain unbroken. They all appear perfectly normal—except Pauley's GMC. It's slathered with enough thick orange mud that it's hard to tell its original color. The only exception is a pair of 180-degree smudges across the windshield where the wipers were used to maintain some semblance of visibility for the driver.

Inside, the seat is all the way forward. The formerly virgin ashtray contains a pile of ashes and a dozen unfiltered cigarette butts much too short to determine the brand much less the previous owner.

"Who the hell did this?" Pauley asks to no one in particular. I exchange glances with a couple of the other Long Lake porch sitters, but no one says a word.

The scene at the take-out repeats the disorder of the put-in with far less due care. Gear is tossed ashore and piled in haphazard fashion in the trucks. It's not unlike the British evacuation of Dunkirk minus the Cockney accents, doughboy helmets, and incoming German artillery shells.

Once all the canoes are safely strapped atop roof racks or tied on a trailer, it's time to hit the road for that night's destination, the Holiday Inn in Bangor. Getting there requires a somewhat convoluted route.

First we traverse fourteen miles of good gravel on the Bingo Road to Route 1. A quick left there points us south toward Calais, but we'll hang a right onto Route 9, the storied "Airline," before we get to downtown.

Named for the Airline Stage Coach line that once hauled people, goods, and mail between Bangor and Calais, Route 9 twists and bends its way due east and west across a hundred miles of Washington and Hancock Counties. It's one of the most desolate roads in Maine, devoid of utility poles and power lines for much of its distance.

Along the way, it intersects with some of the state's legendary paddling rivers, including the Union, Narraguagus, and Machias. Its most notable feature is called The Whalesback, where the road runs atop a high, snakelike glacial sand deposit known as an esker. Over the years, the state has improved much of the route, adding passing lanes that allow smaller vehicles to get around the steady stream of yellow Sunbury tractor trailers going back and forth to Canada.

As we turn west onto the Airline, all thoughts are drifting toward hot showers and a dinner out. A voice comes across the CB radio from one of the other vehicles in our ragtag caravan. "Hey Earl," Keith asks. "How far is it to Bangor?"

In preparation for my response, I attempt to factor the distance, weather, and prospect of having to avoid the odd moose or two. And even with the new passing lanes, it is still possible to get stuck behind a slow-moving truck or a clueless Winnebago.

I reach down with my free hand and key the microphone, pausing to make sure it's on. "It all depends on a lot of things," I reply with a smile. "My best estimate is two, maybe three beers."

SO YOU WANT TO SEE A MOOSE

EVERYONE WHO VISITS MAINE WANTS TO SEE A MOOSE. IT RANKS right up there with visiting a lighthouse, eating a lobster, and actually meeting an old salt who still answers questions by saying "ayuh" and "you can't get there from here."

Senator Angus King, when he was governor, liked to say that a good way to boost tourism would be to plunk an old codger wearing a red and black checkered wool shirt in a rocking chair on the front porch of every small-town store. That might work, but it still can't hold a candle to moose mania. If you stop into any gift shop, you're likely to find a wide array of moosey items ranging from stuffed toys to welcome mats, stickers, refrigerator magnets, light switch covers, T-shirts, towels, slippers, and even wallpaper.

When was the last time you saw a come-from-away walking out of a store with a bag full of old codger merch?

Living in Maine, especially along the coast, you get asked a lot of questions. After "Can I park here?" "Where's the best place to eat?" and "How come all the boats in the harbor park facing the same way?" the most frequent inquiry is "Where can I go to see a moose?"

Those in the know summon their best old codger accent, and after the proper reflective pause, say just one word—"North."

Except for remote offshore islands, just about any place in Maine will have a token moose or two. But your chances of seeing one improve exponentially the farther north you go.

There's no such thing in life as a sure thing, but there are two spots where you are almost guaranteed to see a moose, providing you're there at the right time of day—the bog next to the Maine Department of Transportation garage on Route 15 in Shirley, just below Greenville, and Sandy Stream Pond in Baxter State Park. At dusk, cars often line the road in Shirley waiting for any number of these forest celebrities to trudge out of the woods.

At the pond, which requires a short hike in from Roaring Brook Campground, moose emerge from the woods to eat the succulent aquatic vegetation in the shallows. Like a North Woods version of whack-a-mole, the moose flit back and forth between the woods and the water with more popping out as others retreat. You're just as likely to see three at the same time as you are to be skunked. If you don't see one right away, crawl out onto one of the massive boulders surrounding the pond and wait. Your patience will be rewarded. Besides, the views are spectacular. Bring a camera, binoculars, and don't forget the bug spray.

Over at the Birches Resort in Rockwood on Moosehead Lake, they offer a Moose Safari by water. Passengers are shuttled up the lake in a boat not unlike the *African Queen* to explore the meandering backwaters of Socatean Stream. George Lucas's Industrial Light and Magic special effects studio couldn't create a better moose habitat.

The only other "big game" to keep an eye out for on the trip are the owners of a $15 million log mansion on the shore. The owner, a Texas corporate CEO, bought up the surrounding three thousand acres of forest. That guarantees a lot of privacy. Sightings are rare, but it's not a bad one to add to your life list.

Access isn't a problem for them or their guests; this "kingdom" comes with a private, paved 2,100-foot landing strip equipped to handle private jets in all weather conditions. Still, that holding is modest by Moosehead Lake standards. Billionaire John Malone owns tracts nearby totaling twenty thousand acres—about thirty square miles.

For a while, my brothers and sisters and I owned the equivalent of a sharecroppers' stake on a quarter-acre lot on the Lily Bay Road in Greenville. We dubbed it Green Acres in a nod to the dull green finish on the weather-beaten pressboard siding. Purchased for less than the price of a modestly equipped pickup truck, it quickly became a base from which to launch expeditions deeper in, whether by car, backpack, canoe, or snowmobile.

One of our favorite pastimes was taking a ride up to Kokadjo, a last-outpost kind of place, where the pavement and utility lines end. From there, it's a quick jog down the Frenchtown Road along First Roach Pond to a spiderweb of dirt tracks where moose always seem to gather in abundance.

Douglas Saunders, my brother-in-law and a Master Maine Guide—he technically outranks me, as I'm only a Recreational Maine Guide—likes to brag on those excursions that he can guarantee people will see a moose. Comedian Steven Wright likes to say that everywhere on earth "is within walking distance—if you have the time." Likewise, Douglas's moose safaris can take quite a while if the buggers aren't cooperating and his batting average is at stake.

With a no-nonsense demeanor and a firm handshake that leaves no doubt he believes in an honest day's work for an honest day's pay, Douglas, Spruce Head born, is Mainer through and through. He roots for the Red Sox and the Patriots no matter how bad they're doing. You're as likely to find paint swatches from a local home center and a book about artist Andrew Wyeth in the cab of his GMC pickup (dark green of course, with a cap) as you are his deer hunting rifle or his fly-fishing rod.

Before buying anything remotely resembling a fixed asset, Douglas first contemplates if he might be able to save money by making one in his workshop. If the answer is no, then it's time to spend Thursday evening poring over *Uncle Henry's* classified magazine to see if there might be a used one in good condition for sale—provided the drive to fetch it isn't too far.

Only after coming up dry there will he ponder reaching into his wallet, which happens so infrequently that it's always accompanied by the sound of a creaking dungeon door. If his hand accidentally brushes his credit card when going in for the cash, the diving klaxon from a World War II submarine goes off.

Among outdoorsmen in Maine, there's no greater honor than to be known as "a good man in the woods." It refers not only to one's camping, woodcraft, navigation, and survival skills but also temperament and the ability to be counted on when the going or weather gets rough. In military parlance, a good man in the woods "always has your six."

Douglas is all that and more. And, he's pretty good at finding moose.

One evening in Greenville I ask him if he's willing to test his guarantee with a wager. As the fishing line screams off my metaphorical reel, he offers that if we go out and don't see a moose, he'll kiss my German shepherd, Shadow, full on the lips. Actually, he specifies a diametrically different part of the anatomy, but I'm employing a little artistic license to keep the narrative suitable for prime time.

If we do see a moose, I'll take his turn cooking a big breakfast for everyone in the morning.

Anyway, Douglas knows the odds are in his favor. So after supper, a bunch of us pile into my sister Patty's stalwart Chevy Tahoe, the quintessential backwoods road trip vehicle, affectionately known simply as The Ho. I prop the *Maine Atlas and Gazetteer*, open to map 41, onto the console, and we take a left out of the driveway. As we head north past the rolling lawns of the stately Blair Hill Inn, I add an extra degree of pressure to the bet. "We have to be back to Green Acres by dark," I say.

Moose are the largest members of the deer family, and the bulls can weigh as much as fifteen hundred pounds. The big ones—and believe me, when you come across one in the woods, they're all big—stand up to seven feet tall at the shoulders. For the most part, they're solitary creatures. When full grown and healthy, they have little to fear in Maine. Their name comes from the Algonquin word *moosu*, which means "bark stripper."

Keeping their massive bodies fueled up takes a lot of browse. A cow moose nursing a calf will eat an astounding sixty-six pounds of vegetation in a day. Their favorite foods include aquatic vegetation, such as horsetails and pondweed. They can eat with their heads underwater.

On land, the menu includes grass, lichens, deciduous green leaves, and bark, including willows and poplars. Moose can leave a stand of young striped maple trees (also known at mountain maple) looking like someone came through and cut them all off three feet above the ground. That lends itself to the tree's most common nickname, moosewood.

Mastication on such an epic scale, in turn, generates a considerable volume of material requiring backend disposal. Piles of distinctive moose pellets can be seen just about everywhere in the Maine woods. The apparent freshness can signal if one is somewhere in the area or moved on long ago.

In typically frugal Yankee fashion, fresh moose pellets do not go to waste. They're used for everything from fire starters to jewelry, the latter after they've been suitably sealed with multiple coats of shellac.

Moose are Maine's official state animal, a noble choice to stand alongside the state bird, the black-capped chickadee, and the state flower, the white pine cone and tassel. Fortunately, those selections were made decades ago when legislators actually took such choices seriously.

A recent addition to Maine's "Official List of Stuff" includes the Maine State Treat, the whoopie pie. An attempt to claim the whoopie pie as the official Maine dessert raised the hackles of the Amish community in Pennsylvania, which, despite the reputation of its members for living quiet, stress-free lives, got pretty agitated over the issue. Apparently, it says somewhere in scripture that the idea to put a sugary vanilla filling between two small chocolate cakes originated where people use horse and buggy to get around instead of cars.

The Maine proposal also drew the wrath of the powerful Maine wild blueberry lobby. Wanting to avoid culinary jihad, a compromise was negotiated, resulting in blueberry pie becoming the official Maine state dessert. Whoopie pies were unceremoniously demoted to official snack status.

Oblivious to all the political drama, moose are far less cantankerous creatures. However, when one lowers its head and raises its hackles (the hairs on the back of its neck), it's time to beat feet.

Although usually considered to be somewhat slothful, moose can run up to thirty-five miles per hour and swim as fast as six. I hope never to put that to the test.

Along with their formidable bulk, and noses only the late Jimmy Durante could love, the most significant feature of moose, at least the bulls, is the antlers. Sometimes attaining a span of nearly six feet, a bull moose's antlers can weigh up to forty pounds. They drop them each fall after mating season to save energy over the difficult winter months. It only takes between three to five months for them to regrow when the weather warms.

Along with providing some measure of defense from predators such as coyotes, a moose's antlers are used to intimidate rivals for the ladies' affections when moose go into the rut, and we're not talking the same old, same old. Cows usually accept only one male each fall, but a dominant bull may mate with as many as twenty-five cows. Apparently, bull moose are the biggest cads in the boreal forest.

When bluster and blow don't work to scare off young bulls, antlers come in handy in fights. The jousting can last for hours, with the skull-crunching sound of clashing antlers sometimes carrying for miles. Injuries or death is common in such conflicts.

Once in a great while, two bulls will get their antlers stuck together in a fight. They remain that way until they die of exhaustion or starvation. While running the Machias River once, we paddled over to investigate two unusual rocks. It turned out to be the carcasses of two huge buck deer. With antlers locked, they apparently stumbled into the river and drowned.

Two moose carcasses were found in an Aroostook County swamp in 2006 with their antlers locked. They formed the basis for a full-size taxidermy display entitled "The Final Charge" at the L.L. Bean flagship store in Freeport.

The other weird appendage sported solely by bull moose, who appear to be far more vain than the ladies, is a flap of skin and hair that hangs under the neck. It's called a dewlap, or bell, and reportedly shrinks with age. Some biologists speculate that it helps bulls to establish dominance, although no one has yet to find two moose carcasses with their dewlaps forever intertwined. What they really mean is they have no idea what purpose it serves. Colloquially, it has also been called a moosetache.

Whatever you do, don't call it a wattle—that's what hangs under a turkey's neck.

Moose in the wild live on average eight to ten years, with twenty believed to be the upper limit.

In Maine, the closest living relatives to moose are deer. Another cousin, the caribou, lived in the state until the early 1900s, in the era when shooting a dozen deer or catching two hundred trout in a day was considered a badge of honor, not a shame.

Much has been written about the state's celebrated first Registered Maine Guide, a skilled outdoorswoman named Cornelia "Fly Rod" Crosby. She also held the honor of being the first woman to legally shoot a caribou in Maine and the dubious distinction of killing the last known legally shot caribou—a buck.

The species was considered extinct by 1908.

An attempt to reintroduce caribou in Maine in 1986 ended in disaster. A dozen animals out of more than forty captured in Canada were helicoptered to the rocky, treeless, and windblown Tableland high up on Katahdin in Baxter State Park. After four years and the release of thirty-two caribou in all, twenty-five were confirmed dead. That includes a dozen killed by bears or coyotes. The rest succumbed to disease and starvation. The project was abandoned.

Moose, meanwhile, just keep plodding along. Biologists estimate the size of Maine's herd, the largest in the lower forty-eight states, at around seventy-six thousand. That's one for every seven-teen people in the state. Years of clear-cutting large tracts of forest around Moosehead Lake resulted in a bonanza of young hardwood regrowth—perfect moose habitat that fueled a population boom, although it has leveled off in the last few years.

Either way, Douglas liked his odds.

After passing by the inn where to the west there are spectacular views of Moosehead Lake and Big Moose Mountain, the road to Kokadjo dips and curves past Sandy Bay, through the burg of Bea-ver Cove, and past the entrance to Lily Bay State Park. There are a few signs of civilization on the lake side of the road, but virtually none to the east. Only the stub of woods roads leading to Prong or Mud Ponds punctuates the miles and miles of trees. Before we know it, we are almost all the way up to map 49.

After half an hour, we arrive at Kokadjo, where the bumper sticker sold in the hardscrabble general store there sports the silhouettes of a moose, two adults, one kid, and the slogan "Population—not many." We check out the flow from the outlet dam where water from the Roach Pond system courses down-stream on its way to Moosehead. All in the car agree there are probably some nice trout in the spillway's runout, but we have bigger fish to fry.

Doug eases the Ho onto the Frenchtown Road, and we head east, remarking how different the terrain looks in high summer. We run that road much more often in winter, by snowmobile, when it's part of the main Interconnected Trail System (ITS), which forms a giant hundred-mile loop around Moosehead Lake.

Meanwhile, Patty apologizes for not getting the shocks replaced last week like she had planned.

The rules of motorized moose safari are few. You slow down, proceeding barely above idle. Each person keeps an eye out on their side, taking particular care to scan down side roads and skidder trails. Stream crossings and marshes are particularly good spots.

Windows are usually rolled down except when an oncoming truck approaches. Then, the scramble is on to shut them quickly to keep the ensuing dust storm from enveloping everyone and everything inside.

———

A moose will often just be standing in the middle of the road. They never seem to be in a hurry to get out of the way. One time, a friend from Bar Harbor, Rob Jordan, was driving up late at night on the fabled Golden Road to join the Moose River Camping Club at Roll Dam for a canoe trip on the West Branch of the Penobscot. He found the entire width of the road was blocked by three moose, one bull and two cows. He honked, he blinked the lights, he raced the motor; they wouldn't move. That, and the fact that he later took a wrong turn and drove almost all the way to Canada before realizing it, resulted in him not getting into camp until after midnight, the gas gauge nearly on "E." It might have helped when he stopped at the last store before hitting the woods if he had filled up his gas tank as well as topping off his beer cooler.

Snowmobiling around First Roach once, we came across a moose standing in the middle of the packed trail. Especially during a hard winter, they often prefer walking the trails to avoid wallowing in the deep snow.

We just shut off the motors and waited half an hour or so for the moose to mosey off into a stand of softwood trees. That stands in stark contrast to the behavior of some snowmobilers from New Hampshire who videotaped their encounter with a moose over near Jackman in 2014. The clip shows them chasing the moose down the trail for more than twenty seconds (try holding your breath that long) before it stops. It turns and charges the lead sledder, cuffing him. A woman on a snowmobile behind him pulls out a handgun and fires it into the air.

Eventually the moose wanders off. Wardens investigated the incident and considered filing charges for harassing wildlife and concealed weapons violations.

Fortunately, most of the encounters I've had with moose, outside of seeing them along the road, have been far less traumatic.

One September while backpacking along Baxter State Park's legendary Freezeout Trail, my companion and I became aware of an unusual, intermittent *swoooooosh* sound. As we got closer to an open marshy area, it got louder. But it wasn't constant. It was difficult to pin down where it was coming from. When we finally got to a spot on a low bluff overlooking the marsh, movement caught our eyes as a massive bull moose, standing in the water up to his shoulders, lifted his huge head from under the surface of the water, his mouth full of succulent aquatic plants. The sound was of the gallons of water cascading off his head and antlers.

While camping at Chimney Pond in Baxter State Park once, my wife, Roxie, and I got up close and personal with a good-sized cow moose on a 1:00 a.m. outhouse run—Roxie wasn't comfortable going alone after dark. In hindsight, that seemed especially prescient. So, I accompanied her on the short path from our lean-to as the bearer of a second source of artificial illumination and erstwhile slayer of all potential forest demons, both foreign and domestic.

We arrived at said facility unscathed, and I pondered whether for security purposes we should take a different route back. After my inspection showed no monsters within, she entered, and I did the gentlemanly thing and turned to look the other way. The canopy of stars was spectacular.

It was then that I became aware of the sound of crunching vegetation from right behind the outhouse. There, standing next to the outhouse, with its butt actually touching the side, was a good-sized cow moose. In a calm, soft voice, I explained the situation to Roxie and recommended that when she was ready to exit she should open the door very slowly.

Repeating the words "nice moosey" over and over in gentle tones, we backed away from the privy and returned quickly to our site. The moose never moved.

At sunup the next morning, while we were having a cup of tea in the lean-to, a cow moose slowly and deliberately, as if headed out to pick up the Sunday paper, walked through the semi-open area about ten feet from where we were sitting. Roxie and I just looked at each other, motionless, and didn't say a word.

I am not 100 percent certain it was the same moose we saw the night before, but I swear when I caught her eye, I saw a glimmer of recognition—perhaps we had met somewhere before.

Only once have I been concerned about getting too close to a moose while in a canoe.

As sort of a late honeymoon a year after we were married, Roxie and I hired the folks at Folsom's Air Service in Greenville to fly us in to a cabin on Horseshoe Pond for a relaxing stay. One afternoon while paddling at the far end of the pond, we heard a lot of branches breaking in the woods. We stopped to see what it was, and eventually a bull moose stepped out into the water. We floated motionless about twenty yards away. After a pause, the moose walked farther out into the lake, directly toward us until it was in over his head. Then he began swimming. To the shout of "back paddle!" we began a hasty retreat. The lag between putting my paddle in the water and the canoe actually beginning to move seemed an eternity. Meanwhile, I was racking my brain trying to remember just how fast a moose can supposedly swim.

Fortunately, it was the other side of the lake that was the focus of his attention. Once we were no longer betwixt him and his favorite lunch haunt, he lost interest.

People who take photographs of moose usually have a lot of bad ones. That's because when you first see a moose it's often at a distance. You worry you'll never get a better opportunity, so you shoot away. And then the moose moves a little closer.

So you take a bunch more and relax for a moment, happy at getting some shots. And then it moves a little closer.

That's not a problem when you can just delete the bad ones from a digital camera, but years ago while shooting film, it was a different story.

A group of us were staying in the bunkhouse at Chimney Pond. A cow moose and obviously newborn calf appeared at the opposite side of the clearing in front of the cabin. People were pushing and shoving to get to the door and take a shot that all believed would be the next cover of *National Geographic*. At the least, everyone was pleased they had evidence of an encounter of a moose in the wild. And then, of course, the moose moved a little closer.

Similar scrambles continued for most of the long weekend, although by Saturday afternoon, when the moose and calf reappeared, this time quite close to the camp, many had become bored or had simply run out of film.

On Sunday morning, one of the guys rushed into the common room through the back door and announced with hushed excitement that the cow moose and calf were sleeping in the weeds right outside the front porch of the cabin. "So?" was the universal reaction.

◆━ ━◆

Meanwhile, back in the woods in the vicinity of First Roach Pond, Mighty Douglas is striking out. We've been at bat for nearly two hours and have nary a hoofprint to show for it. We've ranged from Lazy Tom Stream all the way to Third Roach and have even done a loop down by Big Lyford Pond where the Appalachian Mountain Club has a camp. Nothing, nada, zippo.

Considering the downside risk of his wager, Douglas is not about to give up. The sun has already slid behind Big Moose, its slanting rays turning Big Spencer Mountain a golden yellow. It would be dark before long. We come back out on the paved road and turn south toward Greenville. "Is it me, or are we going well below the speed limit?" I ask.

"I'm just being careful. Nobody wants to hit a moose," Douglas says.

I know what he's thinking. Hitting one at least would be proof we saw a moose, thus invoking the wager's payoff provision. But where it isn't his car, the lower speed seems at cross-purposes. Then I realize he's dragging it out as long as possible because the safari isn't technically over until we turn back into the driveway at Green Acres. "Go as slow as you want, Saunders," I laugh. "I think all the moose have clocked out for the night."

◆━ ━◆

Collisions between cars and trucks and moose, however, are no laughing matter. They often turn out as bad for the driver as for the moose.

Each year in Maine, there are an average of 550 crashes involving moose. Two to three of those involve human fatalities. About 80 percent of the accidents occur between dusk and dawn.

Aroostook County sees the most moose crashes, although they can happen anywhere in the state. Collisions on the interstate are often the worst because of the speeds involved.

Due to their dark fur, which is even less reflective when wet, moose are extraordinarily difficult to see along the road. Their eyes do not glow if a light shines on them.

One strategy I've always used is to keep an eye out for a "gap" in the reflective white line that runs down the side of the road. If you don't see an unbroken white line, something's blocking it.

Mostly I've seen moose standing in the road or by the roadside, sometimes attracted to the fresh growth or road salt there. Still, they have been known to dash out of the woods on a dead run.

In a chance encounter between a thousand-pound moose and a four-thousand-pound car, the laws of physics dictate advantage automobile, particularly where it has momentum on its side. The unique body configuration of the moose, however, evens the odds.

Because of their tall, thin legs, moose tend to catapult into the air when struck. Unfortunately, when they come through the windshield or land on the roof of a car, it collapses and the most serious injuries occur.

In the chance encounter between a thousand-pound moose and the thin sheet metal roof of a sedan, advantage moose.

Highway safety officials recommend slowing down at night, especially if you see vehicles ahead of you acting strangely. Remember, if you see one moose or deer, there are often more in the same vicinity, sometimes on both sides of the road. It's not unusual for a frightened moose to run ahead of a vehicle down the side of the road. Don't try to pass it. They often dart unpredictably to one side.

If a collision is unavoidable, officials say, aim for the back legs so the moose spins off instead of going airborne. The advice of what to do when all else fails reminds me of what I was taught to do in grammar school in the event of a Russian nuclear attack—duck.

In the spring of 2014, two moose were hit on the same night in Aroostook County. The second one landed firmly atop the state police cruiser responding to the scene of the first crash. Only minor injuries resulted—to the humans.

—◦—

Heading back toward Greenville, we all have high hopes of seeing a moose around Beaver Cove where the road swings close to the lake by the marina. Lots of shallow water and pond lilies there. Nothing.

We've been more than fifty miles, and if the Ho's fuel gauge actually worked, Patty might be more inclined to ask us to chip in for gas.

We've seen nothing, not even a line of fresh tracks you can often spot paralleling the road in the band of sand along the shoulder.

Sandy Cove comes and goes with the same result despite the fact that Douglas is now driving so slow that we have to start pulling over to let little old ladies pass. Every time he does, all eyes are on Douglas. Poker-faced, he just stares straight ahead.

No one remembers ever seeing a moose along the road atop Blair Hill, so we focus instead on the evening's alpenglow, that rich swipe of undelineated color rising from hard red at the horizon behind Big Moose Mountain to the west to yellow to almost white to blue and then fading to black directly overhead. Venus hangs low in the western sky almost too bright to stare at. The far shore of the lake is speckled with lights from camps where the day's adventures will soon be the stuff of dreams.

As we crest the hill and start down, I can see the line of streetlights reaching up town halfway down on the left. Our driveway is directly across from the second one. No one says a word, preferring to leave the gloating to the bitter end.

Shadow, I know, will be happy to see us.

"What's that?" my sister yells, pointing dead ahead. Douglas instinctively hits the brakes, bringing the Ho to an abrupt, if not somewhat squeally, stop.

Standing on the right-hand shoulder in front of us, less than a quarter mile from home, is a magnificent bull moose, his still-growing antlers sheathed in velvet, iridescent in the light from the headlights.

"Crap," I say out loud as everyone in the car erupts in laughter. Douglas lets out a big rush of air.

The moose, blissfully unaware of the pivotal role it had just played in a high-stakes wager, just looks over its shoulder at us and takes two lumbering steps into the puckerbrush and disappears.

In less than a minute, we're back in the driveway. "It's not that I don't like your dog," Douglas deadpans after shutting the engine off. "Look at the bright side," he continues. "We did get to see a moose."

WHERE'S BOB?

"Where's Bob?" Carl asks. "Has anybody seen where he went?"

It's getting late, and the long, low light of an early June evening is beginning to etch Katahdin's headwall, looming over Chimney Pond, with a glow like that on rocks around a campfire when flames retreat and only embers remain. Water from the morning's rain continues to gush down the chiseled, two-thousand-foot-tall cliffs. Orange tinted clouds sprint overhead, seeming in a hurry to get from west to east before darkness obscures the way.

Occasionally, one dips too low, catching its soft belly on the unyielding granite of the mile-high summit. Churning billows of mist liberated from the site of injury envelop the peak, sending ragged tendrils of white and gray dancing along the stark line of the Knife Edge toward Pamola Peak. That summit, the eastern anchor on the main escarpment of Maine's highest mountain, is the domain of Pamola, the evil spirit of the night wind of Abenaki legend that lies in wait in a cave near the top. Thirty feet tall, with the wings of an eagle, head of a moose, and body of a man, Pamola is not to be taken lightly. Anyone trespassing on his lofty realm, the legend warns, will be killed or eaten, and not necessarily in that order.

In light of the considerable physical effort required to get to the top of Katahdin, the possibility of incapacitating injury, and the fact that weather conditions can change in mere minutes—it snows on the mountain in every month of the year—it was wise of the Abenaki to craft a deity to serve as a deterrent to idle exploration of a landscape ill suited as a place to find shelter or sustenance. Even the broad and treeless Tableland, the abode of alpine flowers, rare butterflies, curious crows, and the occasional wandering moose, is devoid of anything an indigenous culture might prize.

The most popular artist's rendering of Pamola, which is used on the cover of the book *Chimney Pond Tales*, a collection of stories told by legendary Katahdin guide and trailblazer Leroy Dudley, was done by the famous Maine artist Maurice "Jake" Day. In it, Pamola looks kind of friendly and cuddly, which is no surprise, as Day was the man who convinced Walt Disney that Bambi should be a white-tailed deer, not a mule deer. Day's photographs of the Katahdin area formed the core of research for Bambi and inspired numerous scenes in the film.

In modern times, returning unscathed from a trip to the top of Katahdin is by no means guaranteed. Hikers coming off the Hunt or Abol Trails, on the south side of the mountain, seem like understudies for the figures in that famous Revolutionary War painting *The Spirit of '76*. Nearly every one suffers from something, be it blisters, bruises, cuts and scrapes, sunburn, or worn-out, rubbery legs.

Most modern trekkers have no fear of invoking Pamola's wrath while tackling Katahdin, although many veteran climbers offer a tip of the hat to this fearsome spirit just to be safe. People are still devoured by this mountain. Some disappear for days—a few are never found. The forces of their doom, however, are likely more mundane than supernatural—poor judgment, unforgiving weather, adverse terrain, and just plain bad luck.

Standing on the north shore of Chimney Pond, surrounded by towering cliffs, the entire tableau repeated in the perfect mirror of the crystal clear water, you are hard in the mountain's embrace. It is without question one of the most magnificent views in New England, made all the better by the fact you can't drive a Winnebago to it. You have to earn it, and it doesn't come cheap. Prerequisites include a resilient spirit, sturdy boots, and, according to park rules, plenty of water and a flashlight. The fee to enter Katahdin's realm?—sweat, sore muscles, and inconvenienced knees.

Baxter State Park's magnificent glacial cirques, such as the Great North and South Basins and the remote and mysterious Klondike, trackless forests, sparkling lakes, and rugged mountains, including the patriarch Katahdin, have inspired adventurers, writers, and artists such as Henry David Thoreau and Frederic Church for centuries. They continue to do so to this day, thanks to the unique amalgam of philanthropy and legislation and to the dedication of the rangers and staff who hold an almost religious reverence for their mission to keep the park "Forever Wild."

It is definitely a place you visit on its terms, not yours. Forget that, even for just a moment, and there's a very good chance Pamola will set you straight.

The Moose River Camping Club started an annual pilgrimage to this Maine deeper in some twenty years earlier, after a decade or so of exploring the White Mountains in New Hampshire. It was the era of the rise of the Young Urban Professionals, that burgeoning class of postcollege urban folk known as yuppies. Flush with career success and cash, their fondness for in-your-face material manifestations of upward mobility had yet to be tempered by the hindsight of joblessness and recession.

The Whites, while beautiful, we realized, had become a habitualized landscape, a narrative grown stale—not unlike the deadpan of a tour guide bored to distraction after repeating the same tired spiel over and over far too many times. It was no longer about a place where people from all walks of life meet and share a love of nature on its terms. It was now all about how you did it.

The trailhead parking lots were crammed with Volvos, Saabs, and Beamers with nary a rusty pickup truck or dented minivan among them. Inner-city Boy Scouts in camo pants and Wal-Mart T-shirts were shunned as interlopers on the trails, greeted with one eyebrow raised by upper-middle-class families where even four-year-olds sported matching Patagonia jackets fresh off the rack at Expensive Mountain Stuff—EMS for short.

Nothing epitomizes that trend more than the atmosphere in the Appalachian Mountain Club's venerable high hut system. It allows hikers to traverse the peaks of the Presidential Range without need of a tent or extensive provisions. Guests, by reservation only unless you're an AT thru-hiker, get supper, breakfast, and the overnight rights to a mattress and two wool blankets. Bring your own sheets.

It's tight quarters in the bunk rooms, and thanks to snoring strangers, anyone who forgets to bring earplugs is guaranteed to have plenty of time to read or contemplate the next day's itinerary. Yet the high mountain locations—several are above tree line— offer spectacular views and the freedom from having to hump fifty pounds of backpack over the highest peaks in the East.

The logistical effort to keep the huts supplied is impressive, often relying on helicopters, although much of the food is hauled in on backboards a hundred pounds at a time by the extraordinarily fit Ivy Leaguers who double as cooks and waitstaff.

At dinnertime in the huts, casual conversations among guests about the day's adventures gradually became overshadowed by staff lectures on mountain ecology and leaving no trace. We are a captive audience too ripe for indoctrination for the system's high priests back at 5 Joy Street in Boston to ignore.

I'm a firm believer in Leave No Trace and think anyone who goes into the wilds should follow those precepts religiously. Likewise, moving through a natural landscape without knowledge of its intricacies and the interconnectedness of its parts is like tightrope walking blindfolded. For knowledge to be retained, a student must absorb it with a receptive heart. Why not have a separate session or interpretive display that allows hikers to seek out the information rather than force-feeding it to tired guests held hostage by their supper?

The final straw came one night at Lake of the Clouds Hut on Mount Washington. We'd sat through the blanket-folding ditty, the admonition not to waste water, the pitch to join the Appalachian Mountain Club, and the resident eco-commissar's speech on never straying from the trail in the alpine zone to avoid trampling the delicate blooms of *diapensia* or Lapland rosebay.

A year earlier, at Zealand Falls Hut we'd endured the exact same litany. Only there they added an explanation of why the lights in the common room are shut off at 9:00 p.m. We're told it's to save energy. However, when we try to use our own lantern to play cribbage after lights out, we're admonished to shut it off, because it is "against the rules." Meanwhile, in the brightly lit kitchen, the "Croo" is blasting music from their boom box and having a little party. Apparently, that's a lot easier to do if the pesky guests have shuttled off to the bunk rooms.

After the requisite proselytizing back at Lake of the Clouds, it's finally time to eat. A bright-eyed and energetic young staffer approaches the table and announces, "Good evening, I'm Tavis. I'll be your server tonight."

Considering there's just one entree on the menu and it's served family style on platters passed down the rows of long, wood tables, that salutation seems especially pretentious. "That's it," Carl mutters a short time later as he pushes some soggy arugula around his plate with a fork. "I'm done with the Whites. They're all Yupped out."

Katahdin by contrast has always been a blue-collar mountain. True to the dream of its founder, the late Governor Percival Baxter, it offers nature without compromise—minimalist accommodation devoid of affectation.

At Chimney Pond there are just nine log lean-tos scattered about on the uneven ground at the bottom of the cirque. The bunkhouse at the time—it has since been replaced with a newer one much farther back in the woods—sat at the edge of a rough, boulder-strewn clearing that also doubles as a helicopter landing zone in emergencies.

The building itself consists of a central common room with the main door, two small windows facing south, a long wood picnic table, a woodstove, and a web of nylon lines on the ceiling for hanging out damp clothing.

Off to each side are narrow bedrooms with six bare plywood bunks each in two stacks of three. The setup is a powerful inspiration to not be the last member of a party staying in the bunkhouse to make it up the four-mile trail from Roaring Brook.

Stragglers by default get stuck with top bunks that sit barely twenty inches below the plywood ceiling. In summer, the heat and humidity puddles there, just one Jimmy Buffet song and an umbrella drink away from a low-budget tropical vacation.

In colder weather, the eye-smarting output of the woodstove, intermingled with the funky effluvia from wet polypropylene long johns hanging in the main room, leaves one yearning for dibs on the near freezing bottom bunks just inches off the perpetually wet floor. To compensate for that, those stuck in the bunkhouse equivalent of steerage get veto power over whether it's okay to light the woodstove.

The primary recommendation of the old bunkhouse over the new, which is totally surrounded by trees, is that you can see the entire mountain from the wide wooden step that serves as a de facto front porch. Sitting on that perch as the light fades, I can feel the temperature dropping; an incoming high-pressure area brings with it the promise of a cold, clear night. The hustle and sounds of the hundreds of day hikers that had passed through earlier are gone, replaced by the hiss of butane stoves and the quiet voices of our disadvantaged comrades in nearby lean-tos wrapping up camp chores before calling it a day. A few struggle to get their stuff sacks of food onto the mandatory bear bag line, while others shuffle in down booties, flip-flops, or Crocs past the glare of the gaslight coming from the window of the ranger cabin and down the rock-strewn trail toward the edge of the pond. Cue the resident moose and newborn calf grazing in the tall grass on the far shore.

No one has seen Bob Canavan for the last hour or so. "He said he was going for a walk," someone says from one of the dark bunkrooms.

"Which direction?" I ask.

"I dunno," comes the response.

"Was he wearing a jacket or carrying a headlamp?" I inquire. "Nope," someone replies. "He did take his trekking poles."

Wandering off is nothing new for Bob. A man of calm demeanor whose personal vocabulary doesn't include the word "hurry," he has a deep curiosity about everything and everyone.

With a shock of white hair and perpetually tanned face, he looks every bit the rugged outdoorsman.

Bob loves getting out into the woods. Whether it's by backpack or canoe makes no difference. He loves the view from high places and is perfectly content to sit by a rushing rapid for hours, expensive cigar and cold beer in hand.

MRCC trips are a real escape from his job with a giant pharmaceutical company and a fleeting sabbatical, we suspect, from the woman he consistently introduces to everyone he meets as "my first wife," much to her chagrin.

Bob never complains about it, and we know he loves her dearly, but we all suspect she's a little jealous of his passion for outdoor adventure. It eventually gets to the point that we start mixing up the dates for our annual trips so that she can't predict when they might be. Otherwise, Bob will inevitably discover the "traditional" weekend already has been mysteriously scheduled for an overnight visit with his in-laws in New Jersey or an emergency trip to shop for new draperies for the guest room.

Once off his 9-to-5 leash, it's not unusual for Bob to set out on a trail on his own just to see where it goes. Unfortunately, keeping track of time is not one of his strong suits. Asking "Where's Bob?" once or twice on a trip is nothing new. However, with nightfall drawing close and the temperature dropping, I'm not excited about having no clue of where to look for him should he fail to return.

⸺

Three trails radiate out from Chimney Pond. They soon split, increasing the number of routes to eight. Though well marked and brushed, they all pass through near impassable terrain where taking a few steps to either side can leave you seriously lost.

Rangers in Baxter conduct about a dozen searches and rescues each year. People have been struck and killed by lightning on Pamola Peak and fallen to their death on the Knife Edge. Several technical climbers have died in the park over the years, although the most frequent causes of death appear to be heart attacks or drowning.

For all the potential dangers, rangers admit Katahdin is a forgiving mountain. Considering the number of people who climb it who are unprepared or ill equipped, it's amazing more don't get into trouble.

The most remarkable story of survival is that of little Donn Fendler, a twelve-year-old Boy Scout from Rye, New York, who went missing while descending the summit of Katahdin on July 17, 1939. His story was carried by all the major media outlets at that time and later popularized in the book *Lost on a Mountain in Maine*. It remains in print to this day.

As many as six hundred people, including Great Northern Paper company workers and National Guardsmen, searched for Fendler for more than a week. They found nothing. At one point, rangers lowered another boy with a flashlight down a crevice on a mountain slope well above tree line "by his heels," after detecting a foul odor emanating from the hole. Nothing.

As the search dragged on, the Associated Press reported that volunteers had been directed to look for sightings of crows, "as they likely would lead searchers to the boy's body."

Nine days after he disappeared, a naked, bleeding, and barefoot Fendler stumbled out of the woods some thirty-five miles to the north and east from where he had been last seen. He was covered with bug bites. He had lost sixteen pounds. He reportedly told the woman who first saw him when he wandered into Lunksoos Camps on the East Branch of the Penobscot that he firmly believed that had he laid down to sleep just one more time, it would have been his last.

One of the more tragic fatalities happened while the MRCC was spending four days at Chimney Pond in June of 1995.

Jeff Rubin, fifty-three, of Newton, Massachusetts, and a companion started on the trail to the top of 4,143-foot-tall North Brother Mountain, west of Katahdin, about 7:00 a.m. on Saturday, June 3. It rained steady the entire time. By all descriptions Rubin was an experienced and fit hiker, and his goal was one of the toughest hiking challenges—to summit the one hundred highest peaks in New England. He had already bagged ninety-nine.

The two men reached the top around 10:00 a.m. Tired, soaked, and cold, his companion wisely elected to return to the trailhead.

Through breaks in the dense fog, Rubin, who had climbed North Brother previously, could probably see the summit of his hundredth and final prize, Fort Mountain, tantalizingly close to the north. It lay barely a mile away, reachable, he hoped, via an unmapped, unmarked, and unmaintained track. Rubin told his companion when they parted that he would meet him back at the car. He expected to be about two hours making the round-trip traverse.

Hours later when he did not show up, Rubin's companion, who did not have keys to the car, hitchhiked back to the campsite. Rubin was reported missing that evening. Searchers combing the trails found his backpack, containing food, a cellular phone, and some climbing protection gear, propped against a post back on the top of North Brother.

A helicopter crew spotted Rubin's red rain jacket once the weather cleared Sunday morning. It was far down in the bottom of the trail-less valley known as the Klondike. A crew member lowered from the helicopter discovered his body about seventy feet away.

Officially, the cause of death was listed as drowning. According to the park superintendent at the time, Buzz Caverly, Rubin apparently slipped on an algae-covered rock in Wassataquoik Stream and fell, landing facedown, stunned, in comparatively shallow water.

In examining the cause of catastrophes such as airplane crashes, investigators try to piece together a critical path, the sometimes linear series of often minor miscues that together conspire to bring down even the safest airliner. They follow, in effect, the modern version of the old saw, "For the want of a nail, a shoe was lost. For the want of a shoe, a horse was lost, for the want of a horse, a rider was lost, for the want of a rider a battle was lost. . . ."

Stressing that no one will ever know for sure, Caverly said rangers theorize that Rubin, who reportedly suffered dizzy spells and loss of consciousness while hiking before, never made it all the way across to his final Xanadu. Leaving the pack and its survival supplies behind may have been done to make it easier to push his way through the krummholz, the thick, twisted masses of stunted spruce and fir that cover such high mountain slopes. Or it could have been a sign that he was suffering from the first stages of hypothermia, characterized by unclear thinking and confusion.

From his bruises, rangers believe Rubin slipped and fell frequently. He was severely scraped and cut by the gnarled vegetation as he descended in the rain and fog and growing darkness down "near vertical terrain," Caverly said. Getting to a relatively flat spot and realizing his predicament, he spread his red raincoat over a bush, perhaps to signal the air searchers he knew would eventually come.

Some fifty years earlier, much farther down that same stream, young Donn Fendler, remembering his Boy Scout training, followed the life-giving waters back to civilization.

In reviewing Rubin's critical path, some deviation from accepted tenets of wilderness travel that may at first glance appear to be minor and manageable, emerge. Most are probably things Rubin, or for that matter, hundreds of experienced outdoors people, myself included, have done casually from time to time before.

Many times, he had to have hiked in the rain or lost the marked trail, yet suffered little harm. He had probably even been able to bounce back from being mildly hypothermic on previous excursions.

From time to time, he may have split up from a companion with both getting back without mishap. Maybe he had bushwhacked without gear, and like all hikers, he had undoubtedly survived numerous spills on slippery rocks. In the battle of man against mountain, Rubin won ninety-nine times. But on that day, all of the above took a tragic toll.

And then there is the mysterious case of a man who left Chimney Pond to summit Katahdin on a bright and sunny day in 1974. He vanished without trace.

Augustus Aldrich, of Weathersfield, Vermont, a spry eighty-six and an experienced hiker, set out around 7:30 a.m. to climb via Hamlin Ridge. It's one of the longest routes, but it avoids precipitous sections of the Cathedral and Saddle Trails that require the use of hands to make progress.

When he failed to return that night, a search was launched.

A tracking dog followed his scent past the well-marked junction where the trail up Hamlin begins, to an area known as Blueberry Knoll. The hardscrabble nubble with a 360-degree unobstructed view sits at the mouth of the Great North Basin a little less than a mile from the campground as the crow flies. More than fifty rangers, game wardens, and volunteers spent a week looking for him to no avail.

It had always puzzled me how that area could just swallow someone up. As cold as it sounds, after a certain time, you'd think, as those looking for Donn Fendler suggested, the circling crows would eventually provide a clue.

In an ironic twist, Aldrich was not the only person to die on the mountain that July. His nephew, Hollister Kent, died of an apparent heart attack on the trail to Chimney Pond to assist in the search for his uncle. Earlier, in February, Thomas Ketty died while winter climbing on Pamola Peak.

It was the park's deadliest year with the exception of 1944, when six airmen and a passenger died in the crash of a C-54 transport plane. Investigators believe poor visibility and inaccurate navigation resulted in the plane flying at full cruising speed into the side of Fort Mountain, a stone's throw from where Jeff Rubin would lose his way, and his life, some fifty years later.

<hr />

The answer to how someone could just disappear comes to me on my third trip to Chimney Pond while making a short bushwhack to the back side of an obscure body of water called Cathedral Pond. I want to take a photograph from the same angle well-known Maine photographer J.C. Bicknell had used on an old black-and-white postcard some seventy-five years before. My goal is only about a hundred yards off the Cathedral Trail, where the terrain comprises large, moss-covered boulders with a formidable thicket of small spruce, fir, and cedar trees. Each is only several inches in diameter, but they're far older than trees twice their size on more generous earth.

Wearing shorts is my first mistake, as the ragged fingers of long dead branches scrape and cut the skin on my legs. Joyous mosquitoes and blackflies enjoy an open bar as I huff and sweat my way through the damp shadows of this softwood jungle for almost half an hour.

At one point, I slide on my backside down the forty-five-degree slope from the top of a boulder the size of a box truck. My feet stop on the next big boulder over. My butt rests at the bottom edge of the bigger rock on what turns out to be an overhang. Looking down, I realize I'm astride a three-foot-high gap that opens to a broad cavern underneath. The brightness of the sunlight above makes it impossible to discern its form.

Just then, my friend Alan, who is much shorter, shoots past me as he slides down the boulder.

With a long, untrimmed beard, furrowed face of dark complexion, and the hard-edged ears of a man twice his age, Alan looks every part the character from a Tolstoy novel, especially when he's wearing his ubiquitous shopworn leather cabbie hat. Of slender constitution, he possesses both inner and physical strength in excess of outward appearances.

A carpenter and cabinetmaker by trade, Alan lives in an urban homestead of his own creation, complete with organic gardens, chickens, and a three-legged dog, in the middle of downtown Bar Harbor. Along with the compact home he extensively renovated, he designed and built an enormous Victorian-style post and beam barn to house his workshop and to protect his many projects from the elements. In testimony to his ingenuity and skill, he managed to raise the barn's forty-foot-long laminated main beam into position twenty feet off the ground without a crane using only levers, pipe staging, and the occasional assistance of a neighbor.

In the barn's dusty recesses can be found, among the skeletons of other projects and experiments, several full-size trebuchets, model airplanes, antique motors, a three-year supply of firewood, and a beautifully crafted Rangeley boat that Alan built after lofting the plans himself from some original drawings.

He's just as likely to blurt out a quote from Aristotle as he is to hold forth for an hour on the artist Alphonse Mucha's influence on the art nouveau movement. And if he asks you if you want to play a quick game of chess, he means that literally. Be prepared to lose and lose fast.

But best of all, he too is a devotee of the late, great inventor Nikola Tesla, whose seminal work laid the groundwork for the world's alternating current electrical grid, x-rays, radio, neon lights, and more, and whose experiments in wireless transmission of electrical power are still not fully understood.

All of this, of course, is made all the more remarkable by the fact that much of it was done after Alan was declared legally blind.

A degenerative condition has slowly eroded away his retinas over his adult life, leaving him with no more than a small percentage of clear vision in one eye. True to form, he believes it has made him a better cabinetmaker, as he now has to fit pieces together as much by feel as by sight. Apprentices, however, assist when it comes time to operate dangerous machinery, such as the band saw.

Over the years, Alan and I have backpacked hundreds of miles in Baxter State Park and on the Appalachian Trail in Maine. Before his eyes got too bad, he would have someone drop him off in the 100-Mile Wilderness for solo trips lasting ten days to two weeks. Trekking poles, of course, became a necessity as his eyesight deteriorated, although he developed a unique hiking style. He just forges ahead and instantly adjusts to whatever surface or elevation his feet encounter, be it rock, root, or slippery log. It works perfectly on solid footing, no matter how uneven. The only pitfalls are mud holes, with Alan often getting one or two steps into the deep goo before realizing it. His ever-present gaiters, though, keep the mud and water out of his boots. His agility allows him to make rapid adjustments and detour away from the problem.

Flat light in morning or evening provides the best situation for Alan to navigate in the woods. On a bright sunny day, the changing patterns of sunlight and shadow, especially if it's windy, are a particular challenge.

Those are the exact conditions we're dealing with while trying to make our way around the back of Cathedral Pond.

As he slides past me, Alan heads straight for the widest part of the gap. Instinctively, I reach out and grab him by the scruff of his daypack, arresting his momentum just before he drops over the edge.

The look on his face and flurry of expletives leaves no doubt he is surprised by what I have done. I quietly suggest he look down between his leather boots now dangling over the chasm. The push of cool damp air rising from the hole, as much as the darkness of the void, tells the tale.

Fishing a headlamp from my pack, we peer into the abyss. Interlocking boulders, left in ill repose by centuries of avalanches and rockslides, form a shaft about fifteen feet across. At the bottom, nearly twenty feet down, is a floor of ice with pointed rocks protruding Gibraltar-like from the surface. Water dripping from dangling roots creates low stalagmites.

Anyone falling into this pit would be lucky not to survive the impact. There would be little hope of climbing back out while perfectly healthy, much less mortally injured. Unless someone knows precisely where to look, the odds of being rescued before succumbing to injuries or hypothermia are zero. The sound-deadening properties of this jumble of perpetually damp stone with its cap of rudimentary soil and stunted vegetation guarantee that even the loudest calls for help would never carry far.

Ice and cold temperatures in such places linger below ground year-round, portending that in the event of calamity, even scavenging crows may fail to detect anything of interest.

"That was close," Alan says as we continue, taking great care to test every footfall for firmness before stepping ahead. I get the shot, and we carefully work our way back to the marked trail. Like soldiers retracing their steps across a minefield, we try to duplicate our original route as closely as possible.

From the base of the cliffs to the bottom of the basins, the flanks of Baxter's mountain are a geological sieve. Ponds appear and disappear literally overnight depending on what the ice is doing far underground. A thin layer of branches, forest duff, and moss—perfect booby traps for an unsuspecting leg—conceal uncountable openings.

Visitors are welcome to explore any part of Baxter they wish. However, when rangers warn casual hikers to stay on the trail, they are wise to follow that advice.

❦

Calling everyone together around the picnic table in the common room, Carl and I explain that we're worried about Bob. Carl feels especially responsible, being the unofficial cat herder for MRCC's Connecticut contingent. If anything serious happens, he's the one who will have to return home and explain to their loved ones.

Carl's organizational skills and his innate confidence, born in his hard-fought success while working his way up in corporate finance without a college degree, are always a comfort. He sometimes can be impatient with those he views as time sucks and energy vampires. He does not suffer fools gladly. But he is always looking for an angle, and he is an expert at distilling down the fundamental dynamics of any situation. He applies universal lessons from art, science, religion, or economics to whatever problems confront him. Worrying about Bob, he knows, does no good. It's time to do something about it.

The plan is to cover five trails—the Saddle, the Cathedral (to the base of the first difficult pitch), as well as Hamlin Ridge and Blueberry Knoll, and the Dudley Trail to tree line. Each searcher will go no more than a mile and then come straight back. If we don't find Bob, the next step will be to notify the resident ranger, Greg Hamer.

Hamer is a thick-legged fireplug of a man with a perpetually nonplussed demeanor. He hikes so fast he can carry a half-gallon of ice cream from Roaring Brook to Chimney Pond and get there before it has a chance to completely melt. He once set off alone from Chimney with a chainsaw, climbing up and over the windswept Tableland and down to the lean-to at Davis Pond, the remotest campsite in Maine, clearing blowdowns as he went. It is a distance of approximately ten miles with nearly a mile of total elevation gain. The trail is rough, rocky, and muddy, and there were places still harboring patches of snow.

Hamer was gone for only seven hours. Most backpackers take two days to do that same trip.

A wellspring of stories and tall tales from years in the woods, he routinely checks on all campers in the evening, making sure everyone is back safe. Over the years as our friendship developed, he timed his rounds to arrive at the bunkhouse right around dinnertime. He knows we bring plenty of food to share. He insists it's just a coincidence that he happens to have a fork in his shirt pocket.

We're always honored to have him join us and regale us with tales of hapless greenhorns and the human and natural history of Katahdin.

The mood in the cabin is quiet as we gear up to look for Bob. Boots are laced on feet protesting that they thought they were done for the day hours ago. Gaiters are buckled, daypacks stuffed with warm jackets, and bug dope liberally applied. As we gather outside for a final word, I spot a familiar shape in the dusk lumbering up the path from the pond.

I elbow Carl. He looks up and sees it too. It's Bob.

"Where the hell have you been?" Carl shouts.

"I went over to the far side of the pond to get a better look at the moose and calf," Bob replies. "Man, there isn't any trail. It's some rough back there."

"Next time please let someone know where you're going, for chrissake," Carl says.

"Yeah, yeah, I know," replies Bob as everyone laughs. All are happy he's back safe and believe he's learned his lesson and will never do it again—until next time.

———

As the bright band of the Milky Way takes its rightful place in the sky overheard, the bunkhouse windows glow with the light of a lantern hanging from the web of lines above the long wood table. The sounds of a game of cribbage carry through the open windows and across the boulder-strewn field to mingle with the nonstop salutations of white-throated sparrows. At this altitude they sing throughout the night, not wanting to waste a single minute of an all-too-short summer in the push to find a mate.

Pulling a fleece cap down over my ears, I sit on the porch and watch as an incandescent moon rises over Index Rock to begin its slow arc along the Knife Edge toward the summit. Ghostly voices from water falling off the cliffs mingle with the rustle of newborn poplar leaves. In unseen currents, the cold night airs descend the headwall's slopes and call themselves to order on the floor of the basin.

For another night at least, Pamola will have to find something else for supper.

COLEMAN MAGIC

SLEET AND SNOW STING MY FACE AS WE PADDLE EAST ON THE West Branch of the Penobscot River two hours downstream from the put-in at Roll Dam. Cursing the deteriorating weather, I'm beginning to question the wisdom of scheduling these trips for Columbus Day weekend when cruel winds surrender the last color of autumn to looming November's browns and gray.

We've just passed the muddy banks of Northeast Carry and the river has yet to hook around to the north. Usually on the West Branch, the current allows you to make good headway with minimal paddling, at least several miles per hour. The damn headwind has slowed our pace to a crawl.

The original plan was to paddle downriver under the Golden Road Bridge at Hannibal's Crossing and push on to camp two at Big Island. After that it was on to the Boom House site all the way down in Chesuncook Lake. It's what comes after that I'm the most worried about.

Chesuncook, Maine's third largest lake, trends from the southeast to northwest. In total, it's twenty-two miles long and up to four miles wide with few islands in between.

That makes it a difficult paddle in all but the most ideal weather. When the wind and rain howl out of the southeast, the waves have an unobstructed fourteen-mile run by the time they get to the village, just around the point from Boom House. Likewise, when the weather clears and the wind switches around to come out of the nor'west, breakers build in the opposite direction. Four-foot-tall waves with whitecaps are not uncommon.

Today's weather forecast calls for clearing from west to east, but the scud clouds coming in fast from the wrong direction hint that Mother Nature has other plans. It's obvious that the low-pressure system that rattled our tents last night and was supposed to move out to sea and over Nova Scotia has retrograded—spinning back to take another swipe at Maine. Like a line of mindless infantry marching headlong toward formidable fortifications during the Civil War, the befuddled storm is slamming itself headlong into the hard, frigid air elbowing its way down from Canada with no thought to the consequences. There's a term for anyone caught out in such a brew—collateral damage.

A mile ahead on river right is the confluence with Lobster Stream, the last chance to abort the trip on the West Branch. To continue means having to spend today and tomorrow on the river, and then, if and when the weather allows, paddle the length of the lake to Old Dam, where the skeleton of an old log crib dam sits just under the surface, drowned forever when the gates of the much higher Ripogenus Dam were closed in 1916. My biggest fear is that even if we fight our way to Boom House, we'll be pinned there for two or three days because of high winds. Once there, there's no easy way to walk out. Until recently, you could not get anywhere near the place in a motor vehicle. Evacuation by floatplane isn't an option. It's impossible to call in an air strike when you're forty miles north of the last place that has even a hint of cell phone reception.

We can stretch our food rations for an extra day or so, but I have a low degree of confidence that the cigars and Canadian

Club will last. Mutiny in the face of such deprivation is always a possibility.

The decision needs to be made before we pass Lobster Stream. After that, the swift current of the West Branch will make upstream travel without a motor almost impossible. The theoretical point of no return is just ahead.

Rafting up the six canoes to hold a conference, I see in everyone's eyes that no one is having fun. Cheeks are red and raw from windburn and sleet. A thin layer of icy snow is beginning to accumulate on fleece hats, shoulders, and gear in the canoes.

As cold, outstretched hands reach out for the Ziploc bag of Oreos my brother Carl is passing around, I explain my concerns. No one wants to just end the trip at the launch ramp at Lobster Stream landing after less than half a day in the boats.

I suggest changing the itinerary by heading up the stream to Lobster Lake and hunkering down at one of the fine campsites there for two days. On Sunday, it will then be a short paddle back to the landing where we positioned a vehicle for just such an eventuality. Theoretically, the wind on the way out will be at our backs.

To get there, we'll have to cross the big bay of the lake, steering hard into the still freshening wind. But that isn't anything we haven't done before.

There isn't much discussion. The "ayes" have it. Lobster Lake it is.

Depending on how much water is being released from Seboomook Dam upstream on the West Branch, the current in Lobster Stream can move in either direction. In lower water, the flow runs north out the lake. During higher flows, it reverses, raising the lake level. Either way, the stream itself is a relatively short, easy paddle through wild and rugged country.

As we get closer to the lake, the stream curves through a wide marsh of low grass with nothing to arrest the wind. The outlet is in the northwest corner of the lake where today the waves will be at their highest. At least, in theory, they should gradually diminish in height and intensity the farther down the lake we go.

Kneeling to keep our centers of gravity as low as possible, there's nothing left to do but put our heads down and paddle hard. I can't wait for the calmer waters in the lee of Ogden Point still more than a mile out across the gray churning lake.

By the time we're a hundred yards out into the bay, two-foot whitecaps quarter in from off the port bow. About every six or eight waves, a big one comes through. Almost instinctually, we stop paddling as it arrives, go into a brace, and with its departure resume our course.

It's always a struggle in such heavy conditions to keep the canoe from getting spun sideways, increasing the risk of a broach. The irony is that just when you want to make some speed to spend as little time as possible exposed to the elements, you have to devote most of your energy and power just to keeping the boat on course, upright, and into the wind. Intensifying gusts make for excruciatingly slow going. Snowflakes sizzle as they hit the dark surface of the lake, pausing there for an exquisite moment before yielding to the collective.

Even with warm paddling gloves, my soaking wet hands are beginning to cramp. I yell to the others to stay in a rough formation. I don't want canoes spread out all over the lake, especially if one goes over.

Almost inexorably, the far shore draws closer, the tallest pines becoming more distinct in the mist and fog. There are just three things to focus on at times like these: a dry tent, a cozy sleeping bag, and the warmth of a good campfire.

Who can resist the hypnotic, primordial attraction of a crackling fire?

Who among us has not been captivated by the brilliant, swirling maelstrom of flame, overflowing with elemental sentience. Seductive, malevolent, sometimes near white at the core, the fire's shimmering orange caverns pulse with the power of the sun's very core.

Faces to the flames, we are at once too hot on the front and too cold on the back. Especially on cold evenings, our bodies become the transient demarcation between the fire's searing, life-giving energy and the dark, foreboding, frigid space beyond orbiting the warmth like forlorn Mercury.

In some circles, a campfire is called cowboy TV. On a cold night, I'm a big fan of watching all Prometheus Channel, all the time.

Mastering the art of building a campfire is a quintessential skill for any who deign to call themselves outdoorsmen or -women. Growing up, I read Jack London's short story "To Build a Fire" about a man rapidly freezing to death in the Yukon, who, while struggling to light a fire, finds himself down to his last match. I swore right then and there never to find myself in a position of not being able to kindle a fire at any place or any time.

That's the explanation people get when they sometimes ask why I always carry a lighter in my pocket even though I don't smoke cigarettes. It's the same idiosyncrasy that prompted me to rush out and buy a hunting bow and razor-point arrows after watching the movie *Deliverance* for the first time.

The Boy Scout motto is "Be Prepared." Exactly. You just never know when you'll find yourself lost above the Arctic Circle in desperate need of warmth. Likewise, if I ever stumble across Ned

Beatty lost in the woods in his underwear along some forlorn river, I won't be caught unawares.

In scouts, fire building skills are honed by racing against others to see who can be first to get a quart of water boiling with only one match, using only materials collected from the forest. Sometimes the race is against a time limit—ten minutes max.

It's much more difficult than it seems. You can't just push two damp birch logs together and hold a match at one end and expect a roaring bonfire. There's an art to it, even though, in practical application, success comes down to simple science.

The basics require a graduated stack of burnable materials starting with the smallest diameter and working your way up. If you think about it, the head of a match can create a flame that will ignite a piece of wood roughly the diameter of the match. The rule of thumb is that you can't get a big stick to burn with just one small stick. Hold a match against the side of a 2x4 and you'll be lucky if it does anything more than make a smudge.

However, lots of smaller sticks on fire will do the trick. If you ball up the dried remains of dead fir branches, a match will set that alight quite easily. Better yet, look for some material that contains pitch or resin that burns extra hot. Bark from a white birch tree fits the bill perfectly.

Again, don't hold the match on the edge of a thick piece and expect success. Tear off small, thin strips—and only from pieces on the ground, never from a live tree—and layer them.

Above this tinder, place a generous grid of small sticks, working from smallest to largest. I usually add up to finger-size wood before I try to light it. It's also important to have more wood on standby, as the first pile will disappear quickly. If you fail to feed it properly, the fire will sputter out before you can return with more.

Slowly add larger-diameter wood as the fire grows.

The key is to pay attention to airflow. Oxygen needs to get in down low, and heat and smoke need to rise and exit on top. That creates a draft that keeps the embers glowing and the flames on top strong.

Other than dousing it with a bucket of water, the fastest way to put a fire out is to just dump a load of big wet wood on top of it without adequate spacing for airflow.

Any type of dry wood—softwood, such as spruce or pine, or hardwood, such as beech, maple, or oak—will be fine to get the fire going.

Hardwoods will burn down to make a great bed of hot coals. That's especially important if you plan to cook over the fire. Flames are only good for one thing—turning any and all combustible material into ashes. That goes for wood, or your supper.

Dead standing hardwood trees from two to four inches in diameter or branches and tops that have broken off but not laid directly in contact with the ground are the best sources of dry wood. Sometimes you have to walk quite a ways to find good wood, but the effort is nearly always worth it.

White birch, prized for its bark, is one of the worst kinds of firewood, especially if it has been on the ground. The grain of the bark runs perpendicular to the grain of the wood. That wraps it all very tight, meaning it dries very poorly unless it's split long ahead of time. It's ironic, considering the flammability of the bark, but most white birch logs rot quite quickly. The hollow tubes of bark they leave behind are irresistible to Boy Scouts, who inevitably spend an inordinate amount of time exploring a campfire's entertainment potential. Standing straight up in the fire, birch bark chimneys spew impressive columns of billowing gray smoke and flame.

While campfires are a quintessential part of camping in the Maine woods, they're also a lot of work. You don't have to necessarily have one every night. And it goes without saying, you should never start one during times of high fire danger, in an unauthorized area, or without first clearing a wide circle of all combustibles and creating a proper stone fire ring. Using an existing ring helps to avoid multiple scars on the land.

As the unfortunate fellow in London's "To Build a Fire" discovers way too late, don't build a fire directly under a tree branch pregnant with a thick coating of snow.

When it comes to gathering campfire wood, the more the better. A sharp bow saw and trusty hatchet speed the process.

Especially in cold weather, my rule of thumb is to collect as much as you think you could possibly need—then double it. As my camping companions will attest on more than one occasion, I have admonished them with the call for "Mooooore wooooood."

Creating a generous woodpile accomplishes several things. It means you'll enjoy the fire as long into the night as you want. And more than likely, there'll be some wood left over for morning so you can get a smudge going quickly without having to stumble through the woods, brushing spiderwebs off your face, looking for more. That's especially useful in places where the easy-to-find firewood is gone early in the season.

Having plenty also allows you to leave a stash behind. I always assume the next person to stop along the river or hold up at a lean-to on the Appalachian Trail on a cold, wet day will be in desperate need of warmth. Having everything there for them to get a fire going in minutes is not only neighborly; it just might one day save someone's life.

Jack London, no doubt, would approve.

Sometimes, however, conditions dictate abandonment of a traditionalist approach to kindling a fire. Desperate times do, in fact, call for desperate measures.

Dragging the canoes up the gravel and crushed stone beach on Ogden Point, our predicament is far from ideal. A few of the guys are shivering. That could be the early stages of hypothermia, although for some of them, other symptoms such as confusion and a general lack of cognitive acuity are well within the norm.

Just back beyond the first row of trees, the existing fire ring is drenched, its charcoal long grown cold, the entire site abandoned by campers smart enough to leave before it began to snow. Everyone fans out looking for firewood, but everything is soaked, and the pickings that late in the year are slim. There is little or no tinder. I'm beginning to feel a little like the unnamed protagonist in "To Build a Fire."

While a tarp is rigged for a windbreak, we decide to get a fire going as quickly as possible. A foot-tall pile of medium-sized wood accumulates next to the established pit. The exercise required to find decent wood and drag it back helps take the edge off the cold.

The terms *fire ring* and *fire pit* are used interchangeably. Calling it a pit in this case is a bit of a misnomer, as it's actually raised about a foot above the surrounding terrain. Like the seven layers of ancient Troy, decades of occupation have resulted in successive layers of ashes. Charcoal and additional rocks have elevated it to its present prominence.

Using my river knife, I saw the top off a discarded beer can and fill it with some of the Coleman fuel (white gasoline) we use for the cookstoves and lanterns. This is carefully poured onto the overlapping layers of wood in the fire pit.

As you no doubt are already thinking, this is where good conscience dictates I advise you never to try at home what is going to happen next.

Familiar with the explosive nature of such a cocktail, everyone who knows better steps back. Standing about six feet away, I strike a wooden safety match on the side of the soggy cardboard box and fling it with some authority toward the fire ring. The trick is to time it so the tip will be at the maximum explosive fury as it touches down.

The first two fall short and fizzle in a puff of frustrated smoke on the wet ground. The third time is the charm.

Before the match even reaches its target, it broaches the invisible boundary where there is a sufficient mixture of fumes and oxygen for liftoff. A five-foot-tall mushroom cloud erupts, accompanied by a deeply satisfying, ground-shaking *whooooommmfp*. Like the pyroclastic flow from an angry volcano, flames race along the ground for three feet around the fire pit where fumes had settled. A collective cheer goes up as an instant roaring campfire draws everyone close to its promise. "It's like magic," one paddler remarks.

When weather, impending darkness, or whimsy dictate, the ritual that has come to be known as Coleman Magic continues to be summoned forth with great fanfare.

The lowest rank in scouting, of course, is called a Tenderfoot. It's an observable law of the universe that the smoke from a campfire will search out and blow right in the face of the youngest tenderfoot. It took a while for me to realize why. My first hypothesis merely filed it under the unsolved mysteries of nature.

The real reason is quite simple. After anyone has suffered in the downwind spot where the smoke tends to go, eyes and lungs burning hours afterward thanks to the acrid smoke, they know better. Experienced hands naturally gravitate toward the upwind point of the compass or least one of the flanks. That leaves only the campfire equivalent of a seat behind a roof support post in Fenway Park's right field. Naturally, it's filled by an unsuspecting tenderfoot.

Not wanting to be seen as a wimp, and hoping the wind will eventually shift and relieve them of this circumstance, they often resist the urge to flee, blinking rapidly and holding their breath in eye-smarting, smoky silence.

Sitting by the fire, entranced by the hiss of a damp log's stubborn surrender to Einstein's fundamental equation, spirals of sparks shooting high into the night sky, I've often pondered a direct, almost mystical connection with our most primitive ancestors. How fearsome and wondrous fire must have seemed to them. How vital such a force must have been to those for whom mere sticks and stones were implements of great power and advantage.

Myths surrounding how humankind came to possess fire transcend cultural boundaries. Best known, perhaps, is Prometheus, who steals fire and gives it to humanity, sparking the first tentative hallmarks of civilization. In Jewish tradition, Azazel and fallen angels give humans fire. Similar stories abound in Polynesian, Cherokee, Algonquin, Ojibwa, and First Nations lore.

The harnessing of fire was, for all intents and purposes, humankind's earliest energy technology. The ability to use and later actually kindle fire at will provided the capability to oppose the forces of nature, not merely suffer at its hand. It also led to that other great civilizing influence—cooking, which led to the creation of a thousand cable television shows, a million handy gadgets, not to mention the charcoal briquette and gas grill industries, which led directly to the recent fall from grace of Paula Deen, expert of everything Southern-fried.

Yet even before the ancient Greeks included it as one of the fundamental four elements of the universe (the others being earth, air, and water), fire, for all its promise, for all its magic, came with a cost. In this fundamental kindler of civilization also was sown the potential seeds of humanity's destruction.

Fire's progeny, all manner of modern technologies, have allowed us to surround ourselves with an ever-widening circle of light. As knowledge and our ability to shape and control our world expand, the edge of night, both physically and symbolically, is pushed further and farther back.

For primitive man, the devils in the shadows were more literal than figurative. Just outside the reach of the firelight lurked certain danger from cold, isolation, or predation.

By medieval times, those real threats were in full retreat, the demons taking on a more mythical stature. Science was dawning. The warmth of reason and logic, misplaced in the fall of Mediterranean empires, began to return. Yet in the woods just beyond where the flickering light of the castle's torches could not penetrate, trolls, dragons, dwarfs, and fairies still ruled the night.

As the earliest mariners first ventured beyond the horizon armed with compass and sextant, it was the suspected edge of the earth that became the line between the familiar and the unknown, where savage teeth, tentacles, and talons of sea monsters awaited.

By the turn of the twentieth century, fears of unknown beasts of supernatural origin faded. With the farthest reaches of the land explored and many ocean depths plumbed, the demons retreated again, this time taking ethereal form—specters lurking in abandoned houses and seldom-visited, cobwebbed basements and attics. The demons in the darkness found a home for a while during the dawn of the Atomic Age in popular culture's tales of towering nuclear or genetic mutants wreaking vengeance on a society that through ignorance and arrogance had spawned them.

Now, we possess even more awesome technology. Millions of artificial lights peel the darkness back from entire continents. At the same time, they pull a shade down on the night sky, weakening our connection to the stars, leaving our souls the poorer for it.

Computers have opened up the unexplored realms of cyberspace. New demons, we fear, await. They are "out there" on the flip side of computer screens, undetectable and untouchable denizens of the dark, uncharted back alleys of the information superhighway.

Above our planet, the Hubble Space Telescope squints back ten billion years to the farthest reaches of the cosmos. It peeks at galaxies that glimmered when our Milky Way was little more than a chaotic hydrogen fog. Humankind's firelight now flickers at the outer limits of the universe and shines backward in the throbbing hum of particle accelerators toward the beginning of time.

Naturally, that is where the monsters now lurk. "Out there," we say, with a nervous toss of the head skyward: UFOs, brain-sucking aliens, silent abductors, drooling reptiles with a thirst for human blood, or warlike cyborgs bent on enslaving entire planets. As always, however, the biggest evil remains in us.

Astronomer Neil deGrasse Tyson notes that there's a simple reason we worry that any aliens out there might invade or destroy us: that's what we would do if we were them.

Inevitably, by discovery or deduction, we will push the circle of firelight outward farther still. Where, I wonder, will the demons live then? Will they at last evaporate as humanity extinguishes the last flames of ignorance? Or will they forever thrive just outside the range of our understanding? Maybe, if for no other reason than deep down we need them to feel alive, to challenge us to act, to drive us forward.

———

At Lobster Lake, the snow and rain have retreated, although an unapologetic wind shows no signs of relenting.

The insolent fog won't be chased away until morning.

A hearty meal of ziti, meatballs, and marinara, attended by freshly grated Parmesan and accompanied by Chianti, has tempered the memories of the afternoon's arduous slog across the lake.

"Be sure to cover what's left of the woodpile so it'll be dry in the morning," I say to no one in particular as I turn the knob to extinguish the harsh white glare from the Coleman lantern. As the fire burns down, its receding glow illuminates the vacant faces of the few holdouts who have yet to seek the sanctuary of their sleeping bags. Mine awaits as well.

Out on the lake, loons are calling, a final family reunion after the storm's inconveniences. Tomorrow, they'll fly south, but not too far, to winter along the coast. Together all summer, the male and female will separate. The juveniles will be on their own as well until the day they, too, return north to breed.

Along the West Branch, the campsites on Big Island lie empty—the fog alone holds full authority. Devoid of light, the sodden forest stands unrealized and undefined. Not far away on Chesuncook, the waves continue to roll and build, relentless in a rush to rendezvous with a distant, unseen shore.

IN SEARCH OF DUDLEY'S CAVE

Anyone hoping to traverse the fabled Knife Edge trail atop mile-high Katahdin and then return to the campground at Chimney Pond without having to backtrack or dangle from a rope has Mark Leroy Dudley to thank.

Up until his death in the early 1940s, "Roy," as he was known, was the official protector of the mountain, guiding parties of sports to and from the nascent camping grounds at the water's edge, hard at the base of the Knife Edge's spectacular two-thousand-foot-tall headwall.

It's estimated that during his lifetime, Dudley climbed to the summit at least five hundred times and probably trekked above tree line on the Tableland, Pamola Peak, the Knife Edge, Hamlin Ridge, and the North peaks at least that many times again. In an era when most paths up the mountain were unclear, it was a remarkable accomplishment.

Until he blazed the path up Pamola Peak, now known as the Dudley Trail, the only way to include the Edge in a loop hike from the pond was to ascend via a near-vertical route up a steep couloir known simply as The Chimney. Now considered a technical climbing route, The Chimney Trail, which has several massive chock stones blocking easy progress, is no longer marked, maintained, or shown on maps.

In *Forest and Crag*, Guy and Laura Waterman's most excellent guide to the history of trails in New England, a 1920s listing of The Chimney Trail describes it as "a short sporting path to the summit, suitable for ladies, be they sufficiently enterprising."

While still requiring the use of hands in some places, Dudley's much less precipitous route gains nearly eighteen hundred feet of elevation on its run one and a quarter miles from Chimney Pond. At the top of Pamola, it intersects with the Helon Taylor Trail—named for the iconic Baxter State Park superintendent—which ascends Keep Ridge from the campground at Roaring Brook. Along the way, it passes a spectacular, triangle-shaped boulder the size of a small house. Known as Index Rock, its unusual position pointing skyward, coupled with its enormous size and the fact that it's not below any appreciable peak from which it could have become dislodged, raises legitimate questions on how it ended up there.

Its situation no doubt leaves ancient alien theorists salivating at how there is no way it could have ended up there naturally without the aid of advanced technology or "help from above."

Dudley was born in far eastern Maine, in the town of Wesley, a tiny outpost along the fabled "airline" route between Bangor and Calais. As a young man, he moved to Staceyville, east of the mountain, to work in the logging camps. Officials hoping to deter deer poachers later hired him as a game warden. His primary qualification for the job, according to one account, was that "it takes one to catch one."

Eventually, Dudley's knowledge of the wilds of the region resulted in him guiding parties up the mountain. He established a base camp at Chimney Pond, at first seeking shelter in a cave. Before construction of a ranger cabin on the site, he built and quartered his "sports" in a rough log lean-to known as Dudley's Den.

Dudley eventually found himself a "sufficiently enterprising" lady with which to share his passion. He and Abby, who eventually became a Maine Guide, were married at the summit in August 1927. According to historian John Neff in his book *Katahdin: An Historic Journey*, hiking parties a few days afterward reported finding copious amounts of rice at the summit. Sadly, the lovebirds would spend only eight years together. She died in 1935.

Dudley himself was a tall, lanky man who felt more comfortable in the vastness of wild places than he did in the parlors of polite society. Most photographs, including an iconic image of him reclining at the foot of the summit cairn on Monument (now Baxter) Peak, the highest point on Katahdin, show him wearing his trademark rumpled fedora, a curved stem pipe in hand. As was the fashion in the 1930s, he wore long pants with canvas knickers, suspenders, and a buttoned-down white shirt with collar. Having such portraits made at the time was considered a formal occasion, so it should be no surprise that in many posed photos, including those taken high above tree line on the mountain, he's also sporting a skinny black necktie.

A bronze plaque on a boulder at Chimney Pond, as permanent a memorial as one might construct, commemorates Dudley's contributions and cites his "genial philosophy, kindly ways, and droll tales."

Even though Dudley routinely guided scientists, adventurers, famous politicians, and even the park's founder, Governor Percival Baxter himself, it's those tall tales and stories for which he is best remembered. He's credited with popularizing the legends of Pamola, the fearsome Native American deity that supposedly guards the mountain. Many of those stories have been preserved in the book *Chimney Pond Tales*.

Just inside the cover is a fanciful illustration of Dudley sitting with Pamola high on the mountain. Maurice "Jake" Day of Damariscotta, an artist and illustrator for the Walt Disney Studios, drew it. Day and a group of friends known as Jake's Rangers frequented the park and Chimney Pond and befriended Dudley.

Best known for convincing Walt Disney to make Bambi a white-tailed deer instead of a mule deer, Day spent several months photographing in Baxter to develop scenes for the famous animated feature. In fact, two orphaned deer from Maine, christened Bambi and Faline, were shipped to California to assist the animators.

As is the nature of oral tradition, stories about the exploits of previous generations of pathfinders, such as Dudley, are eventually folded into the amalgam of legends shared among campers at Chimney Pond. Longtime ranger Greg Hamer often spoke of Dudley's dedication to helping people enjoy the park's beauty and how his predecessor's success in that regard often resulted in the place becoming too crowded for his tastes.

When the campground at Chimney Pond was very busy, Dudley and Abby would retreat to a cave on the far side of the pond where no marked path in or out facilitated casual visitation.

There are numerous caves in the vicinity of Chimney Pond. None are caverns in the traditional sense. Unlike the massive underground labyrinths formed by the steady dissolution of limestone by dripping water, Katahdin's underground consists primarily of modest-sized voids—slab or fissure caves created by clefts in the hard granite bedrock and boulders unceremoniously abandoned by the Laurentian Ice Shield's disorganized retreat.

Pamola reportedly resides in just such a cave on its namesake peak. The precise location continues to elude dispassionate inquiry. As the last rays of the setting sun fade from the peak in the evening, several dark shadows near the top suggest possible entrances. However, many are on precipitous cliffs too dangerous for casual exploration.

Near the base, a marked side trail off Dudley's path leads directly to an area of slab caves named for the mountain's most fearsome spirit. Within those north-facing recesses, traces of winter ice linger long into summer. The experience of entering them is akin to stepping into a house that has been closed all winter on the first warm day in spring. An unmistakable chill greets you first. Then, as your eyes struggle to adjust to the gloaming, you are enveloped by still, lifeless air through which, it seems, even sound has difficulty finding passage.

The main gallery of the caves is about thirty feet long and fifteen feet high with perfectly perpendicular sides approximately six feet apart. The impressive symmetry and flat precision of its walls are not unlike those of the grand gallery in the Pyramid of Khufu at Giza. That alone more than qualifies this spot for a mention in a future segment of the History Channel's TV show *In Search of Ancient Aliens*.

In contrast, the precise location of Dudley's pied-à-terre is not shown on any map.

Some members of the Moose River Camping Club began to wonder if tales of a cave frequented by the legendary trailblazer were even true. When pressed, Ranger Hamer insisted he had happened upon the place himself, quickly adding that it was a long time ago, and he didn't remember exactly where.

On excursions to Katahdin, our usual itinerary calls for spending four days and three nights at Chimney Pond. The first day is spent hiking in on feet full of confidence. The last day is for stumbling out. Two full days on the mountain provide sufficient flexibility for summit attempts when the best weather conditions allow.

The non-summit day is spent around camp. It allows for day trips to the numerous points of interest in the Great South and North Basins or to do volunteer work, such as helping build new lean-tos, stacking firewood, or brushing out trails.

On one trip, the threat of low pressure moving in from the west convinced us to summit on day two. Many in our party were able to tackle the Knife Edge and return via the Dudley Trail. The best evidence of this accomplishment could be found in the threadbare seat of hiking shorts nearly worn through from butt scooching down so many rough granite boulders.

The morning on day three dawns damp and gray, validating yesterday's executive decision. Clouds hang low over the mirrorlike surface of the pond. The sound of water from the previous night's rain cascading down the headwall provides the only confirmation of something immense looming behind a pervasive veil of fog.

What better day to look for a ghost?

The weather report posted on the porch of the ranger cabin indicates a chance of clearing in the afternoon, so the drizzle is not long for this world. An expedition of some sort to walk off the creaks and stiffness of the previous day's altitude is definitely in order.

My brother Carl has a suggestion. "I think we should search for Dudley's Cave," he says.

While some of the ten-member crew ensconced in the bunkhouse defer to savor the ultimate luxuries afforded by places where cell phones and the Internet can't reach—the chance to nap or just read a good book—four of us sign on for the jaunt to dark territory on the far side of Chimney Pond. The party consists of myself, Carl, friend Kurt from Connecticut, and Carl's son Ryan.

Kurt and I have been pals since we were boys, as our parents were constant companions. At one time, we planned to crew on a cruise ship as ship's photographers, theoretically allowing us to see the world on a budget. That seemed preferable to the other alternative—joining the Navy and potentially being shot at.

College eventually took him south and me north. The fickleness of life put the last stake through the heart of those globetrotting plans, although our friendship has never wavered.

Tall and gangly, a printer by trade, Kurt sports a build and disposition that leaves him just a skinny black necktie short of being a reincarnation of Leroy Dudley himself. On the other hand, a quick check of the EZ Pass in his car will reveal there is no major highway from Bangor to Washington, D.C., that Kurt has not traveled repeatedly. When it comes to surviving rush hour traffic in an urban heart of darkness, he is among the best of them.

During his years in the publishing industry, he has handled and transported original paintings and works of art by all the grand masters alive and dead. He is just as at home in the halls of the Metropolitan Museum of Art in Manhattan as he is on the trails.

Kurt's long legs, veterans of decades of conquering the highest peaks in the White Mountains, are perfectly suited for navigation on Baxter's many trails that often are little more than slots between krummholz lined with knee-high boulders. While others must find a way up and over, or around, Kurt can merely step over most obstacles without breaking stride, resulting in a seemingly effortless transit of even the roughest ground. Like most of us, however, by the end of the day, his knees remind him of the need to dial back from a pace more suited to someone thirty years younger.

Kurt's near perpetual smile has managed to forestall the wrinkles that by all accounts should be on the face of anyone who has been his family's strength through illnesses, job losses, recession, and heartache. On first impression, his perpetually affable and ebullient nature might easily be mistaken as a touch of goofiness. But that would be a mistake. Within his chest beats a heart as big as Katahdin itself—from which radiates an endless supply of love for his wife, family, and friends, which few other men can hope to emulate.

On most MRCC backcountry trips, Kurt is the unofficial photographer. While others cut handles off toothbrushes and tags off tea bags to trim weight from their pack, he never hesitates to throw a full-size Nikon SLR, a mini tripod, and a couple extra lenses into his kit.

If by chance we do find evidence of Dudley's lost cave, Kurt, for sure, will be there to chronicle the discovery.

Carl's son Ryan, a former top-market rock-and-roll radio station personality who now works in the family auction business, goes into turbo diesel mode the moment his boots hit the trail. A few other hikers may be faster, but nobody else can notch more miles and more elevation and at the end of the day set their pack down in camp eager to do it all again.

A natural leader with a confidence born of superior intellect tempered by a compassionate soul, Ryan has one of the strongest senses of humanity I've ever encountered. It's almost as if Rudyard Kipling had him in mind when he wrote his iconic poem "If" about what it means to be a man. The poem opens, "If you can keep your head while all about you are losing theirs . . ."

If you ever find yourself on a ship that has just been torpedoed, Ryan is the man you want below decks leading the damage control parties.

The second verse of "If" is especially descriptive. "If you can dream—and not make dreams your master; If you can think—and not make thoughts your aim; If you can meet with Triumph and Disaster And treat those two impostors just the same; If you can bear to hear the truth you've spoken, Twisted by knaves to make a trap for fools, Or watch the things you gave your life to, broken, And stoop and build 'em up with worn-out tools . . ." Nothing fazes him.

To paraphrase a later passage, Ryan is indeed a man who walks with kings yet never loses the common touch.

Like most of us who got our start in the out-of-doors as Boy Scouts, Ryan is no rookie when it comes to understanding the philosophy behind successful wilderness travel. He's hiked extensive sections of the Appalachian Trail down south and adheres to go-light precepts that require that every piece of gear do double or triple duty. Whenever he returns from a backpacking excursion, he does a post-trip assessment of his gear. Anything that he didn't use, besides some first aid items or season-specific clothing, will never see the inside of his pack again.

The one exception to this minimalist approach is food. Rather than weigh out and preplan his meals, Ryan merely throws fistfuls of entrees into the stuff sack that will double as his bear bag. That is a luxury afforded only to the young, although decades from now his knees will no doubt remind him of the extravagance.

Into the sack go cans of Korean smoked scallops from the Dollar Store, boxes of Annie's Mac and Cheese, and packets of freeze-dried lasagna with meat sauce or beef stroganoff from Mountain House. Each foil envelope holds two servings, which all seasoned backpackers know is just about right for one hungry hiker.

Add to that beef jerky, gorp, PowerBars, a bottle of Tabasco, and multiple packages of what Ryan refers to as "God's gift to backpacking"—shelf-stable, precooked bacon. There is no adherence to tradition when it comes to what is eaten at any given time of day. Appetite alone determines when. Menu choice is mostly driven by happenstance—whatever gets pulled from the bag next.

On the trail, Ryan sees a meal not so much as a chance to refuel as it is a celebratory, near-religious experience. Needless to say, in the way of those who expend six thousand calories a day traipsing through the North Woods, he finds himself four, maybe five, times a day prostate before the altar of Our Lady of the Roaring Iso-butane Stove.

———

From the campground on the north side of Chimney Pond, the far shore appears to be a pleasant and welcoming place. In the alluvial fan created by the outwash of the stream that drains the headwall, there are several flat grassy areas where moose often can be spotted grazing with calves in the evening. The water itself is sharply crystalline and unquestionably cold. In June, when snowfields linger on the heights, much of it was literally frozen just hours before.

With a maximum depth of, at best, six feet, the pond is believed to freeze solid in winter.

Ranger Hamer likes to tell of a hiker who stopped at the Chimney Pond cabin one day, an aluminum tube holding a fly-fishing rod protruding from his daypack. He asked if fishing was permitted.

Ranger Hamer replied that it was.

The man then spent the morning casting from various points around the pond, trying all manner of flies and nymphs netting nary a nibble. As he was leaving, the fisherman, his ego perhaps bruised by the poor showing, stopped again at the ranger station. He offered that he didn't think there were any fish in Chimney Pond. With an air of classic understatement, Ranger Hamer replied, "There aren't."

"Well, why didn't you tell me that four hours ago?" the fisherman asked. "You asked me if you could fish, not if there were any fish," Ranger Hamer deadpanned.

"I asked him if he hadn't just spent a glorious morning in one of the prettiest places on earth doing something he absolutely loved,"

Ranger Hamer related later. "He said 'yes' and admitted it was kind of hard to be upset about that."

Getting around to what appears to be the land of milk and honey on the farside of Chimney Pond is no easy task. The long sloping talus fields on the east and west flanks end in the waters of the pond itself. The boulders are a jumble of sizes and orientations offering no obvious route over or around them. Thick stunted spruce and fir trees poke from any opening. Their dead twisted under-branches tug and tear at any skin or clothing the rough granite itself may have overlooked.

If Dudley had an obvious way to get there, it remains well hidden. Perhaps it waits to be discovered by a group of, as that early guidebook described, "sufficiently enterprising ladies."

We choose to work along the edges of the pond, which requires the skills of an acrobat to make progress. Attempting to do so without at some point getting our feet wet is futile. Whether by slipping on algae or merely having no other options but to wade, sooner or later, dry boots are only a memory. Had we understood that earlier, the first half of the trip would have gone much faster.

The edges of the meadow are sharply defined by the outwash routes of the stream that drains the cirque. Seen from above, the geography is not unlike a diagram of a tree. The multiple channels where it surrenders to the pond are like roots—the distinct main channel above the trunk. As you move higher up the valley, it diverges into multiple routes, each one splitting into smaller and smaller branches until every narrow cleft and ledge that might collect rain or snowmelt is reached.

One of the main branches served for years as the direct route to the base of the Chimney from which climbers could access Pamola Peak and the Knife Edge. The streambed is also used by technical climbers to access the base of the headwall on trips to challenge themselves on the mountain's traditional routes, including The Flatiron and the Armadillo.

The smooth, rounded stones of the streambed provide a wide, clear passage. Their pale bleached color sits in vivid contrast to the dark, sharp-edged granite blocks just a few feet away on either side.

For most of the summer months, there's only a modest amount of water in the stream. The forces required to create these massive cobbles, however, leave no question as to the enormous volume and violence of the flow on other occasions.

The plan is to head upstream looking for any obvious paths that may branch out to the left or right. We work our way nearly a half-mile up the stream with no success. As the sun begins to burn off the fog, we note an increase in the number of avalanches off the headwall onto the jumble of talus slopes below.

To the uninitiated, the rocks appear to be the spoils of some titanic quarry. And in a sense, they are. However, on Katahdin, the quarryman's only tools are the relentless cycles of freeze and thaw.

As massive and as solid as the mountain is, gravity and time are destroying it a bushel basket full of rocks at a time. Water freezes in cracks, expanding and working rocks loose. As the sun increases in intensity in spring, its warmth can melt the ice, which until the very end functions as a de facto adhesive holding the rock together. When a piece is finally liberated, it begins a long tumble and crash down the headwall, often persuading others to join it on its journey.

Hiking into Chimney Pond in spring, you're aware that you're getting close from the sound of repeated avalanches long before you can see the headwall through the trees. Most of these cascades of rocks are small to modest in size, although a few times a day, large ones have no trouble getting your attention.

You only have to look at the massive size of some of the boulders around the pond to realize what theoretically may be heading your way at any moment.

Unsure of the demarcation line between relative safety and the danger zone, we decide to head back. Instead of using the stream, we bushwhack west toward the cliffs that form the base of what is known as the Cathedrals. Maps show a distinct change in topography there, and we suspect it may be a good place to prospect for Dudley's Cave.

With the sun doing its level best to dry out the world soaked by last night's rain, the air in the thick woods is especially steamy. Little sunlight penetrates the canopy, and no breeze provides a vital first line of defense, so the mosquitoes are out in force.

Evolution crafted these kissing cousins to lobsters and crabs into elegantly simple vampires that hone in on a mammal's heat signature and the carbon dioxide in its breath. Invariably, they approach from downwind, tracking your emissions back to their reward.

The more you perspire and the harder you breathe, the easier it is for them to find you. Being overweight and seldom in fighting trim makes me the equivalent of an all-you-can-eat buffet.

Although mosquitoes can be bad in places, Maine and the other states in northern New England are more famous for blackflies. Unlike mosquitoes, which prefer brackish pools to breed, blackflies require clear, moving water. While mosquitoes pierce the dermis with a sharp proboscis, taking a ladylike sip, blackflies use serrated mandibles to rip a tiny gash, then lap up the blood that fills it.

The worst hatches are in the spring.

Ironically, the successful campaign through the 1960s and 1970s to clean up Maine's polluted rivers resulted in vastly increasing the blackfly population. The white-legged species around the Kennebec River at the Forks, where most white-water rafting companies are headquartered, seems especially abundant and voracious. They are the outlaw bikers of blackflies, diving fearlessly into the fray with little regard for the potential of injury or death. Funny how the rafting companies don't include photos of people swatting clouds of these bugs in any of their brochures.

Deerflies by comparison are the F-17 fighters of the insect world. They often attack in a single pass, approaching from behind, seeming to prefer the soft flesh of the back of the upper arm or right behind the knee. Those that miss their first target of opportunity invariably circle your head, becoming so irksome you want to just extend an undefended forearm so they can chow down and get it over with.

Moose flies, which are akin to horseflies on steroids, are the largest offenders. Their buzzing wings are the insect equivalent of the droning engines of a B-17 bomber. With two massive, green eyes, plump, tapered body, and front legs that cross like a carver rubbing his hands while contemplating the Thanksgiving turkey, they are the least attractive members of the North Woods' most repugnant fraternity.

Slower than a deerfly, a moose fly is comparatively large, which makes it difficult for it to land without detection. Watching it preparing to drill for blood is fascinating, as it must first reposition its legs, not unlike a fire engine extending hydraulic braces before deploying the aerial ladder. That instinctual choreography provides ample time to bring its miserable existence to an abrupt end with a well-timed swat.

But be forewarned, moose flies are well armored. You must approach the task at hand with enthusiasm, as it often requires more than a single blow.

Although males and females exist in roughly equal proportions for all the aforementioned annoyances, it's only the ladies that bite—to provide the nourishment needed to guarantee that their eggs make it to adulthood. Their saliva, which contains compounds to prevent the blood from clotting while they dine, produces the itch and swelling of a bite.

When it comes to avoiding that itch and swelling, I firmly believe in living better through chemistry. Popular wisdom holds that Avon's Skin So Soft bath oil can repel blackflies, but only if you can put enough on so the little buggers get mired in it and die of starvation before they can escape.

I love hiking with friends who swear by natural repellents, as it gives me a fighting chance. I see them repeatedly slathering on their eau de citronella, Egyptian lavender, or similar hippy capitalist concoction, in the hopes that sheer volume alone will make up for the fact that it just doesn't work.

When pressed, those preaching the gospel of going au naturel will share that what they're using helps "a little bit." That suggests to me that if you choose a repellent based on political correctness rather than proven performance, all you're really getting is a high-priced placebo effect.

Meanwhile, the best defense is just to stay upwind of me.

Ben's Backyard Formula with 30 percent DEET seems the most effective, although at a concentration of 100 percent, this solvent is capable of melting plastic. One friend swears by those green mosquito coils that burn, emitting a noxious smoke that appears equally effective at repelling other humans as are folk remedies such as eating copious amounts of garlic.

There's probably no repellent, or bug dope, as it is known in the Maine woods, that's not bad for you over the long term. I've always suspected that one whiff of the smoke from those coils equals smoking an entire pack of unfiltered cigarettes.

Before DEET, folks north of the Canadian National Railroad line in Maine swore by a concoction called Ole Time Woodsman, a pine-tar-based formula guaranteed to stain anything and everything. Created in 1910 when anything good for you had to be black, icky, and make your eyes water, it had the added distinction of being nearly impossible to wash off skin or clothing without the aid of leaded gasoline. Of course, that resulted in it being marketed as "long lasting."

Lately, along with packing a small spray bottle of DEET, I've become a big fan of a device called a Thermacell. It uses a small cylinder of butane to heat a pad that releases permethrin into the air, creating a bug-free zone about fifteen feet in diameter. Many companies now offer clothing and gaiters pretreated with permethrin that are especially effective at convincing ticks to abandon ship before they begin to embed in your skin. I figure I have at least another decade or so of using it before some researcher discovers that at concentrations several thousand percent above the recommended amount it "may" cause cancer in laboratory mice.

Granted, anything that kills other living things is undoubtedly bad for you and the environment. But when it comes to avoiding mosquitoes, biting flies, ticks, and the diseases they can carry, this is war.

While spray-on repellents may keep bugs from biting, they don't stop them from buzzing. After you've involuntarily inhaled one through a nostril or swallowed a few just by virtue of the incredible swarm around your face, you'll never hike without a head net in your pack again.

Folks often ask what the allure is of wilderness camping in cold weather. The primary reason is the lack of bugs. All the repellents and all the head nets in the world just can't compete with a good hard frost.

———

Fanning out in the hopes of increasing our chances of finding Dudley's encampment, we soon lose sight of each other as we work our way back toward the pond through thick woods. We retain voice contact with occasional shouts. Carl is working the base of the cliffs while Kurt anchors the opposite end of the line within sight of the stream. Ryan and I work the middle.

"Hey guys, I think I found something!" Carl yells.

Thrashing through the underbrush, we follow the sound of his voice to the base of a thirty-foot-tall cliff. The rock here is undercut, creating an overhang about twenty feet wide, reaching back almost twelve feet. There's height enough inside to stand up. For the most part, it's remarkably dry, despite the previous night's heavy rain.

In the event of wind-driven precipitation from an unfavorable direction, it would be easy enough to close the opening with a tarp.

In front of the cave is a narrow, elevated area running perfectly perpendicular to the cliff. The soil under the leaves and fallen spruce needles there is crumbly and black, riddled with fragments of charcoal like any backwoods fire pit that has been in use over a very long time. It's obvious that many of the stones had been piled up in a deliberate manner to make a hearth. The heat of a campfire, like the echoes of our voices, would reflect off the back wall of the cave, making it downright toasty on chilly days. At night, cold air sinking off the spires of the Cathedral Trail above would create a downdraft that would naturally push any smoke in the opposite direction away from this sanctuary.

Scratching around in the leaves and duff with his trekking pole, Carl discovers the first artifact, the remains of a blue, enameled coffeepot, the lid long gone, its bottom rusted out. Next, we spy a dented tin cook pot.

Elsewhere about the site, there are numerous rusty food cans and a beer bottle or two. The latter appear to be no more than a decade or two old. We surmise that squatters who unceremoniously visited long after Dudley's departure must have left them.

The pile of trash is quite deep with an obvious vintage pedigree. Back in the day, there was no thought about principles such as carry it in, carry it out. Lodges, campsites, and other spots habituated by humans all had their own garbage dumps. As Arlo Guthrie sings in "Alice's Restaurant," the attitude was that one big pile of garbage was better than a lot of little piles.

It's clear that the spot is the perfect natural shelter on a mountain where welcoming places to bed down and escape the weather are few and far between. Agreeing that this must be it, we pause to pay respects to the spirit of the pathfinder.

What curiosity and drive it took to discover this spot in a time when few traipsed these wilds and fewer still strayed from the one marked trail more than a quarter mile away. The minimal yet effective improvements to its situation to make it even more suitable for habitation are similarly impressive.

As the strengthening sun's rays penetrate the dark canopy, glowing shafts stream through the humid air, ending in islands of light that dance and weave across the damp detritus. Ears struggle to comprehend words in the voices of the rustling poplar leaves and tumbling water of the distant stream.

Surely this place is the province of ghosts.

"Leave everything just where we found it," I say as we turn to leave.

Although there's no rule against what we've done, it's hard not feel like somehow we're guilty of trespassing. Still, it's impossible to shake the awe that comes from uncovering a tangible connection to the life of a legend who, prior to that moment, had existed for us only in the pages of books and myths shared around a campfire.

Those who devote sufficient time to exploring Maine's North Woods know that feeling well. The artifacts of times long forgotten are everywhere, hidden away along the riverbanks and cast aside in forgotten mountain valleys.

Some of these touchstones are well documented, such as the massive rusting steam locomotives on the portage between Chamberlain and Eagle Lakes on the storied Allagash Wilderness Waterway. Others are more forlorn, empty cellar holes along the abandoned sections of the Old Canada Road through the Kennebec Valley or the idled farm equipment in former fields reverting to forest at New City, near what geographers have determined is the remotest spot in Maine, in the middle of Baxter State Park.

For an attentive eye, the subtle signs of those who have passed through the wilds of Maine are everywhere. They can be found in something as simple as the grade of a long-abandoned road or an arrowhead liberated from a sandy stream bank in the spring. And sometimes they're as obvious as a stone chimney still standing in the middle of nowhere or a rugged iron eyebolt drilled into granite to anchor booms of logs on a river drive.

Nature's gradual erasure of those insults demonstrates just how temporary and ephemeral life and the works of humankind actually are. Bearing witness to this process is a powerful foil to any arrogant flirtation any of us may have with notions of immortality. When we tread these paths, we walk in the footsteps of others, seen and unseen. And one day, too, others will walk in ours, and wonder.

As much as the majesty of mountains and grandeur of the forests, it's the enterprise of all those who have lived, loved, worked, and died in these places that gives energy to the spirit of the Great North Woods. It's in the magic of the natural landscape, seasoned with the catalyst of cultural history, that the true power of such places is born.

On a large boulder at Katahdin Stream on the south side of the mountain, a modest bronze plaque memorializes the words of Governor Baxter, who single-handedly purchased land over several decades to create the park that bears his name.

It states: "The works of man [and one would hope, nowadays, 'sufficiently enterprising ladies'] are short-lived. Monuments decay, buildings crumble and wealth vanishes, but Katahdin in its massive grandeur will forever remain the mountain of the people of Maine."

Governor Baxter died on June 12, 1969. Long after that plaque has corroded away, the mountain, indeed the entire park, will still defend his memory.

Leroy Dudley died on February 14, 1942. The man who made hundreds of climbs to the top of Maine's highest mountain with nary a spill slipped and fell under the wheels of a moving logging truck on an icy road while heading out to check his line of fur traps.

Dudley has a granite monument—two in fact. One is that memorial at the campground at Chimney Pond. The other, a polished piece of brick-red granite similar to the distinctive bedrock on the summit of Katahdin, marks his plot in a Staceyville Cemetery. Originally, only a simple white wood cross marked his grave. Jane Thomas, one of the authors of *Chimney Pond Tales*, who listened to Dudley tell stories as a child, purchased it in the 1990s with proceeds from sales of the book.

The headstone bears his name, his dates, and an etched profile of the mountain he loved so much. Beneath the image are the words "Katahdin Storyteller."

As long as Katahdin is there, the legend of Leroy Dudley will live on. It will beat in the hearts of those who hike the trail that bears his name. It will linger in the oral legends of his exploits and in "droll tales" preserved in the pages of a book that shares the spark of a remarkable life with succeeding generations. And, unbeknownst to most, his passion for the mountain's wilds will dance like mist on the Knife Edge, in ephemeral images of an animated baby deer romping through a deep Disney forest that looks all so familiar.

And for those whose curiosity invites them to stray off the beaten path to an unmarked cave on the far side of Chimney Pond, he lives on in shafts of sunlight dancing on the forest floor and in the echoes of voices some seven decades gone, whisked away on a chill evening downdraft from Cathedrals of stone high above.

THE WELLSPRING OF TELOS

LOADING UP THE CANOES ON THE GRASSY BANK OF THE EAST Branch of the Penobscot in front of the Matagamon Campground store, I don't like the looks of the river. The gates of the dam on Grand Lake Matagamon, just upstream, are puking water—roaring, wide open, surrendering the lucre it so jealously cloistered all summer, discarding the surplus in the ritual of the annual autumn drawdown. *Matagamon* is Abenaki for "far on the other side." It's definitely on the short list for places in New England that qualify to be considered the back of beyond.

The water is high, technically in flood, coursing knee-deep among the trees and alders along the banks. Pounding rain over the previous three days has filled the entire watershed full to overflowing.

We're off on a three-day, thirty-mile trip down to the take-out point at Whetstone Falls. The excitement of running a river none of us has ever been on before is tempered by the knowledge that there are three unrunnable waterfalls, including one thirty-foot mini Niagara waiting between us and where we'll camp tonight.

While the Columbus Day foliage is just peaking on the coast, here it's well past prime. Trees laid bare to await winter's further insults add to the sense of foreboding.

Passing squalls are spitting snow. The stiffness of my fingers, even with neoprene gloves, betrays that the temperature is steadily dropping. It already has taken two hours longer than it should have to break camp and get ready to get on the river. We need to get rolling. Otherwise, we'll be overtaken by darkness on the other end.

This is paddling in big water, in big country, at a time of year when it's unlikely that there will be anyone else around to help in an emergency.

By all measures, it is going to be a wild ride.

"Nobody gets in a boat unless you're wearing a wet suit," I yell as I finish cinching down the gear in my canoe. "And no sitting on the life jackets. Put 'em on."

One by one, six canoes slip into the river. It's a ragtag fugitive fleet—a couple of patched Old Town Trippers, two newer Discoveries, a cracked and duct-taped fiberglass White, and a square-stern Grumman aluminum canoe affectionately dubbed the "K-whopper" due to its resemblance to the legendary brand of Kenworth tractor-trailers.

The first paddlers who put in are idling impatiently in a small eddy along the opposite shore. My brother-in-law Douglas and I are the last down the muddy slot in the bank that serves as a launch ramp. We'll bring up the rear in the sweeper position, theoretically ready to assist any of the others if they flip or encounter problems.

As we drift south on the swift, roiling current, the northernmost mountains of Baxter State Park loom to the west. Below the clouds lie Bald and Billfish, the latter named for the attractive pond of the same name at its feet. In his book on Maine mountain names, author Steve Pinkham notes that fishing on the pond is quite poor. He explains that the peak was probably named for pioneering lumberman William Fish, meaning today's literation perpetuates at least two typographical errors: one the missing space between the words, the other a lack of capitalization of a proper noun.

Obscured by the mists are the solemn, treeless volcanic rhyolite stumps of the highest peaks in Maine north of Katahdin—the seldom-visited Travelers, both North and South. If Greta Garbo had really wanted "to be let alone," up there she'd have had her wish.

Little did I realize that this view would be the last idyllic distraction before we had to give 100 percent of our attention just to making it down this river.

While distances between campsites on the East Branch may seem modest, there are other factors that must be taken into account when estimating how far you can expect to travel in a day. As the *Appalachian River Guide Maine* advises, "This is a river for masochistic portageurs."

The intention is to head downstream ten miles or so, we hope, as far as Grand Pitch, the highest falls on the river.

First, we need to make it past the aptly named Stair Falls, and then portage twice, once around Haskell Rock Pitch, a sharp series of two-foot ledge drops with a sprinkling of meddlesome boulders, including a twenty-foot pillar of conglomerate in the middle of the river. It's what geologists call an erosion remnant, an obstinate if not vaguely obscene Joseph Merrick–like protuberance laying bare the nature of the bedrock along that stretch of river.

Like so many others in Maine, the name of this rapid is connected with a calamity that occurred in the nineteenth century—in this case, the drowning death of a river driver named Haskell.

The second chance to take our canoes and all the dunnage on a not-so-leisurely walk in the woods will be at the much more dangerous Pond Pitch—a straight, unrunnable tumble of ten feet.

From there, it's less than a mile to Grand Pitch, where we plan to camp.

Carabinered to the thwart directly in front of me is a throw bag, a sack of coiled rope that can easily be tossed to help retrieve someone from the water. There's another in the lead boat.

As they say in the military, no plan survives contact with the enemy. Both throw bags will get plenty of exercise before this day is through.

The challenges begin at Stair Falls, a series of eight distinct drops ranging from eight inches to two feet in height. In most situations, having a generous flow of water makes rapids easier to navigate. With liberal depth, there are fewer rocks to hit, less of a chance of grounding out. When it's too high, however, currents stronger by an order of magnitude offer no measure of forgiveness for even minor indiscretions in technique.

As we scout from the portage trail, we see no hint of the sneak route the guidebook suggests should be on river left. The swift flow today will tend to push any boat into the flooded forest on that side. The straightest shot appears to be hard to river right. As long as we keep the bows pointed downstream, we tell ourselves, we should be fine.

One by one, the teams dig their paddles in deep to get lined up for the first step. On each successive drop, bows plunge into the slower water ahead, the resulting splash showering the paddler in front. As the stern shudders and takes its turn, water pours in over the back a bucketful at a time.

With the remaining drops coming in quick succession, barely a canoe's length apart, there's no opportunity to bail out any water before slipping over the next step. The game apparently will be to get to the bottom of the falls before the canoe becomes a submarine.

Whoops of triumph signal that the first two boats have made it to the eddy pool below, although both have more than six inches of water on board. Watching them waddle to shore as the undesired burden sloshes back and forth inside provides an element of comic relief.

The next two teams meet the challenge as well, although the Crystal Jay, paddled by my brother Dale and his ten-year-old son Jason, looks more like a backwoods bathtub when they're done—nearly filled to the gunwales. Fortunately, all the gear in waterproof bags helps displace much of the water. Otherwise the canoe would be nearly impossible to handle with all the extra weight.

As those crews head to shore to bail, the canoe directly in front of us gets stuck between two barely submerged rocks. Paddled by Jeff Betts, a lumberyard worker, and Keith Nevin, a machinist, both of Meriden, Connecticut, the borrowed White has gotten itself into a precarious situation about halfway down the falls. She'll need more duct tape tonight for sure.

Betts is a veteran of our very first expedition on the Moose River—the MRCC equivalent of a fraternal legacy. A man of carefully manicured mustache, yet brimming with unbridled and ill-apprised suburban enthusiasm, he adheres to the belief that the size of a man's hunting knife signifies his level of prowess in the woods. The sixteen-inch, bone-handled blade hanging in a leather sheath on his belt dwarfs all others on this trip by at least two orders of magnitude.

Real woodsmen smirk at such ostentatious displays of over-endowed cutlery, knowing that even a small knife kept sharp enough to get the job done is eminently more useful. Jeff has no idea that his pride and joy leaves him just a hat adorned with reptile teeth and an annoying "G'day Mate" short of being a stunt double for Crocodile Dundee.

Nevin, by contrast, doesn't even carry a pocketknife. In a screenplay for a 1950s Western movie, his character would be listed as "dude," or "dandy."

A friend since high school, "Knave," as we called him back then, is a skilled tool and die man and part-time antique dealer with superior intelligence and extraordinary attention to detail. A man with no emotional red line, he moves through life at a constant rpm, always a mile or two an hour under the emotional speed limit. It's the perfect strategy for staying off official radar, whether it's the boss, the IRS, or a state police speed trap.

With shoulder-length hair and a recreational fondness for weed, he could easily be mistaken for a stereotypical slacker. But his exterior layer of "whatever" conceals an extraordinarily deep well of energy and ambition. No matter the situation, if the crap is about to hit the fan, he's the first guy who'll have your back.

Despite his impressive résumé as a friend, when it comes to the out-of-doors, Keith has a lot to learn. On the drive up, long after we'd left the village of Patten in the rearview mirror and been on dirt roads for thirty miles and hadn't seen a utility line, structure, or any other sign of human civilization for more than an hour, he got on the CB radio and asked the others in our convoy to "let me know when you see a cash machine."

The good news is that Betts's and Nevin's canoe, while hard aground, is still upright and pointed straight downstream. Its stern is high, so the force of the water will be an ally in getting it free.

The bad news is that the bow is fully awash with Keith, now basically sitting in the river.

Because Douglas and I are already committed to our run, there's no safe stopping to help. While the first canoe in line on a river trip gets to see the most wildlife, the last has the benefit of watching the mistakes of those ahead in the rapids and taking corrective action to avoid them. We back paddle and ease the canoe gently over the lip of each drop to slow our descent and reduce the amount of water coming in fore and aft. We're taking some water, but not as bad as the others who decided to do the entire, adrenaline-fueled run at ramming speed.

We make it to the bottom with only an inch or two of water on board.

Meanwhile, Nevin and Betts, accompanied by the butt-clenching crunch of brittle fiberglass on Devonian sandstone, manage to skid free and are near the end. As they plop over the last drop, they're upright, but the canoe is fully awash. Both sit in water from the belly down; only the tops of the dunnage protrude above the surface.

To celebrate their Pyrrhic victory, they stand, paddles held aloft in both hands over their heads, as if making the winning touchdown in a playoff game.

The shift in weight, predictably, forces the canoe even farther under water. The buoyant gear protests, straightening the metal clips on the bungee cords holding it in place. Like free divers breaking the surface for that first glorious gulp of air, the bright orange rubber river bags pop to the top, swirl a time or two, then bound off downstream like puppies gleeful at having wiggled free of their leashes.

After anchoring one end to a tree, I deploy the throw bag. With a smooth arcing toss it lands behind Nevin, the current sweeping it to him. As rehearsed, he grabs it and wraps it around one wrist. His other hand clutches the canoe as we swing the MRCC equivalent of the *Edmund Fitzgerald* ashore.

Betts manages to thrash to the riverbank on his own, emerging with one hand on his paddle for balance, the other checking to make sure the river has not absconded with his knife.

Fortunately, the wet suits have done their job. After the initial breath-stopping shock of immersion, a thin layer of water gets trapped between the neoprene and the skin, forming an insulating layer. Keeping it on until you make final camp for the day is a bit like wearing a soggy, full-body diaper. At least you'll stay warm—but.

A quick inventory shows that in addition to the disappearance of their personal gear, one of the large, communal nylon tarps used to create a dining fly in camp is missing, as is a watertight drywall bucket holding the ingredients for tonight's dinner—homemade beef stroganoff.

As the designated quartermaster and "cookee" on this expedition, my mind immediately focuses on the possible reallocation of remaining entrees. Nevin's distress, however, is more narrowly defined.

"My vodka's gone," he laments, apparently nonplussed that his missing river bag also contains most of his dry clothing and his sleeping bag.

Back on the river after bailing everything out, it isn't long before the paddlers in the lead boat spot a bright orange object stuck on a small rock outcrop midstream. It's Betts's river bag.

He and Nevin alter course to retrieve it. One found, one still MIA.

Still no trace of the tarp or meat bucket.

Just a hundred yards farther downstream, we pull over on river left at the unmarked portage trail around Haskell Rock Pitch. Time to get out and take all the gear for a walk. After several trips each back and forth over the trail, the boats are reloaded, and we're on the river again. Our relief from what is rapidly becoming more of a forced march than a river trip doesn't last long.

At Pond Pitch, what should be the day's shortest portage quickly becomes anything but routine. The normally placid Kimball Brook that cuts perpendicular across the trail is swollen and in flood. Instead of merely sloshing across in water up to our ankles, we confront a raging brown torrent, waist-deep and thirty feet wide.

The first team paddles across, trailing one of the throw ropes. Once on the opposite bank, they attach another stout line to the bow. We use this rig to pull all the dunnage and people across.

The anchorman left upstream is pulled across in the canoe on the final run. Then it's down past a lower set of rapids deemed this day too risky to run.

Carries two and three complete, it's time to reload and get moving to the next portage of the day at Pond Pitch.

— ❦ —

There were two routes to wealth in the Great North Woods in the early 1800s. Both in a sense are theoretically renewable resources—wood and water. One, businessmen quickly learned, was worthless without the other. You can own all the stumpage rights in the world, but you can't spend potential. It's worth no more than the piece of paper the deed is written on unless you can get those logs to market.

Like every major river system in Maine, the modern abundance of water available throughout most of the year on the East Branch is due to an extensive series of dams originally constructed to store the power needed to drive millions of board feet of logs south to mills on the spring flood. Lumberjacks spent the winter in the frozen north felling trees with axes and crosscut saws and piling logs on the banks of streams and atop frozen lakes, where river drivers could nudge them toward payday as soon as things thawed.

Once that was done, and the water supplies exhausted, it was off to Devil's Half Acre, a section of Bangor known for its whiskey and women, where lumberjacks and river drivers embraced the pursuit of personal vice with the same muscular intensity they applied to toppling the majestic old-growth pines that had stood untouched for centuries.

Whether it was out of a fundamental licentious nature or some unconscious expression of guilt for what they were doing to the land they loved so much, it was not uncommon for men to squander the year's pay, ending up penniless and hung over in just a month's time.

Back then, there were few roads in the far north. There were no rail lines. The primary way out, or in for that matter, was by river. Rudimentary maps of the time contained large swaths of "dark territory," although nearly every river and all the major lakes were accurately depicted.

Dams not controlled by those who owned the land, or who had rights to the timber, were effectively opportunities for legal extortion. Fees were collected on every log sent through the sluices on their way to the three hundred hungry mills lining the lower Penobscot at the head of tide between Bangor and Brewer.

From there, schooners, once described as being so numerous you could cross from one side of the river to the other without getting your feet wet, took the finished lumber to growing cities along the East Coast and around the world.

Prior to the early 1800s, the primary source of water in the East Branch of the Penobscot flowed from a series of modest-sized ponds, including Third Lake, Hudson Pond, and Webster Lake, several miles up Webster Stream from Matagamon. At that time, logs from the valuable pine forests just a few miles away around Chamberlain and Churchill Lakes were driven north, down the fabled Allagash River, the major tributary of the St. John, which serves as the border with Quebec for more than fifty miles before cutting south through New Brunswick and emptying into the Bay of Fundy.

The lumber barons of Bangor who owned the stumpage rights in that area bristled, however, at having to pay duty on those logs to the Canadians. It didn't take long before scouts looking to satisfy the insatiable appetite of mills in Bangor developed an ingenious plan to cut the Canadians out of the loop.

As Archimedes once said, "Give me a place to stand, and I'll move the world."

In 1834, forester Shepard Boody stood at the water's edge on a lake called Telos upstream of Chamberlain and realized it would be possible to make all the water in that part of the Allagash watershed flow backward—south instead of north. A little over fifty years after Lord Cornwallis's surrender to Washington at Yorktown brought an end to the Revolution, Boody made that determination without sophisticated surveying equipment, topographic maps, satellite photos, or the counsel of global positioning satellites. The only level he needed was observing the water itself.

He used his knowledge of the interconnectedness of the lakes and streams in the area to realize that by building a dam at the outlet of Churchill Lake, the water level would rise twenty feet, joining it with Chamberlain and Telos into one massive body of water.

The design was so simple, historian Fannie Mae Eckstrom explained, "Two men with a rifle, a spirit level, and a bean pole could have done all the engineering." The idea, however, was worth millions.

With creation of a short canal below another dam at the east end of Telos, all the water, all the wood, and by extension, all the wealth from nearly five hundred square miles of watershed could be directed to Webster Lake and down Webster Stream into the East Branch.

After leaving Grand Lake Matagamon, the East Branch— swelled by the reliability of the Seboeis River and the generosity of Wassataquoik Stream, which drains the northern peaks of Katahdin and Baxter State Park—eventually joins the West Branch at Medway. From there, it's a relatively straight shot down to Bangor.

"A History of Maine," written for the state's centennial in 1919, cites a mid-1800s source as stating "anyone who knows that country can see that the valleys of the Penobscot and of the upper Allegash [sic] are continuous, and that at some recent period, Chamberlain Lake must have burst out a new outlet at its side. Old lumbermen say that at very high water, there used to be a trickle overflowing from Telos to the Penobscot."

Geologists in later years would determine that the ravine between Telos and Webster, which became known as the Telos Cut, was once the river's original outlet until blocked by debris from the glacier's retreat some ten thousand years earlier. It was only after that southern avenue of escape was plugged that the water from the big lakes found an Achilles' heel in the land, cutting a new outlet to send their prodigious flow north.

For all his success at Telos, Boody had far less luck with subsequent North Woods mega engineering schemes. In 1856, he received a charter from the Maine Legislature to construct a turnpike to Katahdin, but it never got off the ground. He had a few years earlier bought a sawmill in Oxbow and built a timber transport road from the Aroostook River to Grand Lake Seboeis, which eventually drains into the East Branch, so he could continue to ship logs to Bangor, where they fetched a better price. He cleared a farm of some two hundred acres and was considered a model citizen. Unfortunately, he went bankrupt.

An early history of Aroostook County describes him with a good measure of charity as "an honest man, kind and generous to the poor, but unfortunate in businesses."

His days of backwoods adventuring over and career in the timber industry done, Boody lived out the rest of his life as an itinerant Methodist preacher directing his energies to changing the courses of souls instead of streams.

No memorial to him remains save a nondescript stream named for him in the far north of Baxter State Park. Its waters drain into Grand Lake Matagamon, and from there, the East Branch.

Telos comes from the Greek and means "end," or "purpose." For those headed upstream, it was just that, the end of the river system. But like so many things in life, looking at it from the opposite shore provides an entirely different perspective. For those headed downstream, it wasn't the end—it was the wellspring, the beginning, a place of possibilities, a place from which all other things— success, fortune, and fame—flow.

For the lumber barons of old Bangor, it would be the means to the only end in which they had any interest—making more money. With some of the pines in the Telos area described, undoubtedly with some hyperbole, as being six to seven feet in diameter, money was literally growing on trees.

In a century when wilderness was something to be subjugated and tamed, not protected and preserved, there was no Department of Environmental Protection, no required permits, and no regulatory or conservation hoops to jump through. If you owned land, it was yours to do with as you desired. So what if you want to change the course of rivers, inundate hundreds of acres of shoreline, and foul the waters with mud, debris, and dead trees. Good for you.

Enterprise, not respect for what the Abenaki called Nigawes Ta, or Mother Earth, was the virtue most highly prized.

The job of building the first dam at the outlet of Chamberlain Lake fell to Major Hasting Strickland in 1841 after he and Amos Roberts of Bangor purchased tens of thousands of acres of land in the area from the state. Their grand plan included building a second dam at the east end of Telos, it being remarkable in the fact that it was constructed completely on dry land about five hundred feet away from the natural edge of the lake in anticipation of the rise in water level.

When the gates on the new dam on Churchill were closed, water quickly flooded the surrounding woods. The impact could still be seen more than fifteen years later.

Henry David Thoreau, who visited Chamberlain Lake on his third trip to the woods of Maine in 1857, described the desolation. He wrote: "A belt of dead trees stood all around the lake, some far out in the water, with others prostrate behind them, and they made the shore, for the most part, almost inaccessible. This is the effect of the dam at the outlet. Thus, the natural sandy or rocky shore, with its green fringe, was concealed and destroyed."

Thoreau, who described loggers of the time as "ten thousand vermin gnawing at the base of her [Nature's] noblest trees," added, "They have thus dammed all the larger lakes, raising their broad surfaces many feet, thus turning the forces of Nature against herself, that they might float their spoils out of the country."

While much is made about the creation of "The Telos Canal," in fact, very little digging was required. A five-hundred-foot-long channel about fifteen feet wide was created between the existing lake and the new dam. Below the dam, all the trees were "grubbed out" in an area fifty feet wide in the mile to Webster Lake. Only minimal digging, all done by hand with picks and shovels, was needed to direct the anticipated flow of water.

The 1919 history states, "When the gates were raised in the spring of 1842, the water went surging down the hillside and tore everything before it, filling Webster Lake with mud and debris for twenty-five rods [more than four hundred feet] from the shore. It is not a 'canal' in any sense, but a 'cut,' a wild mountain torrent."

That first year, more than two and a half million board feet of pine rode that wild mountain torrent all the way to Bangor. Eventually, a toll of twenty cents per thousand board feet was imposed.

Potential had at last been turned into profit.

⁓

The torrent of water pouring over Pond Pitch is such that the bedrock around it literally trembles. Billows of mist reach far back into the woods along the shore. A microscopic dew condenses back into raindrops on spruce boughs and the tips of the few remaining birch leaves. After a brief taste of freedom, they surrender, bowing to the inevitability of gravity, repentant after their holiday and ready to rejoin the hydrological cycle.

Lugging all the gear and the boats around the second half of Pond Pitch on what has become our third portage of the day prompts a realization that should have been apparent hours earlier at Matagamon. We've brought way too much stuff.

Our canoes are filled to overflowing with every backwoods luxury from collapsible camp chairs to a cooler filled solely with crushed ice for evening cocktails. We're Hannibal's army hell-bent on sacking Rome by sneaking across the Alps with all our household goods in tow. We, however, don't have elephants to do all the heavy lifting.

"This is getting wicked old," says Dave Murdy, another MRCC legacy, as he makes his third trip carrying unwieldy cargo over the rough and unforgiving trail.

If there are several pieces of gear waiting to be portaged, Davy is the kind of guy who always shoulders the heaviest one. Then it's off down the trail on long, confident strides in the high-top blonde leather work boots that appear to be the only pair of shoes he owns.

When the stares of others in the party of twelve go blank when a single check lands on the restaurant table after dessert, Davy is the first one to reach over and pick it up. There is no agonizing over who had shrimp cocktail or ice cream with their blueberry pie. He looks it over, takes out his wallet, and lays down twice his share.

Decades of running his family's construction company, which is small enough that everyone gets their hands dirty, has strengthened his physique. Years of dealing with the emotional dunnage of family and running a business have chipped away at his youth, yet he remains unbowed. The brightness of the baby blue eyes that helped make him so irresistible to the ladies in his bachelor days remains undimmed.

The biggest challenge Davy has on these trips is trying to pronounce Native American place-names. It starts the minute he crosses Maine's border with New Hampshire. The Interstate 95 bridge connecting Portsmouth with Kittery crosses the Piscataqua (pronounced pis-CAT-ah-qwa) River. I was speaking with him via cell phone as they were heading up the previous day and asked him where they were. "We're just crossing over the, ah Pis, ah catack, um, that big-ass bridge," he explained. His distinct Connecticut accent, a lugubrious plagiarization of Tony Soprano seasoned with a hint of Boston Brahmin, makes it all the more amusing.

"What's the name of it again?" I asked deliberately, baiting him. "You know, the ah, um . . . , ah . . . , that pissing taco bridge!" he spits out.

The only things Davy has no patience for are bullies and bullcrap. On a mutual friend's wedding day, Davy, wearing a suit and tie accessorized by his best pair of work boots, was among the enthusiastic attendees talking with other attendees and family awaiting the start of the ceremony. The entire sanctuary overflowed with excitement as dozens of people exchanged hugs and hearty handshakes.

Suddenly, a deep, disembodied voice of one of the priests came over the PA system in an attempt to impose some decorum. "It is customary before the sacrament of marriage here at St. Stan's for the guests to refrain from idle conversation," the unseen scold announced.

The entire crowd fell silent as people looked at each other in disbelief. Davy, of course, put it all in perspective. "Okay everybody, you just heard that direct order from God," he said in a loud, authoritative tone. "So shut the hell up."

The resulting outburst of laughter and smattering of applause left no doubt what folks thought as they resumed their interactions until the organist played the first notes of the introit and everyone dutifully sat down and shut up.

When Davy drinks, he drinks. When Davy laughs, he laughs. When he works, he works. When he extends his hand to you in friendship, you have one for life.

Human nature being what it is, the heaviest, most cumbersome piece of gear has been left for last. Without complaint, Davy, wet suit rolled down to his waist, sweat staining this year's commemorative MRCC T-shirt emblazoned with the phrase "To each his fate," hoists the official MRCC camp kitchen box onto one shoulder. "To each his freight is more freaking like it," he says as he turns and heads off down the trail, a wet sucking sound marking time as each boot is withdrawn from the deep, black ooze.

Under the hinged lid of this stained and splintered plywood box are dented pots and pans, metal enameled plates, mugs, utensils, forks, knives, and spoons enough for twelve. Much like hieroglyphs on Egyptian monuments, the back is inscribed with

handwritten columns tabulating twenty years of MRCC expeditions. When anyone has a question on a trip about when a particular river has been run, or mountain climbed, all they need do
is consult the oracle of the camp kitchen.

Davy's burden, then, is not just the means with which to prepare and serve sustenance. In his care is entrusted our collective
history, an irrefutable chronicle of wilderness exploits. It's a vain
attempt to preserve those deeds for posterity, a three-dimensional
Post-it note to the future, when the inexorable decline of furtive
memory will blend a thousand rapids, a lifetime of campfires, and
uncountable sunsets into one grand adventure.

A surprise find near the base of the falls provides a poignant
diversion. Sitting in the bushes at the edge of the water is the
front half of a twenty-foot aluminum canoe that had literally been
ripped in half by the river. The thick, riveted metal hull has been
torn like tin-foil.

Scratched and faded lettering indicates that the Boy Scout
High Adventure Camp on Grand Lake Matagamon owned it.
How it got here and whether anyone was in it when it met its
demise remain a mystery.

———

The gestation of Telos as choke point of the early logging industry's transportation system was not without its complications.
Almost as soon as river drivers began sluicing logs from Telos
into Webster, arguments broke out over what was a fair amount
to pay for the privilege.

When Telos Dam owner Rufus Dwinel raised the toll to
thirty-four cents per thousand board feet, landowners upstream
cried foul. The dispute launched another of Maine's famous
bloodless "wars."

Dwinel, mindful that in past disputes armed groups of thugs were often sent to dismantle irksome dams, promptly raised the toll to fifty cents as protests morphed into threats. The additional money was earmarked to pay for a gang of seventy-five Bangor Tigers, the North Woods equivalent of Viking mercenaries, to defend the dam with knives, pick poles, hand pikes, and axes.

In his book *Allagash: A Journey Through Time on Maine's Legendary Wilderness Waterway*, legendary guide and wooden canoe builder Gil Gilpatrick describes Dwinel's private army. "These fellows were more accustomed to brawling with fists, teeth, and spiked boots, but they were willing and eager to wield the new weapons in defense of their employer's property."

In areas far removed from the umbrella of civilized law enforcement, nothing says "No Trespassing," like six dozen World Wrestling Federation rejects who haven't bathed in three months, standing tall, armed, and unshaven between you and where you want to go.

Things came to a head when a cast of two dozen river drivers working for competing timber baron David Pingree, unaware of Dwinel's reinforcements, showed up planning to sluice their logs over the Telos Dam without paying a cent. As soon as they got one look at the not-so-welcoming committee, a brief standoff ensued. Negotiations, undoubtedly over a mug or two of rum, resulted in the drivers grudgingly agreeing to pay. The first battle of the Telos War was over before it actually started.

Pingree, however, was not about to capitulate. It seems the paperwork for the Telos Dam was not exactly in order. In fact, there wasn't any. The owners never got a charter to build the dam or use the water. And, it was Pingree who owned the dam on Chamberlain Lake that made the entire system possible, which no doubt exacerbated his distaste for the toll.

Seeking to end run around Dwinel, Pingree affiliates submitted a bill in the Maine Legislature in Augusta seeking a charter to build a dam and canal at Telos. Legislators, however, knew exactly what was going on. A compromise bill gave Dwinel's company rights to the dam and cut but set the toll on logs at twenty cents per thousand board feet. Companion legislation stipulated that if Dwinel tried to raise the rate, his competitors would be given ownership rights to the water.

The final blows in the Telos War were the pounding of the gavel on the lecterns when both bills passed handily in the House and Senate.

In addition to its importance to the flow of the state's history, Telos also holds a unique place in the dominion of Maine geography. From that one innocent impoundment, it is possible, with no portage of more than a mile or so in length, to launch canoe trips to five of the state's largest river systems, and via them, gain access to half a dozen more.

The ties to the East Branch as well as to the Allagash Wilderness Waterway, and from it to the St. John, are direct and obvious. But with a carry of just over a mile to Mud Pond and another short transit from the far shore there to Umbazooksus Lake, the vast waters of Chesuncook Lake, Maine's third largest, and the West Branch of the Penobscot, are yours for the taking.

Just upstream on the West Branch is the storied Northeast Carry, a straight, flat shot that connects that river with the northeastern bay of Moosehead Lake.

A handful of miles down the lake to the south, a tamed and toothless Moose River surrenders to the waves of the state's largest body of freshwater, where Mount Kineo's flinty cliffs guard the narrows at Rockwood.

Farther down the western shore of the lake, low dams at East Outlet and West Outlet give birth to divergent streams that eventually merge at the Indian Pond before spewing from the penstocks of Harris Station Dam, Maine's largest, as the mighty Kennebec.

All those interconnections were not lost upon the Native Americans, the loggers who followed, or the folks who laid out the Northern Forest Canoe Trail (NFCT), which opened in 2006. More than 350 miles of the trail's 740-mile run, from Old Forge on the Saranac River in upstate New York to Fort Kent on the St. John, are in Maine.

Scattered throughout the woods and portage trails of Maine can be found a thousand rusting remnants of abandoned dreams. Nowhere is that more apparent than on the shore of Eagle Lake, part of the Allagash Wilderness Waterway and a stop on the NFCT. There, two massive locomotives that once belched smoke and pulsed with steam sit in abject silence as the forest crowds in around them.

The Eagle Lake and West Branch Railroad, built in 1926, was a continuation of the practice begun nearly a century earlier on Telos of sending logs south, rather than north. It carried the area's timber thirteen miles, from Eagle Lake, across the northwest end of Chamberlain Lake, to Umbazooksus, where it could be floated to Chesuncook and down the West Branch. Once the marketable timber was exhausted in 1933, the boiler fires went cold. Obsolete and too expensive to move, the engines were left in a shed that later burned down around them.

After years of being neglected and vandalized, the locomotives were eventually covered with a shed roof and their condition stabilized by volunteers from the Allagash Alliance. Paddlers, boaters, and snowmobilers make regular pilgrimages to visit them, most approaching in reverence not unlike mourners at a wake hesitant to stray too close to the open casket.

At first blush it's easy to interpret such crumbling heaps of iron as impromptu monuments to the enterprise of men.

Despite the best efforts to forestall further decay, these forlorn locomotives sit only as evidence of the inevitability of entropy. Given enough time, no trace will remain.

Stepping back, looking at their wretched situation from a broader perspective, taking a panoramic view, suggests a much different interpretation. The forest that has regrown around these locomotives isn't guilty of encroachment. It's merely reclaiming that which had been taken from it by force.

The real tale of perseverance here is how well the forests, the lakes, and the rivers have rebounded from repeated assaults of human ingenuity. It is the forest reborn that stands as the real monument, testament to the power, the patience, the resiliency of nature.

———

It's a quick run from the end of the Pond Pitch portage to the start of the next at Grand Pitch. The swift current and penalty for mis-calculation should we get too close have everyone on edge. With the river running so high, the normal landing places that would hint at the beginning of another bypass are inundated. This is not a manicured wilderness. There are no hunter orange signs warning "Stop here." Having not done this river before, it would be far too easy to get too close to the falls before realizing a serious mistake had been made.

Paddlers in the lead boat hug the bank and cautiously peek around each bend before committing to the next set of rips. Depending on wind direction, you can often hear a falls long before you see it. But between the din of near constant rapids and the muffling effect of passing snow squalls, today it's "advantage river."

A worn notch in the dirt bank on river left, just before a sharp bend ahead of another long stretch of rapids, catches my eye. I shout for everyone to stop. Atop the bank is an obvious campsite with a view back upstream. I follow a worn trail from the rear of the site as it trends downstream. When the wind shifts, my ears confirm what the vibration in the ground has already telegraphed—Grand Pitch is close. A little farther on, I reach a large campsite on the cliffs overlooking the falls.

The protest of twenty thousand cubic feet of water per second cascading over a near-vertical drop is overwhelming.

In normal flows, the lip of the falls would be distinct, the change in the angle of the water's surface at the point of no return near perpendicular. But the East Branch is in flood. The sheer push of that much flow shoves the water straight off the precipice before gravity can take its cue. The river free-falls nearly thirty feet, dissolving into a maelstrom of foam on a jumble of jagged rocks in the high-walled canyon below.

Like the sound of gentle breezes in the pines, the white noise of falling water provides the perfect soundtrack for a restful night—especially when your companions all qualify as contestants for America's Top Snorer. The roar of this falls, however, is the acoustic equivalent of a galactic black hole, assimilating all, offering other sounds no hope of escape.

To the westard, the day's light will soon begin to fade. It's late. We're tired. We're sore. It's time to lick our physical and spiritual wounds. We'll stop here for the night.

After changing out of our wet suits, we resume the arduous routine of portage for the fourth time. On my second trip, my eye is drawn to a flash of bright orange standing out among the grays and dark greens of the far side of the river. It's midway down a rapid about seventy-five yards upstream from the falls. I push through the small trees and shrubs between the trail and the water's edge to get a better look. It's Nevin's missing river bag, one of the shoulder straps having snagged a low-hanging tree branch. It's bobbing up and down as the heavy hand of the water tests the strength of the wood.

The question now becomes how to recover it. The force of the river and difficulty of the rapids, not to mention the life-threatening downside if a single mistake is made so close to the falls, preclude a direct approach entirely by canoe.

By now, the others have gathered to check it out for themselves. We decide the best way will be to approach by land. But first someone needs to get to the other side of the river. "Any volunteers?" I ask. The only sound is the drumbeat of the falls.

"I'm in," says Davy after a time.

"Let's do it," says Dale.

They will paddle across the river from the start of the portage trail, and once safely on the other side, work their way down the bank on foot. The current is fast, so I suggest they "ferry" their canoe by pointing the slightly askew bow upstream, paddling primarily against the current. It will bring them to the opposite shore not quite parallel from the departure point, and slightly downstream, but in a much shorter distance than if they had tried to cut straight across.

As they will be taking Dale's canoe, he takes the stern. Davy jumps into the bow.

Wet suits are adjusted. Life jackets zipped and buckled. An extra paddle is thrown into the bottom of the boat just in case.

They shove off into the fast current and dig the paddles in hard.

Everyone holds their breath as backs and biceps strain to defy the will of the river.

Once across, they haul the canoe completely out of the water to preclude another party from finding torn pieces of it thrown up on the riverbank. It takes them twenty minutes to work through the thick vegetation on the far shore to get to the bag. Dale grasps a tree as an anchor and extends his other hand to Davy as he wades in the fast-flowing, knee-deep water to grab the bag. As he does, a cheer goes up from those of us watching vulture-like on the opposite shore.

With the bulky bag it takes them a half an hour to thrash through the thicket to get back to the canoe. The trick now, of course, is to get back in one piece.

Their jumping-off point on the return leg is farther downstream than their start even though they have pulled the canoe upstream along the shore as best they can. My greatest fear is that the canoe could flip as they ferry back across, plunging both men into the torrent just above the falls.

As a fail-safe, we position both throw bags downstream of the transit point with the ends presecured to stout trees. When they're ready, Dale and Davy, both kneeling, the front of the canoe pointed upstream, get the high sign to begin the run. Both the bow and stern painters, quarter-inch floating nylon lines, are allowed to trail in the water to assist in recovery of the boat if needed.

The current where they are on the outside of a bend is much stronger than it was on the inside where they began. They're making progress laterally, but inexorably moving backward as well. An old adage says that the best bilge pump on a sinking boat is a scared man with a bucket. I have a new take on that. No one paddles with greater vigor than two men slipping backward in a canoe in rapids just above a malevolent thirty-foot waterfall.

About two-thirds of the way across, the stern hesitates for a nanosecond as it snags a rock. The unseen hand of the river instantly spins the canoe 180 degrees, pointing it straight downriver toward the event horizon barely a hundred yards away. Directly above the precipice is a large field of boulders where maneuvering will be nearly impossible. Once in there, the canoe will not remain upright for long.

Dale and Davy paddle like madmen, as if lives depend on it. In fact, they do.

They streak past the first throw bag station moving far too fast and too far out for effective intervention. I'm up next, like a net below a tightrope walker, the last line of defense, just fifty yards above the falls.

Dale and Davy manage to weave the canoe through a few tight spots between boulders. The bow finally hits the shore thirty feet above my position, at full, get-me-the-hell-out-of-here, ramming speed. Both paddlers were so transfixed on getting back across in one piece they apparently gave no thought as to what to do once they got there. Getting to shore and getting on shore are two very different things.

The next few seconds unfold in glorious slow motion, beginning with the extra paddle and river bag slamming violently forward.

Like a rookie skateboarder who has not yet perfected his dismount, Davy catapults ass over teakettle onto land. Dale flies over the stern thwart, landing crash-test-dummy-like in a heap in the middle of the canoe.

As the canoe begins to slide backward, bumping along the rocks on the bank, Dale manages to sit up, scanning frantically for a paddle.

I launch the throw bag with unadulterated enthusiasm, sending the business end flying well past him as it is designed to do. The rope drops perpendicular across the gunwales within easy reach.

Like reeling in a prized pickerel, I quickly strong-arm him and the canoe back to shore in a small dead water just above the protruding ledge I'm standing on. He jumps out of the canoe without a word, flashing me a wild-eyed look. "I owe you, bro," he says before turning to give his son the longest man hug of his life.

"Holy #@%! Holy #@%! What a ride!" yells Davy as he paces on shore catching his breath. Keith rushes by both paddlers, grabs the prodigal river bag, unbuckles it, and begins rummaging around inside. He smiles as he unrolls a fleece jacket and inspects his half-gallon "handle" of Absolut. "Not a scratch. Good work, boys," he says nodding his head.

While setting up their tent, Dale and Jason discover one of their river duffels was not as watertight at they had thought. Jason's sleeping bag is soaking wet. He had failed to wrap it in something watertight before putting it in the bag. If there's one thing a river will teach you, it's that single points of failure ultimately will.

Like beach sand that burrows into the innermost recesses of a bathing suit, water on a river trip can and will, if not resisted with guile and vigor, find its way into every last nook and cranny. When it comes to keeping things dry, there's no such thing as too much redundancy. Redundancy is good. Unless you're a writer, redundancy is your friend. You can't say it enough times.

All gear that's marketed as "waterproof" comes with an invisible asterisk. In most cases, it's up to the consumer to guess what *waterproof* really means. Does it mean the contents won't be ruined when left on a picnic table in a gentle summer rain, or while going over Niagara Falls like a daredevil in a barrel?

I get a chuckle when something like an MP4 music player is sold as being "waterproof to a depth of 12 meters." If I unexpectedly find myself forty feet under water, the last thing I'm going to be worried about is whether I'll ever hear my road trip playlist again.

As far as I know, Jason's waterproof river bag wasn't guaranteed to keep its contents high and dry "when submerged for an extended period on the East Branch of the Penobscot River in the wilds of northern Maine."

If something absolutely, positively has to stay dry, first put it in a waterproof stuff sack and then into your waterproof river bag. And, just for good measure, you probably should seal it in a plastic zip bag first. All of that will improve the odds of it staying dry to 50-50.

There's nothing like the prospect of facing a long, cold night in a soggy sleeping bag to teach someone that one layer of supposedly bombproof protection is never enough.

To compensate for the day's earlier involuntary sacrifices to the river gods, a hodgepodge of tarps is rigged to create a suitable cooking, dining, and card-playing sanctuary. One roll-up table off to the side serves as the bar. Three others are set up in a line down the center as the focal point of camp. They are soon covered with slabs of cheese, boxes of crackers, and packages of aromatic pepperonis. With everyone ensconced in layers of fleece and down booties, cocktails and cigars in hand, the day's depravations swiftly fall astern.

Under the stark glare of a propane lantern, the three burners on the white gas stove roar like a jet engine. Backlit steam billows from the large aluminum cook pots. One by one, members of the company draw to the comfort of a campfire quickly ignited with the aid of Coleman Magic.

I have commandeered some of the thick slices of ham originally purposed for breakfast on day two for tonight's supper. Frozen corn in the main cooler arrived unscathed. Brown rice stashed in another food bucket in case of emergency also has been pressed into service.

The cookee holds a position of great power and respect in any camp. With the primary entree for the evening meal MIA, the pressure is on. The wording on the hat I wear while preparing meals says it all. "Earl run Bartertown." Like a post-nuclear devastation alchemist, I stir and season, as the gang of hungry survivors, mouths stewed in anticipation of stroganoff since breakfast, look on with suspicion.

"Just put lots of butter and catsup on it and tell yourselves it's stroganoff," I say to the bread line as I ladle it onto the prewarmed metal plates.

The food disappears quickly and, surprisingly, without exaggerated complaint. After dinner and cleanup chores, the cribbage board can't seem to find a friend. Paddlers, exhausted by the day's exertions, drift off one by one to the refuge of warm, dry sleeping bags with the one aforementioned exception. Using a spare fleece sleeping bag liner to cover their damp sleeping pads and using their one remaining dry sleeping bag as a throw, Dale and Jason will double up tonight.

—◦—

As I crawl into my tent, it takes an attentive ear to discern any snoring over the cacophony of the falls. In a moment of selfishness, I had picked this spot to camp because I love going to sleep being serenaded by a river. But this river's roar, its unapologetic sonic display of sovereignty, its subterranean pulse reaching up through my sleeping pad from the very bedrock below, holds more consternation than comfort.

It doesn't take long for me to realize that the East Branch, harnessed more than a century ago by the mercenary imaginations of hard-bitten and profit-hungry men, and fed this day by a thousand streams pregnant with rain, isn't singing. She's laughing, delighted that she'll get another crack at us tomorrow.

It's only half a mile or so on river to the portage trail around the next unrunnable falls, a fearsome rapid called the Hulling Machine. Here, the river twists and turns at the root of high granite walls. The water plummets over several distinct steps with perpendicular rows of jagged rocks lurking below, like serrated rows of a shark's teeth.

It was named for the propensity of those rocks to bite at the timber sent down its unforgiving maw. Legend holds that log sorters far downstream easily could tell which logs originated on the East Branch. They just looked for the naked ones scrubbed bare of bark.

Once that quarter-mile portage is done, we'll have to run or carry at Bowlin Falls before the river eases for the remaining sixteen miles to the last rapid of any consequence at the take-out at Whetstone.

I lay awake for a long time, unable to tune out the din, disappointed that I've let the river's amusement much too far into my head. But ascribing that intent to it in a moment of anthropomorphological weakness inflates its authority.

Nothing, even an entity as powerful as this river, can know what a new dawn will bring. The wet paint of the day just done is all that's anyone's to know.

That's not to say that it's easy to honestly interpret our own past, free of the blue shift of ego and the natural propensity to embrace a propagandist approach to personal narrative. What matters in the end, however, is the attempt.

The ultimate luxury in this earthly plane is to lead what Socrates described as an examined life. For someone to have the time, the curiosity, the surplus of intellectual energy to ponder the great mysteries of existence, to appreciate the elemental inspiration of nature, or to question and assign degrees of virtue or contempt to the laws of physics and the genetic root of human motive, they first must be unencumbered by the basic biological shackles of struggling to survive.

Interviewer Charlie Rose once asked Microsoft titan Bill Gates how he found the time to fight to rid the world of polio and tuberculosis and juggle all the other responsibilities that come with being one of the richest men on the planet. Gates's matter-of-fact response: "I don't mow the lawn."

Once the need to survive is surmounted to some theoretical minimum degree, the innate quest for something more, to discern patterns in chaos, becomes both a blessing and a curse.

The first sting: acknowledgment of the inevitability of our own mortality. The fundamental blessing: to live above, and see beyond, the fickle dictates of here and now.

Those who aspire to be mindful of their life's path must guard against becoming ensnared in the quicksand of hubris lest they dishonor the gift.

Awareness of where one resides on the metaphysical scale that runs from birth to death and ranges from total selfishness to absolute selflessness comes first. It frees the soul from just being swept along unawares by the great currents of life—to escape being tossed about helplessly in the rapids, to strive, as "Ma" Curtain, one of my favorite high school teachers, said of the great figures of history, "to paddle your own canoe."

For those toiling under wretched conditions in the woods above Telos centuries ago, the last thing they had was the luxury to ponder such intangibles. Theirs was a daily fight just to stay warm, to remain uninjured, to stay fed, just to stay alive.

That did not, however, make their labors, their path of existence, any less noble. In fact, those hardships, their collective sacrifices, made them even more so.

Every moment, every heartbeat, every breath, every raindrop coalescing in the mists above and fighting its way to the sea, everything that has come before and everything that will follow, exists at the edge of time, advances the fluid boundaries of history. Some will always struggle so that others can break free, so that those who sail the seas, run the rivers, and stand tall upon the mountaintops can return with one clear and unmistakable message of hope—that there's more to life, that there's more out there for everyone.

Roar on Grand Pitch. Laugh to your heart's content. For all the day's challenges, for all the day's hardships, for all the day's near calamity, we are fed, we are warm, we are whole.

We remain unbowed. We are ready to do it all again tomorrow.

I drift off to sleep, warm in the notion that as hard as she tried to wrest more, the East Branch has taken all she'll get from us today.

HIKE YOUR OWN HIKE

FOR THOSE WHO MAKE PILGRIMAGES TO THE WILDS CARRYING the essentials of survival on their backs, there is only rule—hike your own hike.

As in life, even though you may spend part of that journey in the close company of others, ultimately, when you shoulder a pack and seek the solace of wilderness, you walk alone.

The mecca of all long-distance hikes in the United States is the storied Appalachian Trail, which stretches 2,185 miles from Springer Mountain in Georgia to the lofty summit of Katahdin in Maine.

Granted, the peaks of the Appalachian Range are mere hills compared to the Rockies. It's their advanced age, however, not youth and inexperience, that dictates their diminished presentation. Atop these ancient mountains that pushed skyward four hundred million years before the Himalayas began their geologic rise, the trail climbs the highest peaks and passes through some of the most scenic and wild areas on the East Coast.

While some of it features highly engineered switchbacks for ease of walking, other stretches are chaotic jumbles of tangled roots and ankle-biting rocks. There are heights to scale, streams to ford, bears and mice to fend off, and extremes of heat and cold to endure—all while carrying forty pounds on your back.

The rewards are more sublimer—views out a hundred miles, the embrace of unbridled nature, a chance for contemplation, a chance to breathe. And there's great satisfaction, as the alpenglow fades each evening in the western sky, in reflecting on how far you've come.

Those who accept the AT's physical challenge quickly come to understand that the route was never laid out to be easy on the feet. It was chosen to be nourishment and inspiration for the soul.

An estimated twenty-five hundred people set out to hike the AT end to end each year. Slightly more than 10 percent succeed. The woods near the first road crossing north of Springer are often littered with cast-off gear, the detritus of poor planning, unreasonable expectations, and the premature evaporation of perseverance.

Some stop due to injury, others when the tangential tug of gravity from lives and loves back home can no longer be ignored.

Some run out of time.

Some run out of money.

Some run out of heart.

For others, vagabond dreams surrender to a new daily monotony and the reality of being at times cold, wet, bug bit, hungry, sore, and tired.

Others depart unable to accept the notion of themselves as sole confidante, needing more entertainment than is offered by the metronome of their own pulse. Not all are comfortable with that powerful rhythm, itself life's primordial soundtrack. Its detection in the womb corroborates a new spark of existence—its departure at the end of life's journey is irrefutable evidence of entropy's inescapable silence. With its acknowledgment comes acceptance that the number of our heartbeats is finite, some say fixed—as fleeting in the cosmic sense as ancient mountains, as the notion of time itself.

Since the Appalachian Trail was completed in the 1930s, more than eighteen thousand people have managed to finish it.

Few among them know that a Mainer is among those they are indebted to for showing the way.

Myron Avery was born in Lubec in 1899, graduated from Bowdoin, and later became a successful lawyer in New York and Washington, D.C. A friend of Appalachian Mountain Club founder Benton MacKaye, who first proposed the AT in a 1921 article, Avery helped pioneer and build the actual route.

MacKaye had a dream. Avery made it a reality.

MacKaye's original plan called for the trail's northern terminus to be Mount Washington in New Hampshire. Avery persevered in his insistence it end atop Katahdin.

When the sign demarking Katahdin as the northern terminus of the AT was about to be erected at the summit, Avery is reported to have made a very brief speech. "Nail it up," he reportedly said.

Thanks to Avery, hikers have an additional 250 rugged miles to cover through the remotest wilderness found anywhere, including Mahoosuc Notch, considered to be the AT's toughest mile, and the renowned 100-Mile Wilderness, the longest section that doesn't intersect a paved road on the entire route.

Author Bill Bryson, in his classic take on the AT, *A Walk in the Woods*, tips his hat to Avery. "In under seven years, using volunteer labor, he built a 2,000-mile trail through mountain wilderness," Bryson writes. "Armies have done less."

Sadly, despite being thin and fit from a life devoted to time in the out-of-doors, Myron Avery died at the young age of fifty-three, of a heart attack.

~~~

There is a well-ordered pantheon of AT hikers. Thru-hikers, those who complete the entire distance in a single season, are the demigods. When encountering thru-hikers confidently striding northward in the late autumn, others of lower station instinctively step to the side, eyes averted. It's futile to attempt to make eye contact. The summit of Katahdin, so close they can taste it, is all that they can see.

Section hikers tick off stretches when they can, sometimes taking years to complete the entire length. Those who eventually finish it all, regardless of how long it takes, are considered to be "2,000 milers."

Myron Avery was the first 2,000 miler, covering it with a measuring wheel to accurately log the distance. He personally laid out, brushed out, and painted the trail's distinctive white blazes on much of the route in Maine and elsewhere.

In an article in the publication *In the Maine Woods*, Avery summed up his affection for the wilds of his native state. "To those who would see the Maine wilderness, tramp day by day through a succession of ever delightful forests, past lake and stream, and over mountains, we would say: Follow the Appalachian Trail across Maine. It cannot be followed on horse or awheel. Remote for detachment, narrow for chosen company, winding for leisure, lonely for contemplation, it beckons not merely north and south but upward to the body, mind, and soul of man."

Life along the trail also has its own vocabulary. People will always attach labels to others, but here, the traditional pigeonholes of rich or poor, conservative or liberal, true believer or agnostic, hold no power.

Thru-hikers beginning in Georgia are called north bounders, or NoBos. While taking "a zero day" off for bad weather is tempting, seasoned north bounders know all too well the need to keep moving, regardless of the weather, to finish on time. Their mantra—"No rain, no pain, no Maine."

A much smaller subset, including those who begin on Katahdin plunging headlong, either out of bravery or naiveté, into the wildest country at the height of blackfly season, are called south bounders, or SoBos.

Those who jump off the trail at some point and head north to do the section in New England before winter snows make foot travel impossible are called flip-floppers, so christened long before partisan politics gave the term a negative connotation.

Yo-yo hikers, perhaps the rarest breed, do the trail, then turn around, and perhaps in the ultimate act of procrastination to avoid returning to the real world, do it all again in the opposite direction.

Weekenders, a term that is entirely self-explanatory, are another distinct class from thru-hikers and are also technically section hikers.

Some thru-hikers hold a special measure of distain for others of their ilk known as blue blazers. Their sin?—occasionally taking side trails (readily identified by being marked with blue rather than white paint) as shortcuts or to avoid dangerous stretches in inclement weather. For the ultraorthodox, it does not count that someone took six months to walk all the way from Georgia to Maine, their entire life in a bag on their back, if they don't follow the trail precisely as mapped. Some disdain, too, is held for those who hike the AT "supported," carrying only a day pack with a crew or helper meeting them with food, supplies, and gear at prearranged campsites and road crossings, allowing them to avoid carrying heavy loads.

All who walk the Appalachian Trail at some point adopt, or discover while on their grand adventure, colorful trail names—the hiking fraternity's equivalent of the literati's noms de plume.

A registry of thru-hiker trail names is kept at the Appalachian Trail Conference (ATC) headquarters in Harpers Ferry, the spiritual midpoint of the trail. Here, the white blazes emerge from the woods of Virginia to cross the Shenandoah River, run straight through the historic village, which is in West Virginia, before crossing a long railroad trestle over the Potomac and reentering the woods in Maryland.

Names on file run the gamut from something as mundane as Mountain Dew or Damascus Dave to Orange Bug and No Pepsi. Characters' names from J.R.R. Tolkien's *The Hobbit* and *The Lord of the Rings* books are especially popular.

A computer analysis of all the trail names registered with the ATC, done by someone who apparently had copious amounts of leisure time on their hands, has identified the most frequently used terms. They include, at least in part, the words *old, man, blue, dog, red, turtle, bear, walker, hiker, mountain, fat, little, mister, boy,* and *girl*.

The list is only slightly more creative than the most popular organized crime nicknames. which are dominated by the words *big* (anything), *animal, fat, little, Sammy, Jimmy, Joey, Tony, Tommy, Whitey, sausage, weasel, bananas, boy, killer, lucky,* and *the bull*.

Curiously, the names of the only two atomic weapons ever dropped in anger include multiple words from the tops of both lists—Fat Man and Little Boy.

It doesn't matter if no one else gets what a trail name means as long as it has significance to you. It is, in effect, the penultimate inside joke. A request for its origins is the perfect trailside conversation starter.

When I first started section hiking, my trail name was Stump Jumper, the formal version of the term "Stumpy," used to describe everyone in the forestry program when I studied at the University of Maine. Years later, I adopted the trail name Voodoo Child in reference to the lyrics in the Jimi Hendrix song (best version—*Live at the Fillmore East*) of the same name. People who grew up during the '60s will get it, as the song is already stuck in their head. The rest of you will just have to Google the lyrics or spend the ninety-nine cents on iTunes.

Perhaps in acknowledgment that long-distance hikers leave the outside world behind, even if only for a while, real names are never used to sign entries in the logbooks found in just about every one of the 250 shelters and lean-tos on the trail. Sometimes knowing that Frodo and Gimli are only two days ahead of you, or that Moon Flower decided to flip-flop and is now in the Whites, can be very useful information to keep track of the temporary extended families that frequently form on the trail.

And regaling coworkers with tales of past exploits involving people with colorful and descriptive trail names is way more romantic than admitting that your current circle of friends consists only of "Fat" Bob from accounting, or "Little" Pauly in quality control.

The first documented thru-hiker was Earl Shaffer from Pennsylvania, trail name Crazy One, who, using only a canvas rucksack, worn boots, and rudimentary gear, completed the hike in 124 days in 1948. Originally, ATC officials were skeptical and scoffed at reports of the accomplishment. Later, that organization would help elevate his holiness in long-distance hiking's hall of saints by becoming publishers of his seminal book *Walking with Spring*.

Crazy One didn't care what any of his critics thought. He hiked his own hike.

It took Shaffer only ninety-nine days to repeat his feat, this time hiking southbound from Katahdin, in 1965. In 1998, at age seventy-nine, on the fiftieth anniversary of his first hike, Shaffer, by then known as The Original Crazy One, did another northbound thru-hike, this time taking 174 days. Out of fairness, reroutes of the trail since it opened had added to its length.

Cancer would take Earl Shaffer in 2003. He was eighty-three years old.

The first documented solo female thru-hiker was the hard-scrabble Emma Rowena "Grandma" Gatewood. She took to the trail first in 1954 and didn't get far before dropping out. She tried again in 1955 at age sixty-seven, wearing Keds sneakers and carrying a denim bag slung over one shoulder. In it, she carried a surplus wool army blanket for a bedroll and a plastic shower curtain for a tent. Among her recommended trail foods were canned Vienna sausages, which are little more than slender pink extrusions of pork suspended in a gelatinous goo.

Along the way, she endured a rattlesnake strike, two hurricanes, and an initially tense encounter with an inner-city street gang afield as part of a rehabilitation program.

She stood atop Katahdin on September 25, 145 days after setting out. Grandma Gatewood went on to repeat her trek twice more, including in 1963 at age seventy-five, becoming the first person to hike the trail three times. She remained lifelong friends with the members of the street gang.

Her most-oft-repeated quote: "Most people today are panty-waists."

What's not to love?

She hiked her own hike.

Grandma Gatewood continued to go on long-distance hikes right up to her death in 1973 at the ripe old age of eighty-five.

One of the most inspirational thru-hikers was Bill Irwin. Legally blind, he hiked with his German shepherd guide dog, Orient, earning them the trail name Orient Express. Between the two, they felt their way north, Bill often on bloodied knees, yet spirits unbent. After a hurricane left behind tangles of blown-down trees across the trail near Rangeley, Maine, it took Irwin an entire day to go just a few miles. Still, he pressed onward.

A former alcoholic and four-time divorcé who had earlier in life abandoned his family, he considered his AT sojourn in 1990 to be an act of personal salvation. When he finally reached the top of Katahdin (without Orient on the last five miles, as no dogs, even service animals, were allowed in Baxter State Park at that time), members of his church greeted him by singing "Amazing Grace."

Irwin went on to write a popular book about his experiences called *Blind Courage*.

After having been lost in life more than once, Bill Irwin finally found and saw the way in life, by taking to the AT, by hiking his own hike.

He married, happily, for a fifth time. The couple built a house in the woods of Maine, with a spectacular view of Katahdin. He passed away of prostate cancer in March 2014 at age seventy-three.

Sisters Susan and Lucy Letcher of Southwest Harbor, Maine, trail names Isis and Jackrabbit, achieved AT notoriety not for what they did, but how they did it. SoBos who started on Katahdin in 2000, they reached Georgia, and then yo-yoed, only donning shoes when encountering heavy snow and ice. Between the two trips over two seasons, they eventually covered every inch of the way barefoot.

The Barefoot Sisters, as they came to be known, went on to write two popular books of their experiences, *Southbound* and *Walking Home*. Their story, like Shaffer's, Gatewood's, and Irwin's, has inspired succeeding generations to hike their own hike.

By the time most thru-hikers reach Maine, they are hardened veterans, forged into fighting shape by enduring a total of more than

450,000 feet of elevation gain over 2,000 miles of wilderness. To cover the next 250 miles or so with an additional 70,000 feet of elevation gain as cold weather breathes down their necks, they need every ounce of strength and stick-to-itiveness they have.

Immediately after crossing the border from the Granite State, the trail plunges into the legendary Mahoosuc Notch—considered the AT's toughest mile. The white blazes take hikers over and under a jumble of truck-sized boulders at the bottom of a narrow pass that trends to the eastard between a pair of thirty-four-hundred-foot peaks.

It's no place, as Grandma Gatewood might say, "for pantywaists."

At times, you must find your way over ten-foot-high blocks of skin-shredding granite topped with thick layers of moss and gnarled trees straight out of a haunted forest. In other places, you must shed your pack and squirm and crawl through damp boulder caves accompanied by the rush of an unseen stream coursing even deeper underground.

Because sunlight rarely touches the notch's innermost recesses, snow lingers here long into summer. At night, cold air settles silently to the bottom before filtering down through the rocks. It never leaves.

For many years, the skeleton of a hapless moose that had wandered into this talus pile on steroids and been unable to escape was among the notch's most prominent landmarks.

Heading north from Mahoosuc's claustrophobic confines to the promise of Katahdin's open, alpine Tableland, the trail summits a bevy of four-thousand-foot peaks, including Old Speck, Saddleback and The Horn, Spaulding, Sugarloaf, Crocker, and Bigelow, both West Peak and, to the east, Avery Peak, named for the iconic trailblazer himself. In the col between them is a modest bronze plaque affixed to a small boulder naming a lean-to in his honor. It's the only permanent monument to Avery's impressive contributions.

The AT in Maine, while wonderfully maintained by a dedicated cadre of volunteers, is not for the faint of heart. It often heads straight up the side of a mountain with no intention of seeking a less perpendicular route. Most stream crossings require fording because the wild spring freshets once used to drive sawlogs and pulp to market rip away all attempts by mere mortals to span them with anything short of concrete and steel.

Thru-hikers who tire of these obstacles air their complaints with chicken-scratched whines in the tattered, spiral-bound registers in the shelters. Many ask, with obvious hyperbole, if those responsible for the trail have ever heard of switchbacks or a "new-fangled invention"—the bridge.

We all know what Grandma Gatewood would have to say about that.

Last but not least, at Katahdin's very doorstep, lies the 100-Mile Wilderness, considered the longest stretch without ready resupply on the entire AT. It runs from Monson, just below Greenville, and cuts north and east to emerge on the storied Golden Road at Abol Bridge.

When Avery originally laid out the trail, the 100-Miles was anything but an empty wilderness. Like the current Appalachian Mountain Club (AMC) system of high huts in the Presidential Range in New Hampshire, hikers pushing north from Monson could avail themselves of the hospitality of numerous sporting camps along the way for shelter and sustenance. Among them were lodges and cabins at Perham's Camps (now AMC's Gorman Chairback Camps) on Long Pond, The Antlers on Lower Jo-Mary Lake, White House Landing on Pemadumcook Lake, and camps on Nahmakanta and Rainbow Lakes, as well as privately owned cabins inside what is now Baxter State Park.

Chairback Camps is no longer directly on the trail. The rotting remnants of Antlers now fade into the detritus far back in the woods at the present AT tent site by the same name. Nahmakanta Camps doesn't market itself to hikers. Rainbow is privately owned by a corporation as a fly-in-only fishing retreat for high rollers.

Today, only White House Landing still caters to AT hikers. It can be accessed on a short side trail that leads to a foghorn on a post at the edge of the water. Blow the horn, and soon a boat will arrive to take you on the short ride across the lake to a fantasy world of clean sheets, cold beer, pizza, and one-pound cheeseburgers.

Hikers tackling the 100-Mile today are urged to pack at least ten days' worth of food and supplies. Those who misjudge or encounter delays due to weather or injury may find themselves seriously hungry toward the end of their transit or praying someone else was kind enough when they passed through to leave some extra TP in the outhouse.

It's often at such low moments, however, when one of the most powerful forces on the AT, "trail magic," suddenly occurs.

Trail magic is the term for unexpected kindnesses often offered by people you don't know—in some cases, people you'll never even meet. It can be found on a sign saying "drink me" attached to a cooler full of ice-cold grape soda sitting in the middle of nowhere along the shore of a lake. It's a lift into town on a dark, rainy night that turns into a hot meal and free place to stay. It's having a total stranger offer you their spare spork when you realize you forgot to pack any eating utensils. Purveyors of trail magic are literally trail angels.

In some respects, trail magic is a metaphorical tip of the hat between members of the long-distance hiking fraternity, even among those who may have long ago hung up their trekking poles but are still drawn to be involved. The hiking community, despite comprising for the most part people who enjoy being on their own, knows how to stick together. When those spontaneous acts of kindness happen out of the blue, on any trail, on any backpacking trip, it's a marvelous thing.

A few years back, a friend and I finished up a thirty-six-mile, partial circumnavigation of Katahdin in Baxter that ended at Roaring Brook Campground, some forty miles by road from Nesoudahunk Stream where we had parked the truck. Before we left, we had made shuttle arrangements. The plan was to have the ranger at Roaring Brook radio park headquarters back in Millinocket. They, in turn, would telephone the Appalachian Trail Lodge for a driver to meet us at the campground to run us back to get the truck.

Shortly after lunchtime, we finished the nine-mile stretch from Wassataquoik Stream. It was a hot day in late June. We were sweaty and tired, and the blackflies left no doubt as to our relative position on the back of beyond's food chain.

On leaden legs, we trudged up the steps to the porch of the ranger cabin to sign out on the trail register and request the radio call. A note on the door left us crestfallen. "Campers: I'm out of the campground until later tonight. Please check yourselves in."

Cell phones are useless at Roaring Brook. We were now faced with the possibility of hanging out swatting bugs for eight to ten hours before we could make that radio call. Even then, the hiker shuttle might not be available at that time of night.

Over in the parking lot, a group of men, graybeards such as ourselves with whom we had chatted on the hike out, were packing up their dunnage. One, Fred Michaud, an engineer with the Maine Department of Transportation, was someone I knew from a project he had worked on in Bar Harbor. I went over and gave him a slip of paper with the shuttle driver's telephone number on it. I asked him if he or someone in his group would call it when they got a cell phone signal closer to town.

He said he'd be happy to.

Overhearing our situation, another member of Fred's party, his former brother-in-law, Paul, stepped up and offered to drive us back to our truck. He said he "didn't have anything else to do" that afternoon.

That's trail magic.

The impressive part is that he agreed to do it even though it would take him sixty miles in total out of his way on rough dirt roads.

But it got better.

As soon as that was settled and copious amounts of gratitude expressed on our parts, another member of Fred's party reached into a cooler in the back of a minivan and pulled out two ice-cold bottles of Budweiser. "You guys thirsty?" he asked.

A badly needed ride on roads where opportunities to hitch-hike are few and far between—and free beer? Now, that's real trail magic!

Fortunately, the lean-tos that anchor the ends of the 100-Mile, Leeman Brook to the west and Hurd Brook to the east, are hot spots for trail magic.

Hikers just starting out who realize they're carrying way too much food often leave some hanging in the lean-to. Likewise, those who finish up their transit with some food left over often leave their surplus behind.

While some armchair purists consider it littering, finding unexpected and unencumbered food when you're ravenous and your larder has nothing left in it but a few spruce needles and half a package of instant oatmeal nibbled by mice your first night out is indeed magic.

Paying trail magic forward is an essential part of the equation. Once while weekending on the AT in New York in early November, we were setting up for the night at the Wiley Shelter just across the border from Connecticut.

We had started a fire in the tall, boxlike stone fireplace as it grew dark and were going about the chores of preparing supper when a short, tired-looking man wearing a $4 camouflage plastic rain poncho shuffled into camp.

Atop his head was a tall, almost pointed hat with a wide, rumpled brim. He had shoulder-length hair and an unkempt beard that reached halfway down his chest. Underneath, he wore four soiled shirts to ward off the deepening evening cold. His pack was vintage big box store, not at all what one would expect from a veteran hiker. A tattered plastic trash bag covered a puffy and stained slumber party sleeping bag. He carried no sleeping pad or tent.

His walking staff was a hollow plastic paddle from an inflatable raft like you'd see floating in a backyard pool. "Good evening," he responded to our hellos. "I'm Montana Skateboarder."

As is the custom in any shelter on the AT, everyone shoved over their bedrolls to make room. No one gets left out in the cold or rain. There's always room for one more, even when a shelter is well over capacity.

"He's a mini-me version of Gandalf," my brother Carl whispered. "Minus the cool wizard staff."

Like all who take to the trail, Montana had a backstory. After accepting a cup of hot tea, he explained he had been working a dead-end job in a photo print kiosk in the middle of a windswept mall parking lot in Montana—in February. He was finding it hard to pay bills with little opportunity for other work. "So it dawned on me," he went on. "I said 'Screw this, I might as well hike the AT.'

"I took off in the middle of my shift; left the lights on, just locked the door, went to my apartment to get a few clothes and skated for Georgia," he continued. The genesis of his trail name was now abundantly clear.

Some of the gear, he said, he found in woods near the first road crossing after Springer Mountain in Georgia. The rest he cobbled together or picked up at thrift shops as he went.

Realizing his pace would not get him to Katahdin before winter, Montana flip-flopped in August and began heading south. He didn't even tell his family what he was up to. "I told them I was going hiking for a while. They'll find out where I went when I get back," he explained.

"I'll see how far I can get before it gets too cold."

To save money, of which he obviously had very little, Montana's cooking gear consisted of a fire-blackened Campbell's Soup can with a piece of electrical wire for a handle. "I just use one until it rusts out, then buy another, eat the soup, and I'm good to go," he said. He found the plastic paddle lying on the trail in the middle of nowhere in Vermont. "No idea how it got there. It wasn't near a lake," he said. "It's lasted longer than any stick."

When he took out his stuff sack of food, he removed a single package of ramen noodles. He then turned the bag inside out and shook out bits of dried leaves. "I'm hoping to get to a town in a couple days," he said.

As he set the can over the fire to boil water for the noodles, a series of hisses and puffs of steam on the coals below betrayed the fact it had already given up the ghost.

There was silence in the lean-to as we all exchanged knowing glances.

In less than a minute, pouches of Mountain House backpacker meals, instant oatmeal, and PowerBars began piling up on the

Deacon Seat of the lean-to. "Here you go," I said, pushing it all toward him. He stared for a minute. Considering the reality of his situation, he made no attempt to politely protest the gifts. "Much obliged," he said as he filled the bag.

One of the Boy Scouts in our group had already finished his meal of Spaghetti-Os and offered up the now-empty can to Montana. He had already declined the offer of a small aluminum cook pot.

A couple of holes were made with a Leatherman to attach the wire handle. Water soon happily boiled in the new can. No hiss or steam on the embers below. "This should work out good," he said.

That night, we sat around the fire, comfortable in our temporary fellowship swapping stories and sharing sips of whiskey.

The next morning, Montana Skateboarder was up before first light. As darkness began to surrender to the blue light of the east, the rhythmic sound of the plastic paddle hitting the ground faded as he disappeared south on the trail and to whatever awaited him.

I could not help but think of the words of J.R.R. Tolkien in *The Lord of the Rings*.

> Still round the corner there may wait
> A new road or a secret gate
> And though I oft have passed them by,
> A day will come at last when I
> Shall take the hidden paths that run
> West of the Moon, East of the Sun.

While he had no idea what his future held, on the AT, at least, Montana Skateboarder was free of the shackles of his past—the undeniable master of his here and now. He was hiking his own hike.

For all the fundamental truth that tackling the Appalachian Trail is a uniquely individual endeavor, there is one place, a stretch of just seventy yards out of nearly twenty-two hundred miles, where hikers cannot do it on their own. To try is to risk almost certain death.

Of course, that part of the trail is in Maine.

In Caratunk, where the highway down from Canada is lined with the ramshackle headquarters of white-water rafting outfitters, the AT crosses the Kennebec River just downstream from the confluence with the Dead. A few miles upstream on both rivers, large dams control the flow of water for rafting and the generation of hydroelectric power. Where the trail ends at the water's edge, the flow can go from just a piddling hundred cubic feet per second to tens of thousands with little or no warning. Anyone caught in that maelstrom of frigid water is in extreme danger.

In 1985, thru-hiker Alice Ference was swept away and drowned while she and her husband were trying to ford.

Because building a bridge big enough to span the river would cost millions of dollars and not be in keeping with the rustic character of the trail, the Maine Appalachian Trail Conference came up with an ingenious solution for safe passage. For several hours a day during hiking season, a ferryman is on duty to paddle hikers across the Kennebec in a canoe. There is no charge.

For many years, the most fabled ferryman on the Kennebec was Stephen Longley, a native of Lewiston. Steve's father was James Longley, Maine's first Independent governor. Steve's brother James Jr. went on to serve in Congress. His sister, Susan, was a state senator.

Eschewing politics, Steve, a Registered Maine Guide, former rafting outfitter, and Wilderness First Responder, found his calling helping other people find theirs. He spent twenty hiking seasons paddling back and forth over the same 210 feet of river. A carpenter by trade, his commute to what he liked to call his "day job" was short. He lived just a mile away. His only tools were a trademark red Old Town canoe, a paddle, life vests, the strength of his arms, his knowledge of the river, and a heart as big as the great outdoors.

In an article in *Down East* magazine he's quoted as saying, "I may not be a governor or senator, but I'll be the best ferryman I can be."

True to his word, his concern for his charges didn't end when they stepped safe and dry from the canoe on the east side of the river. Steve frequently helped hikers find the services, supplies, and equipment they needed. He embodied the spirit of trail magic, often giving hikers rides, feeding them, and allowing them to camp for the night in the woods behind his house.

Officials estimate The Ferryman, as his trail name came to be known, transported more than nineteen thousand thru- and section hikers across the river "without a scratch."

Because each ferry requires a round-trip, he crossed the river more than thirty-eight thousand times. He traveled more than fifteen hundred miles on the AT without ever leaving the town where he lived.

Stephen Longley may have paddled a canoe on the AT, but he exemplified the spirit of all those who strive to hike their own hike.

~ ~

Those making a pilgrimage to the Appalachian Trail today not only walk with spring, they also trod a path steeped in the legends of those who built it, nurtured it, shaped its story, and continue to inspire others to follow in their footsteps. All who seek renewal in wilderness leave something of themselves behind. In that respect, the AT isn't just a well-worn track through misty forests and over inspiring heights; it's a shared journey toward enlightenment and self-realization. It's a constantly changing community, a corridor of kindred souls.

The Appalachian Trail Conference doesn't keep performance records on who has hiked the trail the fastest; it discourages folks from trying to set them. That's because there's nothing about the AT experience that requires or compels hikers to compare themselves to any other. Doing so misses the point. The last thing one needs in escaping the rat race is to enter another.

Don't get out of breath trying to keep up with those walking faster who will not wait. Don't let others convince you to dawdle and tarry when you know in your heart it's time to leave. You alone know your abilities. You alone know your limits. You alone can push yourself to do more. You alone establish the goals.

Shortly after he hung up his ferryman's paddle, Stephen Longley died unexpectedly in his sleep of an apparent heart attack. He was just fifty-six years old. While he had helped thousands safely across the Kennebec, when it came time for his life's final crossing, he took it, as will we all, alone.

It doesn't matter whether you're on the trail or off. There really is only one rule in life—hike your own hike.

ALMOST AS GOOD AS GORE-TEX®

Outdoor adventure gear has come a long way since the days when Grandma Gatewood hiked twenty-one hundred miles of the Appalachian Trail in a pair of Keds with two cans of Spam, a plastic shower curtain, and a cast-iron frying pan in her heavy canvas rucksack. Gear has gotten more reliable, more compact, and orders of magnitude lighter.

What that means of course is not that the packs we use to carry the essentials of survival into the wilds have gotten less burdensome, although those who adhere to a minimalist approach do get by with very light loads. What lighter and more compact gear allows us to do is cram in even more stuff.

Part of the allure of all this cool gear is a desire for greater comfort—to rough it in style. As the weight of most items has steadily declined, the movement in price has been inversely proportional. If you're not careful, going high tech to save weight can mean a substantially lighter wallet as well.

Another paradigm shift is that over the past five decades, our wilderness ethos has changed. Two generations ago, we held up deerskin-wearing and musket-toting Daniel Boone as a prime example of how one should act in the wilderness. Now we strive to tread much more lightly, to be more like bug- and bark-eating Cody Lundin, the barefoot hippie survivalist on the Discovery Channel.

If you peruse a Boy Scout handbook from the 1960s, you cannot be faulted for believing all you need to survive in the wilderness is a lumpy, surplus olive-drab sleeping bag, a large box of strike-anywhere kitchen matches, a ball of twine, a trusty hatchet, and a leaky surplus belt canteen with musty canvas cover left over from the Battle for Bastogne.

Nowhere to be found in the handbook is any mention of the notion of becoming one with the wilderness. The pioneer mentality remained alive and well. Nature was something to be vanquished, subjugated, tamed. We came, we saw, we denuded the area—clear-cut and burn.

Although the admonition attributed to Chief Seattle of Washington to take nothing but memories and leave nothing but footprints had been around for a hundred years, it hadn't yet gained traction.

Mid-century Boy Scouts were closet Visigoths foresworn by sacred oath to do a good deed daily. They were a cross between naïve World War I Doughboys and the horny cavemen who lusted after a scantily clad Rachel Welch in *One Million Years B.C.*, a 1966 movie that to this day is offered up by science-denying creationists as irrefutable proof that humans and dinosaurs once roamed the earth at the same time.

Recommended camping techniques involved constructing Stonehenge-like circles of rocks to contain bonfires capable of luring unsuspecting merchant ships to their doom on unforgiving shores. First, of course, it was necessary to strip mine away all organic soil down to the "bare mineral layer." Once this quest for fire was satisfied, then came the felling of copious numbers of live trees to construct lean-to shelters with piles of evergreen boughs for cushioning.

And it was on to crafting spears and setting up lethal snares and deadfalls to catch unsuspecting small mammals and songbirds just in case you forgot to bring the only backpacking staples available at that time—that astronaut-endorsed, crusty, orange-flavored beverage powder called Tang and Dinty Moore Beef Stew in a can. The stew is still made by the good folks at Hormel, the same folks responsible for Gatewood's beloved Spam.

A well-appointed scout encampment had a deep pit for a latrine and drainage ditches hacked into the soil around a perfectly straight line of canvas pup tents. A prescribed distance away was the mandatory steep embankment over which to throw all broken canteens, Tang jars, and empty Dinty Moore Beef Stew cans.

Although there's no formal merit badge for it, playing with fire was, and probably still is, every Boy Scout's favorite pastime. By the time someone gets to the rank of First Class, repeated trial and error leaves them intimately familiar with the relative flammability and burn rate of every natural and man-made material. If someone you know always carries a lighter or matches, but doesn't smoke or have a darknet–based arson-for-hire business on the side, chances are they were once a Boy Scout.

Yes, brave and trustworthy scouts also are all about tying knots, but while the bowline and the tautline and clove hitches are handy for pitching a tent or tying up a boat, the others are suspiciously more useful for restraining prisoners, hostages, and other undesirables, such as Tenderfeet.

Whenever the boys appeared bored and it was too early to start a fire, adult leaders encouraged them to cut down even more trees to build bridges over any minor obstacle or to lash logs together to create the equivalent of a Flintstone cell phone tower. From the top, semaphore flags and Morse code blinks from a flashlight could be used to communicate with the troop on the next hill over to determine if their subjugation of Mother Nature was complete and total as well.

Today, the attitude of those in scouting, and pretty much everyone else who really loves the out-of-doors, has changed. It has morphed from "leave nothing standing" to Leave No Trace, which prizes traveling and camping on durable surfaces, disposing of waste properly, leaving what you find, respecting wildlife, and being considerate of other visitors.

Now, preferred techniques and gear are aimed at treading lightly on the land, not bending it to our will.

Tents are lighter, more spacious, and actually waterproof. And stoves have improved. But the holy trinity of gear, the three items that have had the most transformative effect, are Thermarest sleeping pads, LED headlamps, and Gore-tex® fabric.

Robert Gore patented Gore-tex® in the early 1970s. It featured an outer layer of nylon for strength, which protects an inner layer of fabric that has more than nine billion pores per square inch. Those pores allow the smaller water molecules of water vapor produced from sweat to pass through while preventing the penetration of the much larger water molecules in drops of rain.

In Maine, if you never go backpacking or paddling when it might rain, you never go. Having unreliable and uncomfortable rain gear is not an option.

Gore-tex® works great. It's God's gift to backpacking and paddling. There's just one drawback: cost.

For casual outdoor enthusiasts such as me, even an entry-level jacket costs around $200 or more. Planning on summiting Mount Washington in high winter? Be ready to shell out thousands more for the full kit.

In an attempt to hold the line on cost over the years, I've purchased multiple sets of rain gear I hoped would be economical alternatives to the name brand. All were guaranteed to be waterproof and "fully breathable." I convinced myself that the savings were worth settling for something "almost as good as Gore-tex®."

There were the camouflage pattern pants and jacket purchased from a national retailer that caters to hunters and fishermen. It cost only half as much as one in the same catalog made of genuine Gore-tex®.

I got exactly what I paid for—it kept me dry about half the time.

A year or two later, I broke down and bought another knockoff set, the store brand from an outfitter in North Conway, New Hampshire, that we refer to with half-assed affection as "Expensive Mountain Stuff." It cost a lot more but was still about 30 percent less expensive than entry-level Gore-tex®.

The seams leaked after an hour or so in a heavy downpour. In warmer weather, it was like being inside a portable sauna, even with the "pit zips" open to allow moisture to escape and mosquitoes an express lane to feast upon unprotected underarms.

Having already shelled out one and a half times the cost of the top-shelf set on "almost as good," I finally broke down and bought a genuine Gore-tex® packable shell and pants from L.L. Bean. Dry at last. Dry at last. Lord God almighty, dry at last.

If I had just bought the better set right up front, I'd have actually saved money.

Prior to the availability of Gore-tex®, the choices in rain gear pretty much came down to a basic bulky PVC or nylon poncho, or a yellow vulcanized rubber rain jacket and bibs. The latter was always just a pair of tall fishing boots and a floppy Sou'wester hat short of a one-way trip aboard the *Pequod* to slay the White Whale.

Without a way for moisture to escape what were known as "oilskins," the wearer soon became wetter from the condensation of his or her own sweat inside the jacket and pants than from any downpour or ocean spray.

Ponchos bring with them their own set of eccentricities. Just one step above punching a head and arm holes in a heavy-duty plastic lawn and leaf bag, ponchos can easily snag on passing vegetation and restrict the movement of your arms—always at an inopportune moment. In a headwind, it's almost necessary to walk in a zigzag pattern and tack back and forth like a sailboat to make any forward progress. If they're too long, it's easy to step on the hem in the front and trip yourself up while ascending steep slopes.

Ponchos are heavy, they're noisy, and the last thing they do is keep you warm.

———

While trekking to the summit of Katahdin from Chimney Pond one drizzly June morning, my high school chum and Moose River Camping Club regular Ray is about fifty yards ahead of me on the Saddle Trail. He's wearing an oversized black nylon poncho and an Indiana Jones fedora. Sporting a robust beard and carrying a massive hiking stick that puts the wizard Gandalf's staff to shame, he's picking his way up a large boulder field on a near vertical slope. Everything is slippery and wet. Heavy mists driven by fickle gusts dance up and down the mountainside as we head for the Tableland and the arrival of clearing skies promised by weather forecasters.

A deep-voiced man of respectable size who played football in high school, Ray is a deliberate hiker. Like me, while he's never in danger of being the first one to the top of the mountain, he has a limitless supply of torque. He's the human equivalent of a turbo diesel motor in a piece of heavy construction equipment. Just throw it in gear, and it happily plods ahead at a steady rpm forever until it runs out of fuel or a hydraulic line bursts.

A professional who calculates risks and returns for insurance companies, Ray is a devoted family man who sees nearly everything in life by the numbers. His very presence on this trip is made all the more remarkable by the fact that he has an overwhelming fear of heights. His willingness to confront that phobia in order to share special time with his son and longtime friends says much more about him than any actuary table or spreadsheet of statistics ever could.

For such an inescapable presence, Ray does have this one tiny, annoying habit.

Much like a male dog that seeks to delineate its domain with strategic lifts of the leg, he marks his territory in camp, in a motel room, in someone else's home, by spreading personal items everywhere. Most guys seek to avoid such disorganized sprawl, to respect common areas, keep them as clear as possible—but not Ray.

Upon arrival, pieces of his gear and articles of clothing become strewn everywhere—jacket over the couch, water bottle on the kitchen counter, boots in the corner near the TV, daypack in the overstuffed chair. No matter how many people are sharing the bathroom, his toiletries soon cover every inch of flat surface surrounding the sink.

The bigger problem comes later when he can't remember where he left things. And when he can't find something, it's always someone else's fault. The usual suspects of the subsequent tirade range from the "mother effing universe" in general to any unfortunate innocent within earshot who may have moved or repositioned one of said toiletries some barely detectable fraction of an inch.

Much earlier that morning, around 6 a.m., several of us are standing outside the bunkhouse at Chimney Pond, eager to tackle the remaining twenty-three hundred feet of elevation gain to get to the top of the mile-high mountain.

In any group such as the MRCC, there's always one straggler. He's the guy who never makes it back to the car at the appointed time when you split up for the stop at the Kittery Trading Post. When everyone else is all packed and ready to hit the trail, he's still in his tent just beginning to roll up his sleeping bag.

So, as usual, we're all just waiting on Ray. We can hear him banging around inside the dark, cramped confines of the cabin swearing loudly.

"What the hell is going on?" my brother Carl yells to him.

Ray stomps outside onto the small wooden deck, waving one of the calf-length gaiters he uses to keep grit and water out of his hiking boots. "I can't find my other gaiter," he shouts, pacing back and forth. "Which one of you freaking guys took my gaiter?"

In Ray's world, the prospect that someone had stolen just one gaiter, perhaps in error, but more likely in an act of deliberate provocation, is at the top of his probabilities list. The possibility that it may have been tucked away somewhere in the recesses of his own pack or accidentally kicked under a bunk never enters the picture. Someone is screwing with him, because as far as he's concerned, someone is always screwing with him.

"I know you guys just want to get going. Don't wait for me," Ray continues. "Just freaking go . . . go, I'll catch up to you."

We all look at each other in disbelief.

"Ray, Ray," Carl says in a calm and soothing tone. "No one took your gaiter. It's got to be there somewhere. We're not in a rush. It's going to be okay."

Ray stops waving the gaiter back and forth over his head. His shoulders relax as he takes a deep breath.

"Ray," Carl continues, a big smirk on his face. "Look on your left leg."

There's the prodigal gaiter already buckled and velcroed in place.

"#@%!" says Ray as he disappears back into the cabin to affix the gaiter in his hand to his exposed leg and to grab his daypack. "#@%! #@%! #@%!"

⌒

While not classified as technical climbing, every hiking route up Katahdin is at some point precipitous enough to require the use of hands to make progress. The upper portion of the Saddle Trail is no different. While it's free of the sheer drop-offs of the Cathedral or Knife Edge Trails that also ascend from the Great South Basin, the risk of serious falls is very real. Opportunities abound to trigger our primal fear of plunging to gruesome injury or death.

Most of the time while hiking in exposed places, that dread is kept on leash, tugging you along awkwardly from time to time, but seldom straying far from the obvious path. But every once in a while, fear slips its tether and turns on its master, snarling, red-eyed, fangs at the ready.

Hitting that point where predisposition and instinct can no longer be suppressed, where your gut tells you not to move a single muscle, seldom involves a clear moment of embarkation. It's subtler, its arrival unexpected—set off by the lack of an obvious handhold on a near-vertical wall, the questionable soundness of a loose boulder underfoot, or something about the angle of an icy ledge and whether your worn-out boots will hold.

Individual breaking points differ. Even within ourselves, it's a moving target that seldom telegraphs its intentions. Like Wile E. Coyote chasing the Roadrunner off a cliff, we zip straight past reason's point of no return, not recognizing our exposure until gravity is all that remains between us and a long, whistling fall to a muted bang and a puff of dust.

The first step on the way back to emotional terra firma is to acknowledge that the most formidable obstacle is in the mind. To escape a prison built of fear, you need to reverse its death grip on reason, float above it, view it from afar.

On any climb, you think and plan far enough ahead to avoid getting into such predicaments, but when prescience and foresight fail, it's up to you to talk yourself down off the metaphysical ledge. You can't stay there forever. The way out is always the same. Take a deep breath, eyes forward, maintain three points of contact with the earth and with reality—plan, execute, move.

⁓

As I attempt to get across a tricky section with difficult footing near the top of the Saddle, I suddenly hear Ray yelling above me on the tumbledown rocks of the slide. "Aiiieeeee, Aiiieeeee, Aiiieeeee!" he screams with the intensity of a vanquished supervillain tumbling from the top of the Empire State Building at the end of a Marvel comic book. "I can't see! I can't see!"

Fifty feet above me on the trail looms a large, fluttering black blob with an arm sticking out holding a big stick. A gust of wind shooting up the headwall has caught the back of Ray's poncho and flipped it up and over his head. Perched precariously on a slippery, narrow ledge, essentially blindfolded, his other hand unwilling to relinquish its grip on a spindly spruce, his panic has slipped its leash.

"Hold on, Ray. I'm coming up," I yell. "Just stay put. Don't move."

As I begin to scramble up the boulders, I detect rapid movement just above Ray on the trail. Despite the fog, I recognize that it's Harry, another member of the MRCC, scrambling to get down to where Ray is experiencing what he undoubtedly believes is the worst moment of his life.

Harry's calm and deadpan demeanor is exactly the opposite of Ray's. An electrical engineer who has traveled all over the world to work on avionics in high-tech helicopters for Sikorsky, he has been an inseparable part of my family's extended clan since he first befriended my nephew Ryan in grade school. With shoulder-length blonde hair and a bushy beard that would put even the most diehard religious fundamentalists and hermits to shame, Harry looks to be just a hoodie, a windowless cabin, and a handwritten manifesto away from being the son of the Unabomber.

A talented guitarist who plays in a popular Connecticut rock band, his Garth from *Wayne's World* diction betrays no hint that deep inside lies the buttoned-down soul of someone extremely proficient with a slide rule and with a predilection for United Technologies pocket protectors.

For all his fondness for modernity and popular culture, Harry is first and foremost a man of nature. While the mental gymnastics of calculating the values of various resistors and diodes and/or immersing himself in a fog of loud music are daily diversions, they only drown out, not calm, his occasionally tortured soul. For that, the only salve is wilderness. Only Mother Nature offers the serenity and order he craves.

For all their differences, Ray and Harry do share a common denominator. Both had long ago been taken under Carl's wing, bestowed with patience and love by a man of frequent annoyance who has no hesitation to curtly dismiss any and all who would try to BS him or waste his time.

That paternal instinct is quintessential Carl. Like a drover working the edges of a cattle drive to see that even those with a powerful predisposition to wander never get too far from the safety of the herd, he's the heart and soul of the MRCC. For him, the group is a natural extension of family, a community of his own creation, another sphere for belonging, the natural expression of his own love of the outdoors.

Carl is the one who chases everyone to set dates for our trips. When someone needs a piece of gear, Carl is there with a spare. A little short on cash for a trip? "I gotcha covered," he'll say, even if his own finances are tight.

Carl's the one standing there tapping his foot and staring at his watch when someone is late getting back to the car during a stop on a road trip. Without him, there's no way anything would be done, as the British like to say, "on shed-ual."

As Harry reaches Ray, the black blob has grown silent. The poncho continues to flap like a tarp tied over the statue of some long-forgotten general in an obscure corner of a public park on the night before its unveiling. Talking softly to keep Ray apprised of the plan, Harry flips the poncho flap off Ray's head. Ray looks around to reorient himself to his situation, eyes blinking rapidly to recover from his descent into darkness.

"Let's just sit down and take a little break," Harry says, pointing to a flat, level area. Joining them at that spot, I fish around in my pack for a couple of extra bungee cords. "Hey Ray, why don't you put these around your waist as kind of a belt," I say. "It will keep it from flying over your head again."

Due to a variety of family obligations, Ray does not have a lot of discretionary cash to spend on gear. That leaves him a little insecure on the subject. While I was only trying to be helpful, Ray takes the suggestion as some kind of backhanded insult to his choice of outerwear.

"It's easy for you goddamn guys with your $200 Gore-tex® jackets," Ray fumes. "Not everybody can afford those kinds of toys," he adds.

I totally know how he feels. While hiking with a group of inner-city Boy Scouts wearing surplus camo pants and T-shirts from Wal-Mart, I've encountered families where the mom, dad, and all three kids are wearing matching jackets and wind pants from Patagonia. They cost the equivalent of half my winter heating bill. The looks of horror on their faces when they saw how the scouts were dressed made their disdain obvious.

"No one's dissing your gear," I reassure Ray. "Just trying to be helpful." With the bungees grudgingly in place, we press on, cresting the lip of the Tableland just as the first gleams of sunshine begin to poke through the clouds as promised.

Like all of New England's treeless alpine zones, the Tableland seems not of this earth. The mountain reluctantly allows little more than sedges, blueberry bushes, and patches of stunted krummholz to grow here. Yet in amongst the lee of lichen-encrusted boulders, small patches of rare *diapensia* and Lapland rosebay bloom, their delicate white and pink blossoms straight up and defiant, their fragility standing in stark contrast to the obstinate granite. Holding on at the edge of the habitable zone, theirs is the ultimate survival story. The fragile moss-like clumps of these plants have persevered for eons in places where the temperature doesn't rise above zero for months and where gale-force winds howl for days at a time. Yet one careless step by an errant or ignorant hiker is all it takes to snuff out their hardscrabble existence.

From the intersection at the top of the Saddle, the paler color of well-trampled rock makes the upward arc of the trail to Baxter Peak readily apparent. The way forward is obvious and clear, just ruts and rocks, no cliffs, little chance of catastrophic failure. Even the wind that harassed us on the ascent has abated, the weather gods deciding to cut us some slack.

As Harry strides toward the summit, Ray and I rev up our motors for the next push. It's his first summit attempt. For me it's number three.

After setting out for the top of Katahdin, which he never reached, Thoreau wrote, "The tops of mountains are among the unfinished parts of the globe." He continued, "Only daring and insolent men, perchance, go there."

The broken bedrock and jumbled boulders surrounding the summit cairn offer little in the way of shelter from the nonstop winds. For all the time, for all the sweat, for all the blood and tears necessary to get there, few tarry for long. The mountain leaves no doubt about who belongs and who will be only a temporary visitor. Only the occasional crow seems to float above that chiseled landscape with ease.

While Katahdin is often referred to as "mile-high," in fact, surveyors long ago determined its true height at 5,268 feet, some 12 feet shy. Over the years, visitors have assembled various tall cairns of stones at the peak, allowing the reference to be cited with a straight face.

Regardless of the elevation, the view in all directions is spectacular. Directly behind the summit cairn, the cliff drops off a thousand feet. To the east lie the dips and heights of the majestic Knife Edge. To the west, lesser mountain deities sprawl all the way to the border with New Hampshire.

To the south, the forest is studded with lakes and ponds so numerous that Thoreau described them as "a mirror broken into a thousand fragments."

The top of Katahdin is the kind of place that, once visited, never leaves your soul.

It's impossible for anyone of true heart to stand atop its ancient granite and not hope and pray to be fortunate enough to stand there once again.

Turning to Ray, I wave my trekking pole to signal to him to take point. "Turbo time," I say as we begin the final slog to the top.

———

While online reviews and word of mouth helps, most true out-doorsmen and women eventually settle on their basic gear lists through good old-fashioned trial and error.

There's a big difference between what looks good in the store or in the catalog and what works really well in the field. The best comparison is to look at what enthusiastic Appalachian Trail thru-hikers set out with from Springer Mountain in Georgia and then see what's still in their packs when they reach the top of Katahdin in Maine six months later. It's amazing the number of heavy steel hatchets and "don't taze me bro" 10 "D" cell cop flashlights that get pitched into the puckerbrush before the first road crossing north of Springer.

If something is still in a pack when a thru-hiker gets dropped off on the side of Route 15 north of Monson to begin a ten-day transit of the 100-Mile Wilderness, you know it can serve several purposes, and that it's reliable, lightweight, and indispensable.

The availability of quality gear—and how it's marketed—has come a long way over the decades. It used to be that hunting supply and sporting goods stores were the only options. The camping and Boy Scout section was always tucked away in a back corner behind the rack of Little League uniforms, just to the right of the jockstrap display and a countertop pyramid of suspiciously greasy bottles of "Doe in Heat" buck lure.

Now, North Face and Patagonia outlets seem to be everywhere. REI and Campmore are giants online. In Maine, we enjoy brick-and-mortar retailers such as Cadillac Mountain Sports, Cabela's, L.L. Bean, and the Kittery Trading Post.

Magazines and websites such as *Backpacker*, *Canoe and Kayak*, and *Outside* regularly rate gear, profile destinations, and share the latest tips and techniques.

When it comes to purchasing outdoor gear, it's important to remember that almost every product description comes with an invisible asterisk representing unwritten yet vital caveats that begin with words such as "if," "but," "unless," or "in the eventuality. . . ."

Take for instance, choosing the right-size tent. All descriptions include tiny diagrams showing how many sleeping people theoretically will fit inside. Usually, they're depicted with small puffy wedge shapes representing an average person in a tapered mummy sleeping bag. I have never gone camping with anyone, including small children, who only took up as much space in the tent as one of those wedges.

The prescribed number of people will only fit if folks lay in alternating rows with each person's face just inches away from their companions' stinky feet. And, because no tent spot is perfectly flat, wedging that many people into a tiny rectangle guarantees most of them will have their heads angled downhill or have a fist-sized rock or root between their shoulder blades all night long.

None of the capacity estimates takes into account the fact that each of those people will want to keep some of their gear in the tent with them, especially if it's raining or snowing. And it doesn't predict how many times each of them will be crawling over the others to get up in the night to pee.

In the end, actually fitting the advertised number of people inside a tent is like trying to get something back into the original packaging to return it to the store. It can be done in theory, but in practice, there's always something left over that doesn't fit.

The secret here is to always round down. A supercompact two-person tent, sarcastically referred to as a honeymoon suite among seasoned hikers, is perfect for one. A four is just right for two. A six is adequate for four.

It's like recommended serving sizes and calorie counts on prepackaged food. When it says "serves 12," and that's how many people you hope to feed, get two.

When the calories per serving or carb count on a bag of chips seems low, look closely. The label will list something ridiculous like "Serving size, about two chips." When was the last time anyone you knew ate just two chips?

And speaking of serving sizes, there's not a single, dehydrated backpacking meal "for one" out there that actually fills you up. Most won't keep a chickadee alive. Your best bet on a solo hike—pack the ones that say "serves two."

When it comes to sleeping bags, the comfort ratings are all extraordinarily optimistic. Several decades ago, when a bag was advertised as rated for 10 degrees, you could believe it. Because sleeping in a tent adds several degrees of warmth, and use of a good sleeping pad ups that even more, you could be confident that you would enjoy a comfortable night at that temperature.

But no more.

Now, when someone says a bag is rated for 10 degrees, the formula they use already presupposes you're in a tent and using a sleeping pad, but also that there's no wind, and that you're probably wearing long johns and a fleece hat. If you are not, all bets are off.

By the way, people, speaking of fleece hats, we don't actually lose half our body heat through our heads. It's an urban myth perpetuated by helicopter moms, overly protective kindergarten teachers, and hat manufacturers.

Researchers for the *British Medical Journal* discovered an early reference to this misleading statistic in a 1970s-era U.S. Army survival manual. That one sentence was apparently based on a flawed arctic survival study done during the 1950s, the same decade that brought us Perry Como sweaters, the Edsel, and Tang. It showed that if someone was bundled up below zero but did not wear a hat, most of the total heat loss in that scenario was from their head. Duh.

But that's not close to half the heat your body is generating. In fact, if you stood naked outside at 0 degrees, you'd lose about 10 percent of your warmth through your head, which comprises about 10 percent of your body's surface area. Of course, if you did stand outside naked at such temperatures, said head would be in dire need of examination.

So, don't expect a 10-degree sleeping bag to keep you warm at anything under 20 degrees. The rating doesn't mean you'll be comfortable, just that you're not likely to die of hypothermia. If it's going to be 20 degrees overnight, you probably should pack a bag rated for 0.

━━━

The hike down from Chimney Pond to the parking area at Roaring Brook on the last day of any Katahdin expedition is always bittersweet. At some point along the way, the urge to stop and glance back fades as the lure of home eclipses the desire to linger in a beautiful place that holds great power over the heart. Still, like horses at a riding stable that will no longer respond to a tug on the reins, there's no turning a backpacker around once they know they're near the end of the trail, on the home stretch, heading back to the barn.

As usual, we take the short side trail to pause at the scenic overlook near Basin Ponds, to grab the last few photographs.

The stark, granite headwalls of the Great North and South Basins loom tall to the westard. The pale green fire of newly sprouted leaves has yet to spread to the highest places. Stubborn patches of snow still cling to the steepest slopes, reminders of the glaciers that once carved these spectacular valleys.

Above, the cloudless sky is a dazzling blue. The mountain's usual crown of mist has decided to take such a perfect day off. As we stand in silence, eyes transfixed, our hearts say our goodbyes to the mountain. We must return to the world of traffic, ringing phones, bills, careers, and responsibilities. Despite the truth before us, we still subscribe to the fiction that our day-to-day lives are the reality, and all this is only a dream.

Without a breeze to harass them, the welcoming committee of blackflies grows thick. We don't tarry long. Packs are shouldered, and it's down the rugged trail, past the iconic Halfway Rock to where the route crosses the stream flush with water that just hours ago was ice.

For the rest of the way, we'll march in tandem with the roar of tumbling water along the former logging road back to Roaring Brook.

After signing out in the hiking register on the porch of the ranger cabin, it's time to pack up and head for home. Boots are swapped for street shoes and packs stacked in the back. Discussion wanders to gear: what worked, what disappointed, and what's in dire need of an upgrade before the next trip.

Often when you get new gear, the item it replaces escapes being relegated to the yard sale box and remains in inventory. In the mind it still has value, if for no other reason than discarding it could be seen as invalidating the justification for the original purchase.

Usually, such items are relegated to backup, or "beater," status, the equivalent of a rusty old car that can still be called upon to get you back and forth to work in a pinch—providing you check the gas, fill the oil, and keep your fingers crossed.

The subtext is that if and when a beater gives up the ghost, you can merely remove the plates, roll it into the ditch, and walk away without remorse.

As Carl begins stashing his gear in the minivan, he notices his beater set of rain gear, folded carefully in the plastic milk crate full of extra stuff he keeps in the back. Among the jumble in the crate are a spare headlamp, shoelaces, water bottle, knife, bug stuff, sunscreen, spork, matches, fifty feet of parachute cord, batteries, and a roll of TP in a Ziploc bag.

No worries. If someone forgets to pack something in the rush to get out of the house, Carl often has a spare. That's just the way he is. Whether it's being a scoutmaster, serving as a deacon in his church, being the best dad he can, tolerating everyone's eccentricities on camping trips, or pulling one more chair up to the table for someone who could use a little more love in their lives, Carl always has everything, and everyone, covered.

Carl stares at the rain jacket and pants for a moment before gently lifting them from the crate and walking over to where Ray is struggling to get a sweat-stained Orville H. Platt High School football T-shirt over his head.

"Hey Ray," he says softly. "I think this will fit you."

After standing quietly for a moment, Ray reaches for the rain suit, admiring the camouflage pattern on the waterproof yet breathable fabric. "Thank you. It's a definite upgrade from what I've got now," Ray admits.

"I never had any problems with it," Carl explains. "It kept me dry hiking in the sleet and snow on the AT on Mount Greylock in Massachusetts last November," he adds.

Carl returns to the van and resumes organizing his gear. When I mention what a kindness it was to give Ray the rain gear, he shrugs it off as usual.

"I don't need it anymore, and he could really use it," Carl says.

"It's definitely better than that freakin' poncho," he says. "It's almost as good as Gore-tex®."

WHAT BEARS DO IN THE WOODS

EVERYONE HAS HEARD THE RUSTIC RETORT REGARDING THE bathroom habits of bears in the woods. When it comes to employing the planet's preeminent English curse word, that expression is only slightly less popular than the deliciously sarcastic comeback concerning Sherlock Holmes's grasp of the obvious.

Anyone who spends any decent amount of time in the out-of-doors eventually needs to do what the bears—and the Pope for that matter—do.

After making preparations to stay warm and stay fed, nothing seems to preoccupy folks about to embark on a wilderness expedition more than going to the bathroom. Look at the top of every packing list. Matches or lighter—check. Knife—check. Toilet paper—double and triple ply check.

Survival experts say that you can live for several days without water and several weeks without food. But there is a deafening silence on how long you can forestall a descent into depraved inhumanity without an adequate supply of sqeezably soft TP.

One of the first questions greenhorn clients ask guides is "Where will we go to the bathroom?" The best flippant response comes from the movie *The Big Chill*. "That's the great thing about the outdoors," actor Jeff Goldblum's character, Michael Gold, says. "It's one giant toilet."

The real answer, of course, is that it depends. After forsaking the thin veneer of civilization that is indoor plumbing, you enter an odious world of outhouses, privies, pit toilets, and cat holes. While each of the aforementioned options may seem unpalatable compared to our own home commode advantages, it's amazing how strong a stench one can endure—and how many bugs, cobwebs, and obscene graffiti we will tolerate—in order to have a comparatively dry, sheltered place in which to skip to the loo.

In the movie *Animal House*, the character Boon implores a receptionist at an exclusive girls' school to help find dates for his awkward friends. "We're willing to trade looks . . . for a certain morally casual attitude," he says. That's it exactly. It's astonishing how little time it takes on the trail for someone's American standards to go from "there's no way I'm going to use that malodorous affront to all that is good and decent" to "Let's camp here. There's an outhouse!"

For those inclined to take a scholarly approach to all things scatological, there's even a guidebook to relieving oneself outdoors titled *How to S**t in the Woods*, by Kathleen Meyer. She's without question the number one authority when it comes being outdoors and needing to do a number two.

The most nagging question not answered by our modern preoccupation with proper poop practices is how did our Paleolithic ancestors know what to do for eons without benefit of such authoritative references?

For those incapable of imagining taking a regular constitutional sans magazine rack or Wi-Fi access, there are a handful of wilderness options.

Least attractive to most, but highly recommended by experts who apparently do know Jack you-know-what about that, is the lowly cat hole.

Creating a cat hole involves carving a depression in the duff on the floor of the forest some six to eight inches deep, then squatting, leaning against a tree or boulder, or hanging your butt off a fallen log to conduct said business. Accuracy, of course, counts. The duff is then returned to cover and disguise the insult. Bacteria and natural processes take it from there.

Some outdoor gear manufacturers actually sell a small trowel for said transactions, but the heel of your boot or a stick works just fine.

Proper etiquette and the dictates of good sanitation require that all cat holes be at least two hundred feet back from water sources, campsites, and trails.

Some places, specifically narrow river canyons out west, require that people pack out their own used toilet paper and waste. I'll leave you at "ewww!" on that one.

One step up from the lowly cat hole is a pit toilet—basically a seat atop a box over a halfheartedly dug hole. There are no walls or roof. Even if set off in an inconspicuous location, a pit toilet leaves the user feeling extraordinarily exposed and vulnerable, particularly when it's raining, the blackflies and mosquitoes are really bad, or a troop of ebullient Boy Scouts rolls in to share the campsite. At least when you're doing what comes naturally en plein air, you're surrounded by wilderness in all its 360-degree glory.

Atop the you-know-what house pantheon are outhouses and privies. There's no rule of thumb when an outhouse, also known as the back house, earth house, or even "the crescent moon room," can be officially classified as a privy. When camping, my dad Al always talked about having to make a trip to the "Shoney," which apparently refers to a popular restaurant chain often found at highway rest areas including in the Northeast, Midwest, and in Tennessee where he served in the Navy in the 1950s.

Whatever the slang, all outhouse terms appear to be inter-changeable. Perhaps a privy is an outhouse with pretentious aspirations of greatness. Fair enough, but it's probably no Shoney.

Outhouses don't need to be anything fancy, just four walls, a sloped roof, a bench with a hole cut in it, and a door, preferably with a latch.

A seat with a lid is nice. But that is often considered to be an after-market accessory—not standard equipment on your entry-level models that qualify for the 0 percent for sixty months financing.

Outhouses are three or four feet square, usually designed to make the most efficient use of standard-size building materials. The majority are made of wood, but some, especially in southern climes conducive to termites, are literally built like brick you-know-what houses.

Builders often include a crescent moon cutout in the door in a nod to tradition. The originations of the practice appear to be lost in the mists of time. The Internet is rife with speculation about the moon, ranging from ventilation to simple ornamentation.

Symbols were used to telegraph gender, one theory suggests, during a time when most people could not read. Luna is a symbol of femininity. Men's outhouses purportedly had a more masculine star in the door.

The reasoning goes that the ladies took better care of the out-houses designated for them, so the ones with the moon survived in greater number, and eventually, the symbol became ubiquitous. All the women I know will go to great lengths to avoid ever setting foot, much less fanny, in an outhouse. So I don't understand a line of reasoning that has them spending any more time there than absolutely necessary.

The notion of separate his and hers facilities most likely is a modern affectation. Even on prosperous colonial farms, it was more expeditious and much less expensive just to include extra holes in one "necessary" than to build two separate structures.

Lacking a definitive answer, I have an answer that may further confuse the issue. In England in the early 1700s, *moon* was used as a synonym for *buttocks*. Mooning, or exposing one's derriere to the enemy during armed conflict, was a time-honored if not somewhat risky tradition, particularly in light of rapid improvements in the accuracy and range of firearms.

It only makes sense that in England's colonies in North America, a cutout of a moon would come to signify the one structure in polite society where people of either gender were permitted to bare their posteriors.

Regardless of mode, going to the bathroom outdoors engenders an extraordinary sensation of vulnerability. Parts of us, highly prized and valuable parts, parts we don't like to talk about, much less show off to the world and the inquisitive eyes of passing woodland creatures, are left naked, exposed. What, we fear, is hiding down there just waiting to take advantage of what for all manner of creepy-crawlies has to be a target-rich environment?

Sure, in urban areas, there are the occasional *National Enquirer* stories about boa constrictors or rodents emerging from toilets in search of an escape from the bowels of an urban sewer system. Fortunately, such incidents are few and far between. Most people don't give using a modern toilet a second thought.

But in an outhouse, there's no water, no barrier between you and whatever may lurk below, whether it's a hungry mosquito about to have the best day of her short, miserable existence, or the slime-drenched homicidal alien beast from actress Sigourney

Weaver's worst nightmare. Remember, in an outhouse, as in outer space, no one can hear you scream.

Perhaps the least attractive outdoor toilet options are those ubiquitous plastic sarcophagi known as porta-potties you see all lined up at concerts, country fairs, and construction sites like General Burgoyne's redcoats waiting to be picked off by minutemen at the bridge in Lexington.

The fastest way on the planet to determine whether you're predisposed to claustrophobia is to step into one, especially after it has been sitting in full sun on a humid day in August. Beneath the flimsy floor lies an aromatic, blue-tinted, organic soup, the chemical kissing cousin of the methane-infused ocean that awaits the first astronaut who sets foot on Europa.

Forget those tiny bottles of hand sanitizer. You need a fifty-five-gallon drum "gigando" size after a trip to a chemical toilet.

Fortunately, porta-potties are seldom encountered except at trailhead parking lots. For all their lack of appeal, almost any bathroom option in the great outdoors is still orders of magnitude better than most inner-city service station or sports venue pit stops.

───❦───

According to the all-knowing Oracle of Google, Maine is second only to Alaska when it comes to a fondness for outhouses. The Pine Tree State has an estimated four thousand homes without indoor plumbing.

And that doesn't take into account thousands more at cabins, camps, and campsites. All are strategically situated in the backyard equivalent of the solar system's Goldilocks Zone—that narrow range of distance from a sun in which habitable planets may be found. In the case of outhouses, it's important that it not be too close for noses to be offended by an unfortunate wind shift in summer, nor too far to pose a midnight commuting hardship during winter.

As is befitting a state where folks embrace the "go big or go back to Massachusetts" philosophy, some outhouses in Maine are candidates for inclusion in the *Guinness Book of World Records*. It was not uncommon on larger farms to have outhouses with two, three, or even four holes.

The allocation of openings was approached from a big, bad wolf perspective. When there were four, you'd find two for men, one for women, and one "just right" for a child. It seems the toilet allocation paradigm that to this day results in too few stalls for women, forcing them to wait in potty dance conga lines, goes way, way back.

The apparent holer record-holder in Maine was at a lumber camp in the Allagash region. It boasted eight. Whether that was a not-so-ringing endorsement of the cookee's cuisine or an acknowledgment that large numbers of baked-bean lovin' lumberjacks were "regular" guys remains unknown.

Most likely, casual conversation was not a part of the social paradigm of multiple hole outhouses, as the obvious discomforts of unmitigated climate and olfactory affront did not invite anyone to tarry longer than necessary.

In addition to supersizing the number of holes, Maine outhouse designers did what the best architects in the world's major cities do when space is at a premium—they built up.

The Town Hall in Bridgewater, Maine, has a two-story outhouse attached to the back. The building is even on the National Register of Historic Places. Apparently, they take their you-know-what very seriously.

There's another two-story outhouse attached to the Grange Hall in Bryant Pond, the last place in America to give up using hand-crank telephones. Not to be outdone, the Masons Lodge next door installed a three-story outhouse. Why? Apparently they'll tell you, but then they'll have to kill you.

Multistory models offset the seats on each level so as to allow unimpeded transit of all effluvia to the honey hole, because, as television mobster Tony Soprano was fond of pointing out to his crooked-nose subordinates, "since time immemorial, money flows uphill and you-know-what runs downhill."

Golfers yell "fore." Prior to a detonation, those who work with explosives yell "fire in the hole." Emily Post remains silent on what proper etiquette requires of the person on the upper levels of towering outhouses to do to warn those below when you-know-what happens.

Most small outhouses are simply moved to a new hole in the ground when the pit below becomes full. But those attached to primary structures require regular cleanouts. Servicing outhouses was once a thriving business, with the practice lending itself to the quintessential Maine expression describing someone who can't leave well enough alone, or who likes to raise a stink. Those rabble-rousers are known to this day as you-know-what stirrers.

Census records show that not far from that two-story outhouse in Bridgewater lived a family with the last name of Outhouse. Records of their primary occupation were not kept, but one can speculate. The family patriarch's first name, of course, was John.

The latest trend in Maine tourism is the establishment of various "Trails" linking together towns, sites, and attractions by interest rather than geographical proximity. There's the Maine Birding Trail, the Maine Art Museum Trail, even the Maine Beer Trail. which, if you're not careful, could easily become the Maine you-know-what-faced trail.

You get the picture.

Why has not some enterprising P.T. Barnum established the Maine Outhouse Trail? At the very least, the online, interactive map would be helpful for those always in search of the next Shoney.

Perhaps nowhere in Maine are there a greater variety of unique outhouses than along the Appalachian Trail. The volunteers and trail crews from the Maine Appalachian Trail Club who are responsible for building and maintaining all the campsites have shown great imagination and even a welcome sense of bathroom humor in their approach to the dirtiest of jobs.

You could say that when it comes to privies, they really have their you-know-what together.

Up on Bigelow Mountain, Maine's second highest peak, at the Horns Pond campsite, there is a two-story outhouse designed to look like a castle tower. Affectionately known as the "solar one-holer," it's located on a side hill with access to the upper-level throne room provided by a wooden drawbridge of sorts.

Waste—and a handful of peat moss tossed in by the user—lands in a series of bins on a carousel on the lower level. The designated you-know-what out of luck caretaker must spin the bins as they become full to expose the contents to enhanced airflow and the heat of the sun. Once "cooked," it becomes compost that's used to help fertilize the forest in high-traffic areas.

Over on the approaches to Saddleback Mountain, near Range-ley, at the Piazza Rock campsite, there's a two-holer with a unique name—"Your Move." That's because a cribbage board is perma-nently mounted in the space between the two seats.

For years, one of the most nicely appointed outhouses anywhere could be found at the Antler's campsite on Lower Jo-Mary Lake in the 100-Mile Wilderness section of the AT. The two-holer was very roomy and well ventilated, with log siding and a double-hung window with curtains. A mirror hung inside on the wall. The white-painted door sported the requisite crescent moon cutout. Christened "Fort Relief," it felt almost like home.

It has since been replaced by a plywood outhouse that is dry and suitably comfortable, although it doesn't come close to matching the charm of the original.

Maybe it just needs a cribbage board.

Don't get me wrong. There are plenty of dark, damp, and stinky outhouses at campsites all over Maine, but it's getting better all the time.

As far as nominations for Maine AT Outhouse of the Year, my vote would go to the one at the Potawadjo Springs campsite, just four miles north of Fort Relief in the 100-Miles. The campsite is named for the largest spring on the entire AT. Crystal-clear, icy-cold water bubbles up in a twenty-foot-diameter, moss-lined pool on the side of a hill. The force of the flow is so strong that large bits of gravel can sometimes be seen dancing on the bottom.

The outhouse here, wisely located a good distance from the spring, is nothing fancy, but it's clean, level, well-ventilated, with a relatively new roof. In that respect, it's the Hilton of outhouses, even if Paris, who thinks her you-know-what doesn't stink, and her little dog, too, would never be caught dead there.

Returning to a previously visited outhouse is like the cuisine at McDonald's. It will never get written up in *Gourmet* magazine, but when you go there, you know what to expect.

One thing you won't find at most outhouses in the backcountry in Maine, except in places like Baxter State Park that require advanced reservations, is toilet paper. Ah, as a more scatologically minded bard might exclaim, "There's the wipe."

Only the arrogant or naïve embark on a backcountry excursion in Maine without their own stash of TP. If you don't, you're likely to find yourself literally up you-know-what creek with or without a paddle.

Even if someone has been kind enough to leave some, well, behind, it is likely to be shredded by mice looking for material to insulate their nests. Rare is the facility that does not sport coffee cans and lids to shield the paper from these furtive, furry thieves.

It's simple human nature when using an outhouse equipped with toilet paper to use what's already there first in order to conserve your supply. That dynamic pretty much ensures that any unclaimed tissue disappears pretty fast.

The time to find out there is no TP in the coffee can, or that you should have tucked the Ziploc bag with yours into your pocket before heading up the side path, is before you sit down.

The rule of thumb for determining how much TP to bring follows the same universal approach as collecting firewood in preparation for a very long, cold night. Get as much as you think you'll possibly need—then double it.

Going by how many sheets are on a roll is no help in determining how much to bring unless you happen to know exactly how many sheets you use each time you go. If you do, in fact, know that number off the top of your head, it's undeniable proof you definitely need to get out more.

When it comes to packing plenty of TP, no one can surpass my friend Lisa, who explained that her mother told her as a little girl always to use plenty.

On a three-day trip to the Fowler Ponds area in the north of Baxter State Park, I notice her backpack is hanging low on her shoulders. It seems bulkier than expected for the length of the trip and the expected conditions. Sure enough, when we get to the first campsite and she begins to unpack, I see the top compartment contains six large double rolls of two-ply TP. And taking the firewood rule of thumb in mind, her dunnage also includes two six-packs of king-size Pabst Blue Ribbon beers.

The abundance of both of those necessities would be of no help later that afternoon when Lisa experiences a close encounter of the outhouse kind. For as long as she can, she postpones making a trip to the privy due to her loathing of spiders and dread of confined spaces. Ever the lady, the smell on this hot summer afternoon is a deal breaker for her as well.

After setting up our tents and getting a jump on the firewood supply, I use the campsite's broom to sweep every cobweb I can see out of the outhouse. Still, Lisa continues to procrastinate. Finally, her roommate Bonnie and I suggest she just use the facility with the door open. It's not as crazy an idea as it may sound.

With the doors left open, some of Maine's backcounty out-houses have spectacular, $1,000-per-night views. The multiple-unit ones at Chimney Pond in Baxter State Park come immediately to mind. Several open directly out to a view of Katahdin's spectacu-lar two-thousand-foot headwall that towers over the small glacial cirque. Throw in sunlight glinting off the rustling birch and poplar leaves and the delightful trill of forest songbirds, and using that privy becomes an almost transcendent experience.

Wide-open doors provide superior light and ventilation. If the facility is correctly situated, there's usually a good line of sight on the access trail, providing more than enough time to swing the door shut should you not be in a chatty mood or especially good at cribbage.

Bonnie and I promise Lisa we'll remain down by the shore of Lower Fowler Pond while she uses the outhouse al fresco. She is only gone a few minutes when we hear her hollering. Bonnie and I sprint through the woods worried that the you-know-what has hit the metaphorical fan.

Neither of us could have predicted what we see. Standing about four feet in front of the open door is a handsome fourteen-point buck. He walked around from in back of the outhouse as Lisa sat there sans trousers and then turned his thick, long neck and head to look in.

Lisa screamed. The deer froze. It was hard to decide who was most embarrassed by the encounter.

As soon as the deer composes itself, it takes flight. Lisa is none the worse for wear, but insists on using the outhouse with the door closed from then on, preferably with one of us standing watch outside.

One time while on a Moose River Camping Club backpacking trip on Mount Mansfield in Vermont, the decision was made to hike to the summit and back at first light to get ahead of severe thundershowers forecast for that afternoon. I awake just before 5 a.m. at Taft Lodge, the oldest and largest shelter on the Long Trail, far above Smuggler's Notch on the mountain's east face. Slipping my weather-beaten $5 camouflage camp Crocs from Wal-Mart onto my feet, I stumble up the rooted trail to the outhouse in an effort to beat what essentially will be the post-breakfast rush.

Reaching the outhouse, about a hundred yards from the cabin, I climb the handful of stairs to the door and pull on the handle. I'm surprised to find it latched from the inside.

Worrying I have intruded on some deep thinker's morning reverie, I retreat the mandatory twenty paces and begin awkwardly staring at the forest canopy above as the first rays of the sun paint the tallest branches. After what seems like an eternity, the door swings open, and a small, older man with thick, round glasses and a free-range beard, one whose entire countenance telegraphs solidarity with the woods, steps out. Following close behind him is a billowing cloud of smoke. As he passes me on the path, he speaks the words that I'd heard countless times before while waiting in the outhouse queue—"You may want to give that a minute to air out."

This time, however, it isn't the usual olfactory amalgam of curry, cabbage, and the two-for-a-dollar special at Taco Bell. What I discover is, as my old University of Maine forestry professor Art "The Fart" Randall (whose nickname was "Backfire," but that's another story) once described it, "the distinctive odor of burning rope."

It's a cloud of marijuana smoke. To my surprise, the pungent odor of pot completely masks any and all primordial emanations from the privy proper. Not a bad morning to leave the door open, I think, as the sunlight and shadows begin to dance on the forest floor.

Back at the cabin, the smoker is sitting at the long, wooden dining table, pot of oatmeal balanced atop his Pocket Rocket stove, making fresh brewed coffee with a French press. "That's a different way to start your day," I say as I walk past with a smirk. I tell him it smelled like some really good you-know-what.

When it came to going to the bathroom in a world without walls, the late, great writer Edward Abbey equated relieving oneself whenever and wherever with freedom and the renunciation of conformity. In his book *Desert Solitaire*, about his adventures in the desert Southwest, he urged readers to take a number of steps to cast off the blinders of conventionality. He wrote: "Brew your own beer; kick in your Tee Vee; kill your own beef; build your own cabin; and piss off the front porch whenever you bloody well feel like it."

Most people wouldn't say you-know-what if they had a mouthful. But Edward Abbey talked it to power at every opportunity.

What red-blooded male hasn't savored the thrill of engaging in a defiant, anarchistic act off a porch or some other inappropriate semipublic venue? It seems perfectly natural, providing your mother isn't looking. Dad's reaction would be a nod and wink in solidarity, providing, of course, he too checked to make sure Mom wasn't anywhere in the vicinity.

The world for Abbey, it seems, was indeed one giant toilet. For him, seeking relief off the front porch wasn't so much about marking territory as it was an acknowledgment of the fact that humans, even in a world of squeezably soft TP and low-flow toilets, are part of nature. His act wasn't an attempt to defile the landscape or stake a claim to it, but rather a meager attempt to acknowledge being part of life.

Once, in a speech to a room full of environmentalists, Abbey shared some insights into his wilderness ethos. It's perhaps the quintessential personal mission statement on how to keep balance in your life.

I keep a worn and tattered printout of it tucked in my dry box on every MRCC canoe trip, often reading it aloud when the last wood of the evening burns down and the conversation around the campfire waxes philosophical.

"One final paragraph of advice," he said. "Do not burn yourselves out. Be as I am—a reluctant enthusiast . . . a part-time crusader, a half-hearted fanatic. Save the other half of yourselves and your lives for pleasure and adventure. It is not enough to fight for the land; it is even more important to enjoy it. While you can. While it's still here.

"So get out there and hunt and fish and mess around with your friends, ramble out yonder and explore the forests, climb the mountains, bag the peaks, run the rivers, breathe deep of that yet sweet and lucid air, sit quietly for a while and contemplate the precious stillness, the lovely, mysterious, and awesome space. Enjoy yourselves, keep your brain in your head and your head firmly attached to the body, the body active and alive, and I promise you this much; I promise you this one sweet victory over our enemies, over those desk-bound men and women with their hearts in a safe deposit box, and their eyes hypnotized by desk calculators. I promise you this; You will outlive the bastards."

When it comes to living with nature, he knew full well what bears, the Pope, and himself, for that matter, needed to do in the woods. And when it comes to acknowledging those oh-so-brief moments in life of not-so-sweet-and-lucid air, he remained unashamed, unrepentant, and unapologetic.

You can bet that Edward Abbey never took any you-know-what from anybody.

WIFE'S SLED

NEARLY EVERY WINTER IN MAINE, THERE ARE ACCIDENTS involving snowmobilers breaking through ice or riding pell-mell into open water, often at night. Many of these riders do not live to tell about it.

The idea of struggling to get out of frigid water, in the dark, while wearing multiple layers of insulated clothing, thick gloves, heavy boots, and a full face-shield helmet, scares the crap out of me. I'll do anything to avoid it.

Riding on ice presents numerous other hazards, including jagged pressure ridges and unexpected canyons where someone has plowed a road out to their ice-fishing shack. Spring holes, where warmer groundwater wells up from the bottom, steadily eroding the layer of ice above, are another danger. The thickness of the ice can go from two feet to less than two inches in just a few yards.

Ice on big lakes is constantly expanding and contracting. Experiencing the echoing booms and sharp cracks of a lake "making" ice requires you restrain the innate instinct to head immediately to solid ground.

Any spot with current is also risky. Fast-moving water at the inlets and outlets of lakes seldom freezes solid. Every year, warning barricades are put up around the area where the Moose River empties into Moosehead Lake. Every year, a handful of riders ignore the warnings and end up in the water.

One of the most prudent things you can do when riding across lakes or along rivers where the thickness of the ice is concealed by snow is to stay on an existing track.

Local riders always know the area best and tend to avoid places that are not relatively safe. At the very least, if the riders preceding you didn't know what they were doing, you'll likely see evidence of some previous catastrophe in sufficient time to avoid a similar entanglement.

Slowing down and never riding alone can help improve your odds of getting back safe.

Most snowmobile accident stories in Maine's daily newspapers seem to share a common denominator. They often begin with the same three words—"A Massachusetts man . . ." They go on to say someone was reported overdue, and later, evidence of a calamity was discovered—a sled smashed into a tree on a sharp curve in the trail, or a snowmobile track dead-ending at the edge of dark, open water.

Time to call in the state police dive team.

Often, these accidents happen at night to people on sleds operating at a high rate of speed. All too frequently, the Maine Warden Service reports, "alcohol was a factor."

In one well-publicized accident in Rangeley on December 30, 2013, five riders in two separate groups, running at night, in whiteout conditions, on a lake that had yet to freeze over entirely for the season, rode straight into the water.

A woman out riding with her sixteen-year-old son died, although he managed to scramble to solid ice before his machine sank. Searchers found her body the next day.

It took four and a half months to find and recover the bodies of the three men in the second group that disappeared into the water that night.

Still, snowmobiling is a relatively safe sport considering the number of people who enjoy it and the millions of miles traveled each season.

Maine has more than 80,000 registered snowmobiles and probably half again as many undocumented ones. That may sound like a lot, but the state ranks fifth in the nation in that regard, coming in behind Minnesota with 258,000, Wisconsin with 238,000, Michigan with 205,000, and New York with 116,000.

The backbone of snowmobiling in Maine is the Interconnected Trail System (ITS), a web of numbered routes totaling more than three thousand miles. ITS trails are wide and regularly groomed to smooth out bumps and bare spots, allowing traffic in both directions simultaneously. More or less the recreational equivalent of the Interstate Highway System, the ITS reaches every corner of the state and provides access to more than twelve thousand miles of local trails maintained by volunteers from local snowmobile clubs.

One of the most active clubs in the state is the Moosehead Riders, headquartered in Greenville, the gateway to majestic Moosehead Lake. For a time, my brothers and sisters and I were members when we owned a small house on the flank of Blair Hill in Greenville. Dubbed "Green Acres" for the color of its pale and weather-beaten Masonite siding, it had a generous, if not somewhat ramshackle garage in which we stored a motley collection of nine snow machines. One of the club trails went right by the house, providing the perfect jumping-off point for exploring the wilds of the vast Moosehead region.

Heading west down the hill brought you to the edge of the lake and the network of trails that fanned out across the ice to every part of town and beyond. Heading east, the trail followed an old woods road past the obligatory abandoned and rusting pulp truck and cut through a big patch of sugar bush before twisting and turning its way to the Moosehead Riders clubhouse.

There, it intersected with ITS 85/86 providing access north to Kokadjo and Millinocket and south toward Monson and Dover-Foxcroft.

One of the more popular excursions when all the bedrooms at Green Acres were at full occupancy was to do a hundred-mile loop around the lake. Usually, we traveled in a clockwise manner, gassing up the sleds in Greenville before pointing the skis north on the trail up the west side of the lake toward Rockwood, where the Moose River ends its run from Jackman after a brief interlude at Brassau Lake. There, looming Mount Kineo stands guard as the trail cuts three-quarters of a mile straight across the narrowest part of the lake, the way marked by a line of evergreens set up in holes drilled in the ice.

Riders brave enough to pull up on the ice at the base of the cliffs on the east flank of Kineo can experience the overwhelming sense of insignificance that comes from having seven hundred feet of rhyolite towering directly over their heads. The fact that directly under the comparatively thin layer of clear ice at their feet the jet-black water plunges to the lake's deepest depth—some 246 feet—heightens the vertigo-inducing effect.

While you may be in the middle of nowhere in such places, you're never really alone. Game wardens who track such things have counted as many as three thousand snowmobiles making the dash across the ice at Rockwood in a single day.

From Kineo, a site prized by Native Americans for its flint-like rock perfect for fashioning stone tools and arrowheads, a trail arcs over to Kokadjo, a place where pavement and power lines end, and where bumper stickers note the year-round population is "Not Many." The tiny store and restaurant at the outlet of First Roach Pond there is surrounded by a six-acre parking lot that in winter is always full of the whine and blue exhaust plumes of snowmobiles.

We always pit at Kokadjo to top off the tanks, hit the restrooms, and grab a bite to eat at the lunch counter, where the crooked cylinder of ash on the end of the short order cook's cigarette always seems to hover precariously above the chowder. As my brother-in-law and fellow Maine Guide Douglas likes to say, "In this country, you don't drive by gas pumps without stopping."

From there, it's a comparatively straight shot down the French-town Road and through the woods south along the east side of the lake, past Lily Bay, and through Beaver Cove to get back home.

Sundays at Green Acres were often reserved for exploring new territory. It was a chance to check out the hundreds of miles of less-traveled tracks that often lead to quiet remote ponds or stunning mountaintop vistas bypassed by the ITS. Such trails are often steep and rough, and they seldom get the maintenance attention lavished on the ITS.

Single track is where the adventure really begins.

One weekend, while everyone else decided just to enjoy their coffee and the Sunday paper, Douglas and I decide to check out an enticing track we've seen diverging from the ITS in the vicinity of Big Moose Mountain, so christened when the state replaced every cartographical use of the word *squaw* with the word *moose* some years ago.

"I've always wondered where that goes," says Douglas as we wait in line to gas up at Breton's Store in Greenville Junction.

As I turn onto the main route, my thumb clamps down on the throttle button. There's always a split-second delay, like a quick inhale when jumping into icy cold water, before the motor roars in response to that command. The hands of gravity pull back on my shoulders as the sled rockets ahead, the track sending a rooster tail of snow shooting straight out the back.

After a short run through thick woods where the side trail leaves the ITS, the route follows an old tote road for a time, gradually ascending the mountain's north side at an oblique angle. As the elevation increases, the slope becomes more aggressive, falling away steeply toward what appears to be a small stream in the bottom of a rocky ravine. The trees thin, and we encounter a broad snowfield where the nearly obscured track of a previous rider's intrepid transit crosses perpendicular to the angle of repose. I estimate there are two feet of snow here, the top sealed by a glistening one-inch crust of ice.

Out of habit, I check that the coiled line of my safety tether is clipped to my jacket. In the event that I become involuntarily separated from the sled, it will kill the motor, reducing the possibility of a major mechanism of injury or the prospect that the sled might continue on without benefit of an operator.

As we begin to ease our way across, I notice the track changes. The slope is now so steep the front ski on the downhill side of my sled no longer touches the snow. Avalanches in situations such as this, while rare in Maine, are not unheard of.

Too bad there's no safe way to turn around or go in reverse.

Like so many situations in snowmobiling, the circumstance requires the suppression of any tendency toward timidity. If you begin to bog down in slush, wallow in deep powder, or lose momentum climbing a hill with no place to turn around, and the next sled is coming up fast behind you, the only way to extricate yourself from the predicament is by a judicious application of throttle, never the brake.

I take some comfort in the fact that someone before us apparently made it across, but the prospect of my machine, and me as well, barrel rolling down the mountainside into the stream is all too real.

To improve our chances, Douglas and I instinctively move to stand on the running boards on the uphill side to distribute the center of gravity more favorably. With steady nudges of the throttle, we work our way across, finally reaching more level ground about a hundred yards farther on.

We shut off the snowmobiles with a tap to the bright red kill switches on the handlebars. The silence is deafening. We remove our helmets, quickly donning fleece hats as steam rises from our sweating heads in the 15-degree air.

People often complain about how they look with "hat hair." You haven't seen anything until you've had to deal with "helmet hair."

"Well, that was interesting," I remark while handing Douglas a cigar. "I'm really not looking forward to having to go back that way," Douglas says.

I agree, noting I am in no rush to see a snowmobile accident story in tomorrow's paper beginning with the words "A Bar Harbor man . . ."

After turning our cigars into a respectable amount of ash, we push on, the trail steadily climbing through stark stands of leafless hardwoods that gradually give way to a moonscape of stunted spruce and fir. We pass only one unlabeled intersection, deciding not to continue straight in favor of turning hard right to follow the route that appears to continue to gain elevation. I marvel at the perseverance of whoever first blazed this trail so that folks like us could enjoy the undiscovered reward that awaits at the end.

Suddenly, we emerge from the thick conifers and find ourselves on the summit of the mountain's north peak, where there's just enough flat area and depth of snow around the ice-encased granite ledges to turn the sleds around.

Our perseverance is rewarded by spectacular views out over the lake's monochromatic winter landscape. Everything that in summer is open water is now bright white. All land and forest appear starkly black.

To the north is the distinctive hump of Kineo, and some fifty miles to the east is the sparkling white mass of Katahdin. The morning sun, shining down from a cloudless, cerulean sky, dances off the ice and snow-covered landscape from every direction.

To the south, white smoke and steam rises in lazy columns from chimneys in the heart of the village of Greenville. On West Cove in Greenville Junction, the snow has been plowed from the ice in preparation for the weekly stock car races. Farther out, lone snowmobilers seem like rocket cars on the Bonneville Salt Flats, shooting down the broad, flat surface of the lake at what seem to be insane rates of speed. From here, theirs are silent victories. The ear-piercing wail of those sleds running wide open dissolves long before scaling these heights.

Even sitting in the lee of the trees with the sunshine, it doesn't take long for the cold to penetrate the redundant layers of our riding gear. "I need to get moving again," I say to Douglas as I adjust the choke on the carburetor and turn the key. After a few coughs of complaint, the motor roars to life, the luxury of electric start once again freeing me from the onerous task of repeatedly yanking on a pull cord.

Douglas eases his sled alongside, pushes open the visor on his helmet, and makes a suggestion. "When we get to that intersection, let's go right instead of left," he suggests. I concur with a nod.

As we descend, the spruce and fir gradually surrender to hard-woods. At the intersection where we will resume our exploration of dark territory, Douglas stops and turns back to look at me. I give him a thumb's up. He gooses the throttle, kicking up a spray of snow from his track, as we turn right, away from the devil we know in the hopes that the one we don't won't be as bad.

For a while, the trail twists and turns due north over relatively level terrain through sun-dappled open woods—an altogether pleasant route. We're making good headway until I notice the unexpected glare of Douglas's brake light. We come to an abrupt halt at the edge of a steep drop. Getting off the sleds, we crunch through the snow in our thick, insulated boots to contemplate the track that drops without hesitation over the edge of a precipice. The slightly less-than-vertical slope is so steep that there will be no getting the sleds back up once we commit. The trail continues down through thickening woods, well past our ability to discern where it goes.

"The way I see it," Douglas says, "is that this is either a way out or we're going to find a bunch of rusty snowmobiles with skeletons on them at the bottom."

Still, the prospect of nosing straight down into the unknown seems preferable to attempting to high side the hill we barely managed to cross on the way in. "I'm in," I say to Douglas as I trudge back to my sled and reattach the tether. "I'll be right behind you," I shout.

＊＊＊

One thing a snowmobiler can do to increase his enjoyment is to own a machine tailored for the type of riding he does most. There are racing sleds more than capable of going 120 miles per hour—or faster. Long tracks are ideally suited for breaking trail in deep powder. Lumbering touring models set up for two include comfy backrests, saddlebags, and heated handgrips for the passenger.

Newer sleds now sport four-stroke motors that pollute much less, get better gas mileage, and free the last rider in line from being sentenced to spending the day enveloped in an eye-smarting blue fog of half-burned gasoline and oil.

When the time comes for a new snowmobile, frugal Mainers naturally explore the possibility of finding a good used model, providing they don't have to go too far afield to find it. And for that, there's just one place to look, the weekly bargain-hunter's bible to buying and selling all things Maine—*Uncle Henry's Weekly Swap or Sell It Guide.*

Its plump, unassuming appearance provides little hint of its dominance of the classified advertising market in the region. But once you've perused this micro capitalist compendium of tiny type on dull newsprint, there's no question that *Uncle Henry's* sits atop the buy-it-and-sell-it food chain.

The genius lies in the fact that the ads are free. Oh, how we love to get something for nothing. The only way to take out an ad, however, is to send in the form on the back cover of the booklet— which costs $2.

People of every station in life line up at convenience stores and markets all over Maine on Thursday mornings just waiting for the truck to drop off the latest edition, hoping to get a jump on the thousands of other people hoping to do the exact same thing. You know you've got a motivated buyer on the line when a caller answering your ad begins the conversation with "Have you sold it yet?"

In an effort to protect their evolutionary niche from Craigslist and other Internet competition, *Uncle Henry's* does have an online component, but the print version is still king. It has even spawned a short-lived reality television show, *Down East Dickering*, where a handful of crusty yet endearing hagglers buy and sell their way to fortune and fame in the state's robust underground cash economy, presumably far, far away from the prying eyes of the Internal Revenue Service.

Under the "Snowmobile" heading, ads are grouped mostly by manufacturer. Unlike cars, model year and mileage are not always good indicators of value. Simply unplugging a single wire can disable the odometer.

How often a sled has been ridden, and how hard, make all the difference.

In calling about a sled that's more than ten years old, your first question should be "When was the last time it ran?" It's a bad sign when you go to look at one in the fall, and it's sitting in the dooryard surrounded by a foot of uncut grass and weeds.

The ads run the gamut of all the major brands, including Skidoo, Arctic Cat, Yamaha, and Polaris. Descriptions range from the mundane to the fanciful, mostly centered around the desire to convey that they have not been overused or abused. But as Douglas likes to note, when it comes to snowmobiles, "If you're gonna ride 'em, you're gonna break 'em." That's to be expected from something with that many moving parts operating in extreme conditions over rough and sometimes rocky terrain. Snowmobiles basically have just two speeds—all ahead and stop. But for most of the year, they just sit where they were shut off on the third day of mud season. None of the above is a recipe for longevity for any mechanical device.

To attract buyers, many ads say "low miles," "used only one winter," "dealership maintained," or "always stored indoors." The one that always makes me chuckle is the phrase "wife's sled."

The intonation here is that the sled was not driven hard or abused by some daredevil wearing Day-Glo green gloves with matching boots and a flame-accented Godzilla helmet. The impression of the wife's sled is that of a low-mileage Buick Skylark owned by a little old lady who only drove it two miles to the grocery store once a week and to church on Sunday.

There's no question that women tend to be safer and less aggressive riders than men, but as with any advertising claim, let the buyer beware.

———

My first introduction to snowmobiling came while I was studying forestry at the University of Maine. My roommate, George Davis of West Baldwin, had a bunch of us over for a long weekend in February. He managed to corral enough sleds from other family members that a bunch of us could go for a moonlight ride.

George cut an intimidating figure among the "Stumpies" in the class of '76. Tall and thin, he walked into the lecture hall on the first day wearing a faded jean jacket with a giant marijuana leaf emblazoned on the back and the words "Cannabis Sativa." It was the era of "Have a Nice Day," and he advertised what he thought about that sickly sweet sentiment with an anti-Smiley button of his own. It sported one swollen eye, a tongue sticking out, and the words "Have a Crappy Day."

Attached to his belt was a silver-handled sheathed dagger with a blade about ten inches long. He called it Sting in homage to Bilbo Baggins's weapon of choice in Tolkien's *The Hobbit*.

George rode a Harley-Davidson motorcycle and felt nothing but pity and disdain for those who did not. Someone once asked him what the difference was between his Sportster and a 750

Honda. "A Honda's a Honda and a Harley-Davidson is a motorcycle," he announced with authority.

A big fan of what he liked to call "both kinds of music—country and western," George wore cowboy boots so pointy he could play soccer with a BB. His trousseau was topped with a rumpled felt crusher hat that seemed never to leave his head even while sleeping. Due to the multiple stains from years of liberal application of Ole Time Woodsman's Fly Dope, you could barely tell the original color was once a bright blaze orange.

With a full, robust beard and photo-gray glasses that seemed perpetually dark, George was a poster child for badass. Yet he was soft-spoken and gentle. He seldom dispelled the uncertainty over what he might be thinking by engaging in idle chatter. But when he removed the curvy-stemmed tobacco pipe that seemed perpetually at his lips and he spoke people paid attention.

George liked to call everyone he knew and liked "Joe."

The habit caught on among forestry students, and soon everyone simply started referring to everyone else as "Joe." It would make for humorous meetings in the halls. "Mornin', Joe," one half-awake student would say. "How you doing, Joe?" the other would respond. Two voices saying "Joe" at the same time, accompanied by an upward tilt of the head, was a common ritual in passing. "Joe" is a marvelously ubiquitous salutation—a metaphoric acknowledgment that we were all equals in each other's eyes.

Once admitted to the universal fraternity of "Joe," no further social vetting was necessary. There was no application process or pledge committee. Anyone who was a Joe was deemed perfectly capable of bestowing Joe status on anyone they deemed worthy. Someone was either a Joe, or they weren't. We all knew what it meant. Nothing more needed to be said.

I still use it among close friends to this day. George, however, as the progenitor of "Joe," occupies a special place in the practice's mythos.

As far as "Joe" was concerned, when it came to tractor-trailers, Peterbilt was the only good brand. And when it came to snowmobiles, George was a Skidoo man through and through.

It's important in understanding the context of that first snowmobiling adventure to remember how different society's attitude toward drinking was at that time. Most snowmobilers carried a flask of some kind of liquor in their inside jacket pocket. George and his buddies on the west side of Sebago Lake referred to these libations as "snow snake antidote." George's antidote of choice was Bacardi 151-proof rum. It had the added benefit of having such a high alcohol content you could use it to light a fire in an emergency.

The story goes that riders were at risk of being bitten by invisible yet deadly poisonous "snow snakes" at any time during a trip. Of course, the bites were painless and undetectable. Snow snakes could be seen, however, out of the corner of someone's eye if the light was just right.

The only hope of survival when someone shouted out that they had detected a snow snake was to quickly consume some antidote. Apparently, snow snakes are quite common in those parts, as someone seemed to spot one every time we took a break.

Little did anyone realize at that time, the biggest danger to life and limb was in our pockets the entire time.

As we got ready to ride the first night, I was assigned George's mother's sled. It was an old Skidoo Elan, an entry-level model of uninspired design with little power and minimal suspension. Because the motor had been running rough, the air cleaner on the carburetor located between the rider's knees had been removed, allowing me a good view of the mechanism's inner workings. As I later discovered while running with the throttle wide open across a big field, it also had the disquieting habit of backfiring great balls of blue flame out of said carburetor toward my crotch only inches away.

My brother Carl was assigned George's brother's wife's sled, which, he was assured, had been barely ridden all year. Off we went into the night to explore with George leading the way on a sled so fast his taillights frequently disappeared into the distance.

It didn't take many stops for snow snake antidote before our unfounded yet growing confidence in our nascent riding skills collided headlong with diminishing hand-eye coordination and dulled reaction time. As we headed down the trail, Keith Schultz from Connecticut started racing up behind to give the back of Carl's sled a nudge. This bump and run went on for five minutes or so until one particularly forceful hit caused the sleds to hook together on a curve. Both went straight down an embankment, with Carl being bounced off just before his sled hit a small tree.

One of the front skis on Keith's machine hit the back of Carl's seat, sheering off the mounting bolts and continuing on to smash some gauges on the dashboard.

I hate to think what would have happened had Carl not been ejected when he was.

George quickly turned around, helped extricate the machines, and offered that the damage wasn't all that bad. He would fix it before his brother's wife even knew, he promised.

The snow snake antidote was put away for the rest of the evening, and we returned home without additional mishap.

Even decades after alcohol ceased to play any role in the enjoyment of the sport, mishaps and minor crashes are not uncommon. A friend, Paul Paradis, took Douglas's wife's sled off into the puckerbrush while on a weekend excursion along the East Branch of the Penobscot River from Medway to Bowlin Camps, just south of Grand Lake Matagamon.

We were headed south from the camps after spending the night. It had snowed about eight inches, making conditions on the old logging road that serves as the trail just about ideal. There isn't all that much traffic early on a Sunday morning in those parts, and we were riding on virgin cover. None of us was going insanely fast, and Paul, just ahead of me, was gradually floating from side to side in the soft powder. Suddenly, his sled made a sharp left hook, crested the low banking of snow pushed up by the grooming process, and sailed about six feet through the air before coming to an abrupt halt in a ditch where a culvert passed under the road.

I came to a tail-skidding stop and ran to the edge to see Paul getting up from the deep snow next to the machine, waving that he was unhurt. The only damage to the sled was a crack across the bottom of the fiberglass cowling.

Douglas, who had been on point, and my brother Dale, who had been next in line behind him, came roaring back after noticing no headlights in their rearview mirrors.

Maine Guide and Bowlin Camp owner John Smallwood pulled up on his sled and stopped, surveying the situation, and remarked with an air of classic understatement, "How'd you boys manage to get that sled down there?" The truthful answer, we explained, is that we haven't a clue.

Paul, an experienced snowmobiler, was riding in a perfectly safe fashion at an appropriate rate of speed. "I was going along and—*zing*—off she went," Paul said.

A ski may have gotten stuck in an icy rut hidden by the fresh powder. We'll never know. After an hour of shoveling, pulling, and pushing, we finally get the sled back up to the trail and finish the thirty-mile run back to Medway.

Dale too is intimately familiar with what it's like to make a hard landing on a snowmobile. Granted, accidents do happen. His exuberant nature and fondness for maximum acceleration and speed when it comes to riding snowmobiles, however, suggest a higher degree of culpability on his part.

Growing up in a family that included a set of older twin brothers (Carl and me) and younger twin sisters (Patricia and Barbara), Dale is the classic middle child in constant search for attention. We teased him mercilessly about his habit of spending twice as much time and energy trying to get out of doing something than he would have used just doing it right in the first place.

Dale cannot resist a dare. And he quickly grows bored with any mechanical contraption or tool in which he has not personally exceeded its actual or theoretical red line.

As an adult, he explored a wide variety of careers and business opportunities, ranging from being a roofing contractor to commercial cleaner to director of warehousing for a credit card giant to amateur stock car racer, paramedic, and part-time deputy sheriff. It all turned out to be perfect preparation for that at which he would ultimately excel—managing and expanding a series of KOA campgrounds in beautiful places all around the country.

Like a shark that must remain constantly on the move to drive oxygen to its gills, Dale is a study in motion. There's no such thing as having a phone conversation with him when he's not doing three other things at the same time. His long days are filled with dealing with employees, customers, plans for new construction, and the spreadsheets needed to keep the corporate types back at headquarters happy.

Even when he sports yesterday's stubble on his cheeks, the crowning quality of his appearance is his perfectly smooth shaved head. One of the few men who can make a golf shirt in KOA yellow look good, Dale is ever ready to greet a friend or stranger with a handshake, or a hug, and sometimes both.

With a predilection toward having a handful of vanilla sandwich cookies for breakfast, Dale is the first to admit his diet could use some refinement. Yet he and his wife Jane's priorities in life have always been straight. No people on earth are more devoted to family. Every spare dime they have—and some they don't—goes to help their kids and grandkids. They are just as generous when it comes to spending time with them as they are with their treasure.

And, even though they give so much of themselves to family, friends, and coworkers, they have more than enough love left over to care for a constantly changing menagerie of pets in their home.

One February, on a guys' ride around Moosehead Lake, we decided to have some fun zooming about the golf course at the base of Mount Kineo.

Dale had just purchased a new Skidoo touring sled for Jane. It had electric start, reverse, and all the bells and whistles. It was faster and more powerful than his old Arctic Cat, which coughed and died on the side of a trail one time because there was a huge mouse nest in the air cleaner. We liked to tease him his Cat was a "low rider" because the suspension was so worn that the back end often dragged on the ground.

The lure of the new, plus the fact that Jane wasn't there and would probably never find out, led to his decision to take hers that day.

One of the long, narrow, artificial hills on the course at Kineo is transected by a twenty-foot-wide golf cart path. Unfortunately, Dale didn't know that before zooming up one end and across that ridge. Seeing the ten-foot drop in front of him too late to stop, he and the sled shot off the crest, catching spectacular air. In less than a second, it pancaked, skis askew and track down, onto the forty-five-degree slope covered with deep powder on the opposite side. The force of the impact sent Dale up and over the handlebars. He landed ten feet farther in front of the sled, on his back, feet pointed uphill, like a giant upside-down snow angel.

That was the scenario presented to me when I came around the corner an instant later. It took a few seconds after I stopped to realize what I was looking at, and that it was Dale.

Running over, I'm frantic because he isn't moving. I kneel beside him, calling his name and gently opening the visor on his helmet. Inside, a dusting of snow from the impact still lays on his cheeks.

"Just give me a freakin' second while I finish taking inventory," he says, opening his eyes. "I'm just trying to make sure I can still feel everything, and nothing is broken."

"What the hell were you thinking?" I scream at him once I realize that the odds are he'll live.

Douglas, my other brother-in-law Gary, and the others quickly appear, and we all help Dale to his feet. Other than a sore wrist, he appears to be fine.

The sled is extricated from the drift that fortunately cushioned both impacts. The only obvious damage is that the handlebars are bent to the right even when the skis point straight ahead.

"I think that shouldn't be too hard to fix," a suitably chastened Dale said as he reattached his tether, turned the key, and hit the start button to bring the sled back to life.

Turning his head to me just before shutting his visor to continue our ride, he shouted, "Don't tell Jane!"

Not long after that, and after Dale's visit to a doctor two days later where he learned he had broken his wrist, it dawned on me the term "wife's sled" has the potential to be one of the greatest deceptions of all time.

Almost universally, "wife's sled" in an advertisement is taken by prospective buyers to mean "gently used." But in reality, it's just as likely to be the sled most often loaned to a guy's inexperienced and reckless beer buddies, making it one of the most used and abused snowmobiles out there.

⁓

Dropping down the steep side of the valley north of Big Moose Mountain, there's really no need to hit the throttle. The engine idles as gravity does all the work. I pump the brake occasionally but don't want to build up a pile of snow in front of the track. The term "controlled crash" comes to mind as I resign myself just to steering between trees and keeping the front end pointed downhill.

The main thing is to stay far enough behind Douglas so that I won't smash into his sled should he be forced to stop abruptly, perhaps in shock at first spotting that pile of rusted snow machines and skeletons at the bottom of the pit.

More likely, we might be blocked by something much more mundane, like a fallen tree. With no hope of going back up this trail, I take comfort in the collapsible bow saw I always keep strapped to the back of the sled for just such a contingency.

After about four hundred feet of descent, the trail levels off and passes through a thick grove of hemlocks along a stream. It soon joins an old tote road and trends farther down the mountain in the general direction of the lake. At some point, I reason, we'll connect back up to civilization.

Douglas slows to a stop. I pull up beside. We've reached the ITS.

We watch as a bunch of sleds from New Hampshire go shooting past at a reckless rate of speed. For many years, we had been wondering why most of the aggressive riders we seemed to encounter had prominent New Hampshire stickers. Then it dawned on us—New Hampshire had registration reciprocity with

Maine. That meant anyone with a New Hampshire sticker could ride in Maine without paying another fee.

Riders from Massachusetts had caught on and purchased a New Hampshire sticker and got to ride in Maine for free, too.

"Those guys are just another *Bangor Daily News* snowmobile accident story waiting to happen," I say to Douglas.

When the coast is clear, we punch it, heading south back toward Greenville. The grooming crew has been out the night before, and the trail is perfect despite the best efforts of the previous party to tear it up. The sun sparkles off the snow on the ground and the ice in the trees. Patterns of light and shadow race across our faces as we enjoy the quick response and rush of acceleration of each push on the throttle.

While at times like these you're perfectly alone in your thoughts, snowmobiling is an inherently social sport. There's an instant camaraderie that forms between folks who brave the elements to get to visit places and see nature's wonders that others can only dream about.

With the sleds safely stowed in the garage back at Green Acres, the talk over lunch turns to what different model of sled might be better suited for the backcountry conditions we experienced that morning. Douglas notes it would be ideal to have a long-track sled when the unpacked snow gets deep and extra power and traction might be needed.

"It would be nice to have one," I say as I pick up a four-day-old copy of *Uncle Henry's* sitting on the coffee table. I had been thinking of replacing the heavy Grand Touring Skidoo I'm riding now. It's total comfort and luxury—so much like a Cadillac I named it El Dorado. Built to cruise what amount to the highways of snowmobiling, it can bog down in deep, untracked powder or slush and is difficult to extract once it does.

Seeing as the "bible" has already been out for four days, I know full well the best deals may be long gone, but if something hasn't sold after four days, you can usually drive a harder bargain.

I see an ad for a long track. It's a Skidoo. It's in Monson just south on Route 15. I can stop by to check it out on the way home that afternoon.

A man answers when I call. I automatically blurt out, "Have you sold it yet?" He says "nope" and begins his by-now well-rehearsed sales pitch.

"It's in great shape—low miles," he says. "It has the heated grips, electric start, and electronic reverse." I begin to think I may have hit the jackpot.

"And best of all," he continues, "it's the wife's sled."

INTO THE REALM OF LIGHT

THE LIGHT IS DIFFERENT IN THE NORTH, FAR ABOVE BANGOR, UP beyond Greenville in the realm of townships with numbers rather than names, where moose outnumber people, where thundering double-trailer logging trucks reign supreme on tracks of dirt, dust billowing behind them like the wake of a nameless ship fading across the surface of a deep and unexplored sea.

North is where the waters of the great lakes of Maine spill out of the endless verdant forest to form the headwaters of the state's most fabled rivers—the Allagash, the St. John, the Kennebec, and the East and West Branches of the mighty Penobscot. They were once the highways, prized for their power, their majesty unheeded and ignored. For generations, they suffered the indignities of industry, restrained, abused, polluted, and spurned until a combination of shifting economics and flannel-shirted activism restored them to their proper position among the pantheon of wilderness deities.

We leave from the landing on Lobster Stream for an unhurried four-day trip on the West Branch down to Chesuncook Village on the lake, Maine's third largest, of the same name. The landing itself is ideal for backcounty departures. The state maintains a large parking lot and concrete boat launch ramp here. On either side, there are broad, grass-covered areas for organizing the dunnage. The forest along the stream crowds in close along the low banks, trees tilted ever so slightly over the water, like people on sidewalks waiting for the big parade, eager to see what amusing diversion will be passing by next.

The channel is always calm, the current betrayed only by observing which direction the eelgrass is pointing just below the surface of the dark and tea-stained water.

With a quick shove from shore, all the canoes in the Moose River Camping Club's annual flotilla are equally prepared to head south up into Lobster Lake or north under the sagging logs of the Lobster Trip Road bridge for the short paddle to join the West Branch.

Lobster Lake is a perfect canoe camping retreat, one we have frequented before. But on this trip, we choose north.

Where the stream joins its larger cousin, the greater current muckles onto the canoe. Like the mysterious force propelling the pointer on the Ouija board, it automatically conducts the bow in the desired direction—downstream. For most of this section of the West Branch, there's ample flow with progress of several miles per hour possible with little more than an occasional pry of a paddle from the stern to keep the entire enterprise midstream.

We glide under the fabled Golden Road Bridge at a place called Hannibal's Crossing. Because there's little chance that the great Carthaginian general ever got this far on his way to attack Rome from the rear, all manner of wild suppositions about the name stand with equal probability. On the applicable map in the *Maine Atlas and Gazetteer*, the name appears in large, bold type, like a small town, further adding to the mystery, as there is nary a structure nor old cellar hole in sight.

Did some hapless homesteader once operate a ferry at this spot in Victorian times? Was it named in honor of Hannibal Hamlin, a former governor, Lincoln's first vice president, and one of Bangor's leading citizens?

Curiously, Henry David Thoreau made no mention of this spot in his detailed account of a trip on the West Branch.

The mystery deepens with the realization that in the timeline of the Great North Woods, the Golden Road, supposedly named because of its prodigious construction cost, is just a tyke. The Great Northern Paper Company didn't begin construction of the ninety-six-mile dirt highway from Millinocket to St. Zacharie on the Canadian border until 1969. It was finished in 1972.

The road was put in to allow logs to be hauled out by truck instead of being sent downstream on river drives with their resulting expense and environmental degradation. In that respect, it was the road as much as anything that saved the river.

Further inquiry, including an exchange of communication with television journalist Bill Green, a loyal son of Bangor who skillfully shares his unbridled affection for Maine with his viewers at every opportunity, reveals that the name Hannibal's Crossing was born in a television weatherman's subtle sense of humor.

It seems Lew Colby, a meteorologist at WCSH 6 in Portland during the late 1960s and early 1970s, would often report during his forecasts on general conditions in the imaginary town of Hannibal's Crossing. His colleague, Jim Bigney, with all solemnity, reported nightly in season on the equally fun yet fictitious Blackfly Index.

Every mention of Hannibal's Crossing, of course, sent scores of viewers scrambling to their maps of Maine to find out just where that might be. Perhaps while doing so, some other interesting spot on the map might catch someone's eye and inspire a weekend road trip or spark further inquiry. Today, people would probably just give up after not being able to find it on Facebook.

The Golden Road's bridge over the West Branch was the largest and most difficult challenge on the entire route. According to construction worker Howard Weymouth, crews at the time liked to joke that tackling the project was akin to Hannibal's crossing of the Alps.

When the steel beam structure was completed, the Golden Road's construction crew decided to name it for Colby's imaginary town. They even put up a sign.

Despite the fact that, legally, there really is no such place as Hannibal's Crossing, it has become a vital reference and waypoint in nearly every account of trips both over the road and along the river.

On this expedition, I'm one of a party of twelve that I would soon come to lament includes a couple of free agents who believe that standard operating procedure in wilderness travel requires inordinate amounts of yelling. Within the first hour on river, there are repeated shouts of "Rock!" as if the possibility of boulders lurking just below the surface on any river in Maine is some kind of an epiphany.

In a court of law, opposing counsel could just stipulate to the fact that those paddling canoes will encounter all manner of submerged obstacles be they rocks, logs, or even a kissing cousin of the Loch Ness Monster. But here, we're apparently going to litigate each and every complaint.

There's also shouting from the shore up the riverbank to camp ("Have any of you guys seen my life jacket?!") and from one side of camp to the other ("Anybody have any extra TP?!"), along with the expected bursts of unimaginative profanity when a tent has the audacity not to set itself up correctly or a king-sized can of beer experiences an in-flight malfunction, unabashedly discharging its frothy contents into a sealed river bag full of clothing.

The only thing that yelling guarantees is that you won't see any wildlife. The sound of an excitable human voice is the animal kingdom's equivalent of Paul Revere riding to Lexington warning "The morons are coming!" Anything with the ability to flee or hide will, not as much out of a sense of mortal danger as a desire to avoid exposure to gratuitous banality.

Perhaps it's an inability to comprehend all that open space, a disquiet when surrounded by nature's delicious disorganization, that engenders a subconscious need in some people to turn up the volume. Maybe there's an instinctual craving to carve out one's personal space with noise when confronted with a vastness not constrained by walls or fences or traversed by well-trodden paths with obvious beginnings and ends.

When I'm in the woods, I want to feel nature's embrace, not slap her in the face. The ideal method of communication out here is not a shout; it's a whisper. I'm here to listen, not repeatedly proclaim my arrival with all the pomp and pageantry of the sergeant at arms at the State of the Union announcing the entrance of the president.

Considering present company, I have no illusions of this being a transcendental "wilderness" trip. But in the back of my mind, I promised myself to look for the ghost of Thoreau, who journeyed here himself in September 1853.

On the first night, we camp quite by accident on one of the many islands that bear Thoreau's name; it's almost 132 years to the day after he sought shelter at the same spot. Late that night, long after the sound of the last logging truck rumbling across Hannibal's Crossing has faded, I strain to hear him. Only the murmur of the river rippling over the occasional rock as it tiptoes past breaks the stillness.

Overhead, moonshine glares across the sleeping camp, its pale intensity betraying the hard edges of a soft landscape where the coming frost will soon steal the last spark of life from the leaves.

I wonder the next morning, sitting out a passing rain shower, drinking a second cup of coffee under a trusty tarp, if people from more than a hundred years ago would recognize this place today. The forest along the river, once nearly trackless, is now only a few hundred yards deep. Behind this legislated spruce and fir "beauty strip," clear-cuts, logging roads, and skidder trails stretch endlessly in almost every direction. Dams on Chesuncook Lake long ago drowned the only big rapids on the upper river, although the broad grassy lakeshores of those bygone river-driving years remain. After each generation of cutting or road construction, the land has forgiven the insults, the forest has come back. But would these woods and waters be familiar now?

One of Thoreau's most oft-cited quotes is "In Wildness is the preservation of the world." As unmanicured as these woods and waters appear today, they are far from untrammeled and untamed. Are they truly wild?

Most places in Maine are on their third or even fourth cutting rotation since industrial logging began in earnest almost 150 years ago. Few vestiges of unmolested old-growth forest remain, overlooked in inaccessible microclimates high on rugged slopes or deep in tight valleys where the sum total biomass failed to offer sufficient return to warrant the bulldozing of an access road.

Granted, today the call of a chickadee or the buzz of a locust as the sun beats down on a humid day is indistinguishable from that of their ancestors. But at some point, the landscape itself remains at risk of becoming little more than an aging ingenue struggling to retain the luminance of her youth.

Compared to today's sprawling cities of concrete and steel, these woods definitely qualify as wild. But would Thoreau recognize it?

In his essays about expeditions to Maine, which were later compiled into the book *The Maine Woods*, an almost innate sense of place comes alive, not just in descriptions of natural wonders and wildness, but also in vignettes of the people who populated that country. He understood that the history and spirit of Maine lies not just in a pristine landscape shaped by glaciers and fierce winters, home to beaver, moose, and bear. It resides also in the lives, character, and heart of settlers, loggers, farmers, and Indians who are the messengers through which the land here reveals its story.

For those for whom the spiritual sustenance of these woods is essential, spending time here is as much a chance to feel a kinship with those ghosts as it is a need to escape the great, droning, background hum of civilization, that ghastly orange streetlight haze that poisons the night sky, starving unsuspecting souls in urban environments.

Everyone has heard the question "When a tree falls in the forest, and no one is there to hear it, does it make a sound?" It is one of the great philosophical debates of history.

In Maine's Great North, the rugged landscape and raw climes test the mettle of all living things, giving and taking life without malice or regret.

The people who settle there share resilience with the trees. Those of weaker ilk barely manage to hold on to an oft-times miserable existence. Those of stouter constitution grow tall to loom above the rest.

Such spirit resides in the pluck and grit of Burt and Maggie McBurnie, who for forty years tended out on North Woods travelers at remote Chesuncook Village, accessible for the most part only by boat, canoe, or floatplane.

On an earlier trip to the West Branch, we had the occasion to meet Burt, who led a proud, hardscrabble existence on the northernmost windswept shores of mighty Chesuncook.

He and his wife catered to three generations of hunters, fishermen, and canoeists who found their way to their door, a rare and beautiful location not reachable by car. Burt had lived in the village since he was two. He left as a young man and returned in 1957 after a stint in the corporate world.

Bested only by Moosehead Lake and Sebago Lake, Chesuncook's present eighteen-mile long outline, like the others, was determined by design not by accident. The tall bulwark of Ripogenus Dam, an eight-story-high, solid concrete edifice completed in 1920, harnesses its waters.

Rip Dam, as it is known to those who frequent the north, was not the first to impound these waters. Another, a rock and cribwork structure, was built across the narrows between what is now Ripogenus Lake and Chesuncook in the 1800s. The old dam was left in place and was submerged when the gates to Rip Dam were closed and the water level rose. At low levels, it can sometimes still be seen, an ethereal shape just below the surface.

When that happened, several distinct lakes merged into one large body of water. While other lakes may have bays, these bulges in Chesuncook retain their original names, including Caribou Lake and Ripogenus Lake, even though there are no landmarks delineating that fact when moving from one to the other.

While many of Maine's largest lakes run roughly due north and south thanks to the glaciers that helped carve their basins, Chesuncook's main axis runs from the northwest to the southeast. This is the least favorable orientation when it comes to finding a lee for paddling in both good weather and bad.

When winds whip up giant waves from either direction, there's little that paddlers hoping to transit the lake can do but wait it out. Sometimes, paddlers can choose to start early before the waves mount or wait until dusk when the wind eases and waves subside. But there's no guarantee that will happen.

Rather than tempt fate by paddling into the teeth of white-caps, people hire Burt to shuttle everything down the lake in his powerboat. For a fee, he can load two canoes, all the gear (always too much in his opinion), and four people besides himself and his faithful dog, for the hour-long run south to the Allagash Gateway Campground marina.

Meeting Burt McBurnie was not something that any wilderness traveler was bound to forget. Those who paddle the river in search of the ghost of Thoreau, hoping to stumble across any semblance of a wilderness philosopher, meet instead a strong, clear-eyed man with a weather-beaten face whose swearing and near endless use of salty epithets could make even the toughest Marine drill sergeant blush.

On the day we pulled in at the Chesuncook Lake House Lodge, the southeast winds were gusting near gale force. Six-foot breakers roamed freely down the lake. We thought we had been smart to hole up behind a ledge just north of the property to unload the gear out of the wind. The first words from Burt's mouth when he heard we had stopped there instead of continuing to his dock were "Jesus! Jesus! Jesus!" A barrage of additional expletives, some I had never imagined could be strung together in such inventive ways, and none that can be reprinted here, immediately followed.

Despite the marginal conditions and complaints (justified) that we had way too much "@#&%$" stuff," he delivered us safely and skillfully down the unforgiving lake, his twenty-four-foot fiberglass boat skipping from wave top to wave top in a bone-jarring carnival ride that left us all somewhat bruised if not slightly shell-shocked.

When the first run got to the comparative calm of the marina, the outboard motor shuddered as the propeller kissed a submerged rock. The autumn drawdown of the lake had already begun, so the water was much shallower than normal.

"Jesus! Jesus! Jesus!" McBurnie yelled. "These #@@$% people don't know how to run a @#(&$ marina!" He then escalated the invective from there, drawing pained expressions of incredulity from two unshaven and slightly hungover men fishing from one of the floats.

When it came to swearing, even a skeptical East German judge would have given Burt a perfect score of 10.

The entire episode is now something everyone present remembers fondly, if not for its energy, then for its originality. We all have since found occasion to use Burt's commentary on the operation of a marina on other expeditions when a lack of proper preparation or imperfect logistical execution becomes painfully obvious.

It took me a while, but I eventually came to understand that Burt's swearing was not a primitive manifestation of a profane or stunted intellect. He was by all accounts a generous, courageous, and extremely smart man. Rather, it was his way of rejecting danger, inconvenience, and discomfort, a way to wrest even a smidgen of moral advantage in a daily struggle against an all-too-real and often unforgiving environment.

On the last trip that day, Burt seemed to soften. He confessed that he had an appointment to see a doctor in Bangor the next day for tests. I learned some weeks later from a mutual guide friend that the results were not good. He had cancer.

A little more than a year later, Burt lost his greatest struggle. He died far from his beloved lake in a room at Charles A. Dean

Memorial Hospital in Greenville. No doubt during his stay, he let the doctors and nurses know in no uncertain terms what he thought of the situation. "Jesus! Jesus! Jesus!, these @*$#% people don't know how to run a @#(*% hospital!" he must have said more than once.

And they, like legions of wilderness travelers, probably didn't take it personally, acknowledging in their acquiescence the indomitable spirit and soul from which it originated.

On the point not far from Burt's beloved Chesuncook Village, a stand of towering white pines keeps watch over the lake. From time to time, the unrelenting wind fells one of these giants, sending the mighty stalwart to the ground with a resounding crash. Such an event in this country is no less traumatic than the news of a legend's passing.

If he had been there to hear it, Burt McBurnie would have undoubtedly emptied another magazine of "Jesus! Jesus! Jesus!" Another string of expletives would follow close behind. But he, more than most, would understand in his heart that it is the laws of nature, not the desires of mere men, that hold sway in this realm.

———

With everything soaked from the morning showers, it takes longer than usual to break camp on Thoreau Island. There's no rush, however, as our next expected stop is Big Island, only ten miles or so downstream. The West Branch flows fast here. Even with the delayed departure, we should be ashore in plenty of time for a fashionably late kielbasa-dog lunch.

Big Island, which sits slightly to river left, with the narrow western channel on that side much shallower than the main one to the east, sports campsites at both ends. The darker and damper site at the north end has good views downstream. But no site on this river is more coveted than Big Island South.

It sits atop a high gravel bluff studded with ancient pines. There's ample shade, but sunlight warms and dries the camp for most of the day.

The ground, a sedimentary gift from a retreating glacier, is nearly perfectly flat and well drained—ideal for pitching multiple tents. There are two picnic tables, an outhouse of unremarkable construction, a sturdy ridgepole, and numerous trees for erecting the mandatory amalgam of tarps we have come to refer to on these trips as Bartertown.

A long, stout branch that extends over the stairs from the shore is ideal for raising the club's official colors—a white smiling skull and crossed canoe paddles on a field of black.

From a seat at the fire, the view stretches a quarter of a mile back upstream, the perfect vantage from which to watch the comings and goings of the many guides and sports that stalk the fabled landlocked salmon in motorized, square-stern canoes.

As we approach the site, we're relieved that there are no canoes already pulled up on shore. Our boats are quickly unloaded, and the gear is carried to the top of the bluff with minimal protestation.

At sunset, long golden rays illuminate the bottoms of branches in the grove of trees towering over our tents. It gives the illusion that an otherworldly light seems to be issuing from the earth itself. After dark, I stare at the campfire as snapping spruce sends sparks spiraling skyward to mingle oh so briefly with a million pinprick stars, each point ephemeral in its own way.

The next morning, dawn's first light refracts in the fog, casting long fingers of light and shadow across the still waters. I wait at the water's edge on this first true frosty morning half-expecting Thoreau's spirit to materialize out of the mist. Around me, the steamy breath of the river silently coalesces into a delicate frozen shell on everything, including paddles and the gunwales of our canoes pulled safely up on shore.

His specter does not show itself, but I sense that he is near.

By the time we break camp, the fog has retreated, although a thick overcast has formed, demoting the sun to a mere bright spot in an unbroken mantle of gray overhead. With collars turned up against the chill, we push off into the current immediately running the first of many easy Class II rapids we'll find on this stretch.

In higher water, many of these drops are flooded out, run with barely a notice. But today, the river is low. Canoes seem to scrape and bang as much as float down through the riffles. I wince as multiple shouts of "Rock!" once again begin to be heard from the paddlers on point.

——

The high point of our third day on river is passing the confluence of Pine Stream, a major tributary of the West Branch and the scene of one of Thoreau's most epic adventures, when he accompanied his Native American guide on a moose hunting expedition. The backwater stream meanders south for miles through low marshy country ideal for hunting the North Woods's largest herbivore.

In the essay "Chesuncook," Thoreau, mostly a vegetarian—he did eat moose meat on at least three occasions and reportedly compared it to "tender beef"—revealed a fascination with hunting, softening somewhat from his earlier moral pronouncements on that and fishing in a chapter called "Higher Laws" in *Walden*.

Often lost in the beatification of Thoreau to some sort of wilderness saint was the fact that in no way was he capable of planning and pulling off three backcountry trips in Maine on his own. Some of those trips covered more than two hundred miles.

He seldom left the familiarity of Concord, his trips to Maine comprising the most ambitious expeditions of his adult life. Even his stint of living deliberately at Walden comes with an asterisk. His cabin, located near the edge of the village, enjoyed a steady stream of visitors. On many nights, he walked one and a half miles to have supper at his mother's house or to visit the home of close friend Ralph Waldo Emerson, whose land the cabin was on.

His mother and sisters kept him well provided with cookies, pies, cakes, and other baked goods. Without them, many believe, Thoreau would have starved.

Thoreau was far from a natural pathfinder. He failed to find the summit of Katahdin when he climbed it, spending a cold, lonely night above tree line. After heading north from Chesuncook, Thoreau lost his way while trying to navigate the Mud Pond Carry from Umbazooksus.

On a canoe trip with a friend on the Sudbury River in Concord in 1844, Thoreau managed to stay found but started a campfire in an old stump that got out of control and burned three hundred acres of forest.

Getting him safely home from the Maine wilderness fell to his Native American guides, Joe Polis and Joseph Attean. Both were skilled woodsmen, well educated—men of quiet power—natural leaders.

Joseph Attean, Thoreau's guide on his second expedition that included the West Branch, was an experienced river driver. He went on to become his tribe's first elected chief.

Polis was a guide on Thoreau's third and final trip to Maine. He surprised the writer by living not in a rustic abode but rather a two-story house painted white "with blinds." He later went on to represent the Penobscot Tribe in Augusta and in Washington, D.C.

Both men worked hard to teach Thoreau the Native American place-names along the traditional tribal canoe routes they followed.

The importance of the relationship Thoreau developed with these men cannot be overstated. In his eulogy at Thoreau's funeral, Emerson said his friend admired three men the most—abolitionist John Brown, Walt Whitman, and Joe Polis.

In his last days, Thoreau showed no fear of death. When his aunt asked him if he was right with God, he reportedly replied, "I did not know we had ever quarreled." As he lay on his deathbed, his final thoughts undoubtedly included memories of his canoeing adventures. That suggests that it was on a river, surrounded by nature and people he loved and respected, where his heart truly dwelled.

An earlier essay, "A week on the Concord and Merrimack Rivers," was written in honor of his older brother John, who died suddenly in 1842. It recounts an idyllic canoe trip the two took prior to Henry David's visits to Maine. The poem that serves as the essay's preface reveals the depths of the writer's grief over losing his brother—his closest traveling companion through life.

> Where'er thou sail'st who sailed with me,
> Though now thou climbest loftier mounts,
> And fairer rivers dost ascend,
> Be thou my Muse, my Brother — .
>
> I am bound, I am bound, for a distant shore,
> By a lonely isle, by a far Azore,
> There it is, there it is, the treasure I seek,
> On the barren sands of a desolate creek.
>
> I sailed up a river with a pleasant wind,
> New lands new people and new thoughts to find;

> Many fair reaches and headlands appeared,
> And many dangers were there to be feared;
> But when I remember where I have been,
> And the fair landscapes that I have seen,
> Thou seemest the only permanent shore,
> The cape never rounded, nor wandered o'er.

As he breathed his last, Thoreau seemed to be alluding to that trip and to his later adventures in Maine. "Now comes good sailing," he said to those at his bedside. He then whispered, "Moose." After a pause, his last word—"Indian."

Past its confluence with Pine Stream, the West Branch widens considerably, becoming more or less the broad jagged western arm of Chesuncook. This stretch is not so much a river as it is a long, narrow lake.

It doesn't take long for the traditional welcoming committee, a relentless northwest wind, to make our acquaintance. While a breeze from that direction holds the promise of sweeping away the overcast, it also whips up three-foot whitecaps slowing forward progress to a bicep-busting crawl.

Times like these remind me of why I hate paddling on lakes with a headwind. You have to fight to keep the bow pointed into the blow and avoid getting sideways at all costs.

The problem arises when the heading you want to take is anything other than parallel to the direction of the wind. At best, you can quarter it, take it at an oblique angle, providing that tack doesn't get too sharp. The natural predisposition of any canoe is to bob broadside to the wind, aligning itself to the waves. That, unfortunately, is the craft's precise plane of minimum stability. In such situations, you can almost hear actress Bette Davis warning to "Fasten your seat belts, it's going to be a bumpy night."

The sharper the angle to the wind, the more power that must be applied to keep that from happening. If the waves are big enough, or the center of gravity of said canoe's contents, including occupants, is high enough, the entire system will seek equilibrium via the only path possible—it will roll, often without warning. Like a speed trap, a bite on the ear by heavyweight Mike Tyson, or moose flies when the back of your shirt rides up—it's the one you don't see coming that always gets you.

With the wind pretty much dictating our course, we soon find ourselves hugging the eastern shore. At least if we flip, we won't have long to drift before reaching land.

Working our way along against the wind's advice, we marvel at the impressive sandy expanses of beach. It has obviously been low water all summer. Most of the light brown sand, normally underwater, is covered with a carpet of tall, slender beach grass, itself rippling in waves at the whim of the wind. The stark, silver skeletons of dead trees and stumps pepper the shore, not unlike ghostly figures that have wandered down from the darkness of the woods to luxuriate in the last rays of pastel light at sunset.

For the final night, we set up camp where the river widens farther still, at the place called Boom House. It's just around a peninsula from Chesuncook Village, where we'll end our float tomorrow. The site, which sports a squeaky, cast-iron hand pump well, is hidden behind a wall of alders, backed by a row of towering white pines, the type of giants that first lured those in search of timber riches to this country.

Thoreau visited the village during his second trip to Maine. He wrote, "I was interested to see how a pioneer lived on this side of the country. His life is in some respects more adventurous than that of his brother in the west; for he contends with winter as well as the wilderness."

A huge house once stood on this spot, bivouac of the river men who tended the massive strings of logs connected by chains that corralled wood on the lake. Once contained in the booms, it was easy to move great rafts of wood down the lake with the push or pull of a steamboat.

Not far away to the northeast is Umbazooksus, where Thoreau endured arduous portages on his way to the promise of Telos Lake, that mystic nexus from which can be inaugurated all manner of adventures on the Allagash, St. John, and the East Branch of the Penobscot.

At Boom House, our camp is quickly established, the process of unloading the boats and distributing the gear automatic. Picnic tables, the camp kitchen, and a collapsible table that will serve as the bar, are neatly arranged under the main tarp at the ridgepole. Our assembly of ragtag tents is arrayed around the grassy site in haphazard fashion, the fantasy of finding some semblance of nonlumpy ground being the primary determination for their final orientation.

It doesn't take long for a large block of cheddar and stick of pepperoni to join the deck of cards and cribbage board on the table. The call of "Who's in?" accompanies the official unfurling of the colors, as the hiss of the three-burner Coleman stove announces the official start of supper.

The last misshapen ice cubes from the bottom of the cooler tink into metal cups and await rendezvous with what's left of the rapidly diminishing supply of Canadian Club.

After enjoying a supper of fire-cooked pork chops, green beans, and real mashed potatoes, followed by strawberry shortcake cooked in a reflector oven at the edge of the fire, I walk the short path through the alders from camp to the open shore of the lake. Dark, billowing clouds continue to reign overhead despite a low band of clear sky far across the water to the westard. That growing gap glows with increasing intensity as the sun slips ever downward, by all appearances surrendering to gravity, when in reality, it's the Earth that is the prisoner of its influence.

Almost imperceptibly, the most distant edges of the clouds begin to glow a fiery white.

Far up on shore at what had been the high-water mark in more well-watered seasons, the red, green, and blue canoes are all rolled over, side by side, enjoying a well-deserved rest. The scratched and dented bottoms bear mute testimony to the multiple indignities suffered during numerous encounters with submerged rocks that lacked the good graces to broadcast their negative intentions in advance.

Just around the side of this point to the eastard, hidden to all save those with the enterprise to look, Katahdin looms in the distance, the dark, naked granite itself surrendering to the increasingly golden glow.

The excitement and energy of yet another card game wafts down the shore from camp. Chief among the chorus of familiar voices is that of my brother Carl.

A man who moves freely between a world where money can buy nearly everything and this one where attempting to put a price on intangibles of inestimable value is pure folly, Carl lives for the chance to hike, or camp, or canoe in Maine.

While I, too, celebrate any chance to get out into the wilds, I always embark with an underlying sense of trepidation, a palpable yet unquantifiable measure of reserve—never quite comfortable with humanity's right to declare itself an equal part of the landscape.

Along with reaping the rewards of being in the North Woods, I'm constantly mindful of the risks, the challenges, the "what-ifs," the physical and emotional tribulations that are a part of even the most routine of expeditions.

Carl, meanwhile, rushes right in, savoring each long, cold drink without a pause to swallow. Like an ocean swimmer fearlessly confronting a towering wave about to break, he plunges in headfirst, never doubting he will emerge on the other side unscathed. Despite being the root of his compassion, his patience, his generosity, it's a part of him that I, or anyone else, seldom get to see.

Tomorrow, as is the nature of all things, this trip will come to its preordained end. For every spring, there will be a fall.

There's a bittersweet feeling when breaking camp for the last time, when even a new day holds only endings. Like a pause before finishing a good book, or writing one for that matter, the heart does not want the journey, the reverie, to end.

—◆—

Alone upon the shore, I watch as the first slim crescent of the sun drifts below the overcast. The light becomes full vertical, scratching the tattered bottoms of the clouds, the entire landscape now bathed in a warm, intense yellow radiance that pours like honey from the sky.

I watch, transfixed, as the almost alien glow invigorates a proud, patient landscape, object, admittedly, of many insults, but which has never fully capitulated to the affronts of axe, plow, or chainsaw.

Knowing such sorcery will only last for a few more minutes, I race back up the path to camp to summon the other members of the group. Engrossed in their cards, their cheddar, their cigars and CC, the artificial glare of the Coleman lantern erasing lengthening shadows, they're less than enthusiastic to drop everything and come down to the shore to see the incredible sunset.

"You heard the guide," Carl finally says sarcastically, plopping the deck of cards on the table. "Let's go check it out."

Single file, they tromp down the trail and fan out across the sand shoulder to shoulder, their faces painted in the rich golden palette, islands of light stark against the still-black clouds overhead.

"Look at it. It's incredible. Have you ever seen light like that?" I ask. Only the wind whispering through the waving beach grass breaks the silence. It's clear they're only humoring me, if only to ensure that strawberry shortcake remains on the menu for the next trip.

After the obligatory minute of feigned interest, Carl removes the stub of a cigar from his lips and uses it to punctuate the air. "You know," he says with exaggerated sincerity, "you can't buy light like that."

The spell of the moment broken by such a keen observation of fundamental truth, the company disbands. Each walks quietly back up the trail to their suspended diversions. I stay behind, determined to remain until the sun fully abdicates its authority to the flat, featureless dimness from which the night's first stars emerge.

In that moment, I see there is indeed a timelessness to this place where the trees, the shore, the sky are never the same, yet where the landscape and the light that reveals it to us in each glorious, vivid detail, remain constant. In a world that never seems to have enough, time is the one thing here that is never in short supply.

Light. Time. These, I understand, are the North Woods's greatest gifts.

Turning back toward the sunset, I realize at long last how Thoreau might know this place again. In order to really breathe, one needs fresh air. To really think requires gentle whispers of silence. To really see, one must perceive illumination in every color, in every dimension.

As the sun dips behind jagged black silhouettes of pointed spruce and fir, the present retreats, first from the swaying blades of beach grass stretching down to the water and finally from the tops of the white pines behind me on the point.

At last, I sense the presence of Thoreau. He is smiling in that fading glow, abiding in a realm not built of rock or wood, or ruled by water, but in a dominion of light—a fire of ageless intensity, born in the searing heart of an aging autumn sun, not yet ready to surrender to the pale white ardor of winter.

OH SHENANDOAH

Not all of the Moose River Camping Club's adventures have been expedited in Maine. There have been backpacking and canoe trips in Nova Scotia, Connecticut, Massachusetts, New Hampshire, Vermont, and beyond. We've climbed Mount Mansfield and Camel's Hump in Vermont, stayed in the high huts in the Whites, canoed the Connecticut River in the Nutmeg State in February, endured November snows in the Taconics, and swore never to return to tick-infested lean-tos on the Appalachian Trail just south of the Adirondacks in New York.

In early May 2008, we headed for Harpers Ferry, West Virginia, to hike area trails and to float on tubes on a section of the Potomac River. My brother Dale and his wife, Jane, are managing a KOA campground next to the National Historic Park there, so it's the perfect chance to visit and explore.

My twin brother, Carl, and friend Kurt drive down from Connecticut, about a six-hour run through the heart of the Eastern Seaboard's metropolis. Rob, Mike, Tim, and I fly down from Maine.

The contrast in weather when getting off the plane at Dulles is remarkable. The leaves are barely out on the trees back home where the first hatch of blackflies is still buzzing aimlessly about, not yet acquainted with their bloodsucking predilections.

Along the Down East coast of Maine, a last pathetic snow shower is still not out of the question.

Here, it's nigh on summer.

The sun's glare seems almost harsh, the air thick and humid. A verdant forest covers the rolling hills with a near-impenetrable carpet of green. It's like we've stepped off a time machine that only goes six weeks into the future.

That night, after racing through the property on golf carts and enjoying the swimming pool, we sit around the cribbage board in one of the campground's "Kabins," reviewing the next day's itinerary. From the local outfitter's headquarters, it's only a short bus ride to the put-in. But, thanks to a unique accident of geology and geography, we'll pass through three states. As the Potomac nears the confluence with the Shenandoah at Harpers Ferry, river right is West Virginia and river left is Maryland. The way the road runs, you leave town, which is in West Virginia, cross the Shenandoah into Virginia, go a little over a mile on the highway, and cross over the Potomac into Maryland. It's no wonder with such a convoluted arrangement of roads, railroads, rivers, towns, and states that the area turned out to be a major objective for the armies of the Union and Confederacy during the Civil War. Control of these few square miles changed hands fourteen times in six years.

From the put-in, we'll float downstream on truck tire inner tubes to the appointed take-out spot. Along the way, we'll run under two railroad bridges and past remnants of another, and drift by the attractive village much of which clings to a steep hillside. At the foot of the hill, where the rivers meet and rail lines diverge, is the storied brick armory where abolitionist John Brown rocketed into the national spotlight during his ill-fated raid in 1859.

His body may still lie "a-mouldering in the grave," as the hymn notes, but it's not here. He was returned home to be buried on the family farm back in upstate New York.

Once in Maryland, a narrow, winding back road skirts the edge of the river and ducks beneath the two railroad bridges on the way to the starting point about a mile upstream. Standing on the sandy riverbank, the thick, sweet scent of sycamores surrounds us. Here, the storied C&O canal, another national historic park, parallels the river's course. The park is more than 185 miles from end to end, yet in most places, it's less than a hundred yards wide.

We cross the former towpath, now a bike trail, to get to the water.

On the opposite bank runs the Norfolk Southern railway line, one of several that converge on Harpers Ferry, passing first through a wide yet short tunnel under the imposing cliffs of Maryland Heights. Near the top of this edifice are the faded white letters of an advertisement where the cliff face was turned into a giant billboard in the early 1900s. Where we now see a home for roosting raptors, some enterprising huckster saw an ideal spot to tout the benefits of Mennen borated talcum powder.

After posing for a group photo with our life vests and inflatable tubes, we walk to the river's edge, get situated in the rafts, and use our hands to paddle off into the current. Carl is all decked out for river adventure. He sports his signature Bula baseball hat with neck shield to ward off sunburn, new sunglasses, and a small waterproof case carrying some post-trip celebratory cigars tethered to his life vest.

———

As always on these trips, Carl projects a relaxed air of supreme confidence. Ever mindful of the potential for calamity, I always approach our adventures with a constitution averse to risk. What can go wrong is always in the back of my mind. Not that I'm paranoid, but I'm just the kind of guy who never enters an unfamiliar room without making a mental note of all potential means of egress in the event of a fire.

RETURN TO MOOSE RIVER

As a journalist, I hate to be interviewed. I know from thirty-five years on the other side of the pen and notebook how many things can go off the rails either by oversight or design. In journalism, it's seldom the major or controversial stories where the biggest problems occur. It's usually the simpler, more mundane subjects where things go south. Beware the no-brainers, the kinds of stories you've done a thousand times before and thought you could do in your sleep.

As a Registered Maine Guide, part of my job is to anticipate potential dangers, take steps to avoid them, yet be prepared to respond accordingly and quickly if things should go awry. Folks like to say that you can't call something an adventure if everything goes according to plan. Just how far afield it strays from the expected can be the problem.

Many folks who run rivers become complacent about the risks. Too often, people fret when preparing to run a tough Class III rapid, but fail to review all the gear and procedures when shooting an easy Class II. When swimming in a lake, they don't hesitate to ask how deep the water is, equating greater depth with a corresponding elevation in danger. But you can drown in a bathtub in two inches of water.

Part of being prepared is learning everything I can about outdoor recreational mishaps, not just to know where the potential dangers lie but also to understand what went wrong, what mistakes in judgment were made, so preventative steps can be taken. Like any knowledgeable general, I'm bound and determined to be totally prepared to fight the last war.

Some years ago, six experienced paddlers were canoeing down Carrot Pitch, a set of rapids on the Machias River in Down East Maine. Depending on water flow, that rapid can be a tough Class II or full-blown Class III. On this trip, one of the boats capsized, and one woman drowned.

Although the current was swift, the water was only waist-deep. Everyone had been wearing life jackets.

On hearing the news, my first reaction was disbelief. What a horrible experience for the others on that trip to watch their friend die and be helpless to do anything about it.

Some months later, the Maine Warden Service issued a report that detailed the mishap. Paddlers in two of the three boats decided to portage instead of running the pitch. On its run, the third canoe had gotten nearly all the way down through when it went sideways and hit a large, partially submerged rock midstream.

As is the natural reaction of people in that situation, the occupants of the canoe may have leaned away from the rock at the moment of impact. Doing so, however, strengthens the river's hand and seals your fate.

The tilt upstream multiplies the force of the water in rolling the canoe out from under the paddlers. The current then exerts incredible force on the extended ends, breaking the canoe's back, causing it to wrap nearly inside out around the boulder, bow and stern both pointing downstream.

Both paddlers had been kneeling, which is recommended practice in heavy water. It lowers the center of gravity and allows for better application of power with each stroke.

The paddler in the stern successfully bailed out as the disaster unfolded in relatively slow motion. The one in the bow was not so fortunate. As the canoe doubled around the rock, her feet became pinned between the floor and the forward thwart just behind her. She was trapped, facedown, partially under the boat. There was nothing anyone could do. The woman's companions tried to reach her but were hampered by the swift current.

Wardens were not able to free her body until several hours later.

She was just twenty-four years old.

The incident gave me a newfound respect for the authority of moving water and helped me to understand that the damage to a canoe in a pin and wrap should be the least of my concerns.

Pondering that case got me thinking about how I would react if something like that happened. I've been involved in life-and-death emergencies before, including pulling a drowning young summer camper out of a murky cove and providing first aid and comfort to a coworker in a steel mill who had his leg torn off by a piece of machinery four stories above the concrete floor of the warehouse. Discovering an instinct that compelled me to run toward places others are fleeing most likely laid the groundwork for my eventual career in newspapers.

Someone once asked me how much I charge to guide people into the woods. "That's free," I explained. "Anybody can get themselves into the woods. You pay me to get you out." Becoming risk averse, I realized, was ultimately a better safety strategy than endlessly equipping oneself to deal with the aftermath. Getting out in one piece after all is the most important part of the deal.

Instead of the "What if?" Carl, in contrast, always embraces the "Why not?" He is by no means an adrenaline junkie, but for him, a challenge such as a difficult rapid is first and foremost plain and simple fun. A big fan of *Animal House*, Carl claims there's a line in that classic film for every situation in life. He's right about that, of course.

He loves to quote John Belushi's character "Bluto" Blutarski trying to rally his down-in-the-dumps fraternity brothers. "What's all this lying around #@%!?" he often says. Spurring them to action, Bluto yells, "Nothing is over until we decide it is. . . . Let's do it!"

Hesitant to try something new? "Oh no, Bluto, we might get in trouble," Carl likes to deadpan. "Was it over when the Germans bombed Pearl Harbor?" "Double secret probation." "Fat, drunk, and stupid is no way to go through life." "Seven years of college down the drain." "My advice to you is to begin drinking heavily." "Hey, you parked it out back last night. When we got up this morning, it was gone." "Ramming speeeeed!"

And then there are the classic rock-and-roll songs in the soundtrack. "Shama Lama Ding Dong." "Louie Louie." "Shout—A little bit louder now . . ." That's Carl.

He doesn't take foolish risks. He always wears his life jacket and/or a wet suit in cold weather. But he does not let anyone, or anything, intimidate him.

Carl is never about just going with the flow. The vanity plate, WHITEWTR, on his Sequoia SUV, is displayed in homage to his love of the thrill of places where the water moves fast and the way ahead is often uncertain. A staunch Republican, in marked contrast to my own left-of-center leanings, he takes pleasure in the inquiries the plate attracts about whether it refers to the trumped-up land deal scandal of the same name during the Clinton administration.

———

The Potomac at the launch point is an impressive three football fields wide. It courses and falls over scores of one- and two-foot drops created by the hard bedrock ledges that run perpendicular to the flow like giant ragged steps stretching from one side of the river to the other. Viewed from above, that geological feature continues straight under the village of Harpers Ferry, emerging to form parallel impediments in opposition to the direction of flow in the Shenandoah.

The water itself has a greenish tint, nearly opaque, much of the surface coated with a fine, yellow powder that appears to be tree pollen.

Just downstream loom the impressive cliffs of Maryland Heights, where remnants of Civil War fortifications remain.

The water in the river isn't particularly cold by Maine standards, but the flow is fast—too fast, I worry. Lying on your back in the tubes (there was no way to sit up) makes it almost impossible to see where you're going. Craning your head and neck to see anything but sky compresses your windpipe, making it uncomfortable to breathe.

With only your arms and hands for maneuvering, it's nearly impossible to follow the outfitter's pretrip safety instructions to keep your feet pointed downstream in the constant rapids, much less move left or right to avoid rocks and snags. The speed of the current leaves no room for indecision.

This is far from the idyllic float trip I had expected. I'm upset at myself for not knowing more about it before getting to this point.

The outfitter warned us to hug the left bank when reaching the first railroad bridge. The prearranged take-out spot is just around that bend on river left in Maryland. But the resolve of the river keeps pushing us away toward Virginia, where there really is no place to stop safely. The prospect of being uncontrollably swept far past the appointed take-out spot seems frighteningly real.

A few minutes after launch, Rob hollers that he's going to stop. Uncomfortable and not having any fun, he decides to paddle to shore and walk out on the towpath along the canal. My neck already sore, breathing rapidly, and with even more intimidating rapids ahead, I worry about making it all the way to the end myself.

Spinning around to check, I see Carl is about ten feet behind me off to the side. I notice him trying to get off his tube. "I'm having trouble breathing," he gasps with a bewildered look in his eyes.

Slipping off his raft, he struggles to stand up in the cloudy, waist-deep water. He as much as anyone knows, I say to myself, abandoning ship in these circumstances is a last resort. With sharp rocks, deep holes, snags, and hidden underwater obstacles that can injure or entrap you, there's much more danger, even while wearing a life jacket, when you're in, rather than on, such fast moving water.

After a couple seconds, he slumps, unconscious, his life jacket barely keeping his head above the surface. Swept from his head, his beloved Bula bobs over the next drop, spins in circles for a moment in an eddy before disappearing down another relentless set of standing waves.

I try to scull closer and hold position against the flow to reach him. But the current and repeated drops over the incessant rapids conspire to push me farther away. He sweeps past in the foaming water just beyond my grasp.

I yell to the guys ahead to help. Kurt and Tim, who are closest, position themselves directly downstream. They lurch to grab a hold of his life jacket.

"Carl! Carl! Carl!" we all shout over and over.

There is no response.

They struggle for what seems like an eternity to get him and themselves to safety on the Maryland shore. The rest of our company, alerted by the commotion, begin to try and get to land as well.

After several minutes of Herculean effort, they reach a narrow patch of sand below the towpath. I land about twenty yards upstream, run over, and help pull Carl fully out of the water.

We shout his name.

We slap his face.

Nothing.

He is unresponsive, the pupils of his Nordic blue eyes fixed and dilated.

I clutch at just one glimmer of hope. He appears to be breathing.

There is no cell service in this gorge. Mike and Rob go for help in the hopes of flagging down a passing car on the nearby road. All I can do is hold Carl's hand—and hope.

My heart drops when after a few minutes of shallow breaths, Carl's chest stops rising. Dale, a former emergency medical technician, and I, with a moderate level of first aid training, immediately begin CPR.

Under the rules of CPR, you're instructed that once you begin, you cannot stop until the person revives, more skilled medical personnel arrive, or you're physically unable to continue.

Not able to contemplate the incomprehensible, stopping is the furthest thing from our minds.

We swap off over and over, one of us doing chest compressions, the other pinching Carl's nose, covering his lips with our own, and exhaling to force oxygen into his lungs. The amount of air it takes to make his cavernous chest rise surprises me.

As we swap places, Dale and I exchange knowing glances but dare not speak of our darkest suspicions. We check repeatedly, but cannot detect a pulse.

The thirty minutes until local and national park emergency responders arrive seems like an eternity.

A million things flood through my mind. I convince myself that it must be some kind of transient attack. Maybe he's just dehydrated. He'll be back to the campground by supper, tired and suitably chastened by some doctor to take it easy for a couple days.

This isn't it, I assure myself. He can't be dead.

No panic. No negative thoughts. It's not over, as Carl himself would say, until we say it's over.

Despite incontrovertible evidence right in front of me, I refuse to acknowledge the obvious. I rationalize. I deny. I can't admit that the only flicker of life left in my brother, someone I've shared my entire existence with, someone who shares my exact same DNA, comes from a stilled heart grudgingly complying to compressions on his chest and air that must be forced into him by passing first through someone else's lips.

Through it all, I silently curse the growing heat and the humidity.

And everywhere is the sickly sweet smell of the sycamores.

Where is that time machine when I need it?

Volunteers from two fire departments, National Park Service rangers, and an ambulance crew arrive. They hook Carl up to a portable defibrillator. The unit's cold, dispassionate computer voice announces, "Heartbeat detected." No shock is in order. I want desperately to believe that as a good sign.

I'm surprised when a paramedic hands me a mask and bag to ventilate Carl, but I'm relieved to be able to stop CPR. It takes eight of us to lift him into a wire stokes litter for the carry up the steep embankment along the former canal. The trail is narrow, and people on both sides thrash through the thick vegetation. It's ironic, I think, that in evacuating someone on a trail like this, the only good footing is under the litter, where no one actually steps.

Intent on getting Carl to the ambulance as quickly as possible, no one stops to notice that the lush, knee-deep greenery we're crashing through in shorts and sandals is poison ivy.

Although he insists that it's my place to go in the ambulance on the twenty-mile run to the hospital in Frederick, I beg Dale to do it. I barely know where we are here, and the prospect of descending alone further into dark territory both physically and spiritually, without even the flimsy anchor of geographical familiarity, is too much to contemplate. My heart already knows what my mind cannot acknowledge—the stark realization of the final declaration that lies at the end of that ride. Like a child covering his ears and shouting gibberish to avoid listening to a parent's directive, I pray that my reluctance to get into the ambulance will somehow alter the inevitable.

At the same time, I am ashamed of my inability to accept the reality of this moment. I surrender to my fear of becoming lost as well, not wanting to be surrounded by strangers on a long ambulance ride to an unknown place, to an uncertain end. My spirit founders in the hesitancy of indecision.

I'll have years to wrestle with the soul-crushing guilt of not bearing my brother's witness to the very end.

The ambulance pulls out, lights and sirens blazing. I rationalize that they would not have transported him if they thought it was hopeless. Still, I know from decades of writing stories about accidents that few people are listed as having died at the scene or in the ambulance on the way to the hospital. It's an artifice of deliberate construction meant to reinforce the notion that emergency medical personnel do everything they can in difficult situations. Many EMS personnel are volunteers. Publicly putting the blame for someone's unavoidable death on them does nothing to reinforce their desire to help people or encourage their continued participation in the system.

It's also an acknowledgment of the miracles that can happen once someone gets to an emergency room within "the golden hour." Only someone with the expertise of a doctor should make the final determination. You're not dead until you're in the emergency room and every avenue of treatment has been exhausted and a doctor says you're dead.

Jane arrives to take us back to the campground, where we try and figure out what to do next. A short time later, my phone rings. It's Dale.

"He's gone," he whispers in the resigned voice of a soldier acknowledging the last desperate battle of the war has been lost.

I open my mouth but cannot speak. The others gather around, worried eyes probing for a sign. I shake my head side-to-side, chin down, tears streaming down my cheeks. My questions to Dale, as much if not more so than the answers, leave no doubt in the minds of those who can hear only half the conversation exactly what has happened. The downtrodden looks on their faces confirm that they too now know.

— · —

Later, the doctor would explain that a blood clot that had likely formed in Carl's leg on the long drive down the previous day dislodged, went to his lungs, and cut off the blood supply to his brain. His generous heart continued to beat for a time on reflex, but eventually surrendered as well.

Cold comfort comes from the doctor's assurance that even if it had happened in the emergency room with a surgeon standing right there, they would not have been able to save him.

The calls to family back in Connecticut and Maine are the hardest I've ever had to make. I do not want Carl's wife, Mary Ellen, to be alone when she hears. They were high school sweethearts and have never been apart for long. I remember their wedding day, some thirty-four years ago, my memories illuminated by a soft and gentle light. I was best man. We wore rented tan tuxedos—cheesy by today's standards, but considered high style back then.

The wedding party posed for photos in Meriden's Hubbard Park after the ceremony. We all felt so grown-up. But looking back, we were so young, just a few years out of high school. It was a day and story so filled with love, with hope, the future still a blank page as they embarked together on life's grand mystery. And here, on this day, in this place, Carl's final chapter has been written.

Carl and Mary Ellen shared the inevitable ups and downs of the middle class's struggle to resist downward mobility—careers stopped and started, foreclosure and financial rock bottom, the joys of four bright and beautiful children, the suicide of their youngest son, Blake, just four years earlier.

I call their son Ryan to ask him to break the news to his mother in person and to tell his brother and sister. I know it won't be an easy thing for him to hear, but as the oldest, it now falls to him to shoulder such burdens. "You need to prepare yourself," I say when he answers. "There's been an accident. Your dad's gone. He's dead."

First, a long pause.

"What?" "Get out!" he repeats over and over. "He didn't suffer," I say softly, recounting the day's events. Ryan's questions continue in rapid succession as he struggles to comprehend the answers. And then the silence of stark reality.

"I love you," I say at the end of the conversation. "We'll all get through this together."

The next call goes to my mom back in Maine. She answers and is immediately suspicious when I ask her to put my stepdad Chuck on the phone. "Oh no," he says when I ask him to tell her the worst news any parent can hear. When he finally hands her the phone, I can sense the growing shadow over her heart. "Oh no," she says. "Oh no, oh no, oh no."

My sisters, themselves a set of twins, are next.

And then another difficult one—back home to Bar Harbor to my wife, Roxie. I try to be strong and manage to blurt out what happened. But just hearing her voice asking me if I'm okay unleashes a flood of pent-up emotion. I sob, the tears of the bitterness of loss mingling with those falling in acknowledgment of the precious sweetness of our love in the here and now.

"I love you," I say as I hang up the phone. And then there's no solemn duty left to divert my mind's attention from the emotional monolith that is this day's dark truth.

While going through the contacts on my phone, I rediscover a voice mail Carl left me the day before as we all arrived. He was so excited about the adventure ahead. No one could have known about the time bomb already ticking in his leg.

In a quiet moment, I hit play. A moment of soft static is followed by his energized voice: "Yo-man, we're at the campground. . . . Can't wait to see you." I play it a second time. And then a third.

———

Jane and I join Dale at the hospital. In the lobby, it seems strange that others are going about their business oblivious to our family's great loss. "A man just died here!" I want to scream.

We're ushered to a private waiting room while preparations are made. Tubes are being removed, equipment wheeled away, paperwork filed. I stare at pictures on the wall, annoyed that they all depict bright, sunny days.

After a half an hour, a doctor ushers us into the dim emergency room alcove where Carl lies on his back on a gurney, arms straight at his sides, seemingly asleep. His hair is combed back, a clean, white sheet tucked up to his broad shoulders and across his barrel chest. "Take as much time as you need," he says softly and leaves, pulling the curtain closed behind him. The kindness and compassion of everyone here are a true comfort.

Arms around one another, Dale, Jane, and I just stare. No words. Despite all the activity of a busy emergency room on the other side of the curtain, I recall no particular sound.

Of all the parts of this day, of all the scenes that still play out in my mind like an endlessly looping video that never fades and never changes, this one stands out. I don't remember how long we stood there, my hand on Carl's shoulder.

I wonder who will be taking care of him now, where they'll take him, how he'll get home. I pray, too, for the spirits of our dad, of our grandparents, and of Blake to guide him on his journey.

I am terrified to think that someday the loss of his physical presence will allow his spirit to fade from my heart, that the connection we've shared for so many years will become like an old letter, left to become brown and brittle in a forgotten box in a dusty attic.

I worry, too, about preserving the bonds of a family split between two states now that the patriarch of the reigning generation has fallen.

The lyrics of a Pearl Jam song repeat over and over in my head. "Hearts and thoughts they fade, fade away . . . hearts and thoughts they fade, fade away." "I'm not going to let that happen," I swear to myself. "God," I implore, "you can't let that happen."

Turning to leave, I lean over and kiss Carl on the forehead. There's no holding back the tears that fall from my cheeks to his. "I love you," I whisper. "We'll meet again, my brother; we'll meet again."

That night, as I lay awake back at the Kabin, my head on the pillow I took from the bed he slept in the night before, I toss and turn. I'm now adrift in a cold, cruel universe that has no cardinal directions, no clear sense of up or down. I have no awareness of time and place.

The only light comes from the glow of my cell phone. My finger slides across the smooth glass, stopping at Carl's voice mail. I hit play and listen to his message from a world that no longer exists. I hit play again, and again, and again.

Just after midnight, I hit delete.

＊＊

I realize now that the light is different on the day a loved one dies. Somehow, all the edges are crisper, the colors more vivid, the chaotic choreography of billowing clouds in a hurry to go nowhere comes straight out of a magnificent Maxfield Parrish print.

There's an obvious poignancy when someone dies escorted by windswept rain or under the dark of night. But it borders on malice when someone, as Shakespeare said, departs on a trip to "that undiscovered country" on a bright and sunny day with summer in full bloom and the scent of sycamores in the air. How cruel is it for the world to be awash in warmth and light and life when your heart is gripped by a cold and ever deepening darkness?

There is no good way to die. But of all the possibilities, Carl's passing was better than most. No machines. No weeks in a coma. No heroic measures undertaken with no real expectation of success. No mourning family crowded around a bed in a darkened room, exchanging nervous glances wondering if the next long, labored breath will be the last.

He was surrounded by his brothers and his friends, outside on a river, doing what he loved to do in a place that turned out to be a spiritual confluence of all the great currents of his life.

It seems almost natural for a man who loved history and who made his living from buying and selling all things old to die in Harpers Ferry, home to the iconic stand of abolitionist John Brown and one of the most contentious crossroads in the country. In fact, in his professional capacity, Carl had assumed the auctioneer's honorary title of "Colonel," which originated after the Civil War when officers of that rank were authorized to dispose of surplus equipment by bid.

Because he was an avid backpacker, it is undoubtedly no coincidence that he left us in a place that is home to the Appalachian Trail Conference headquarters. The white blazes of the AT itself guide hikers across the railroad bridge just yards downstream from where he passed. Follow those blazes far enough north, and you'll reach the very trails and high summits he frequented and cherished his entire life.

On warm summer nights in South Meriden, Connecticut, where we grew up, Carl and I would lay in our bunk beds listening to the sound of freight trains in the distance blowing their horns. That piqued an interest in railroads that prompted us both to be lifelong model railroaders.

Harpers Ferry, with its historic tunnel, multiple railroad bridges, and busy commuter rail passenger station, is one of the best rail fanning locations in the country.

As Carl lays breathing his last on the cool sand of that riverbank, a freight train pulled by four throbbing diesel locomotives rumbles north on the opposite bank, oblivious to the drama on the far shore. Its horns sound over and over. The echoes of those bright, brassy notes race across the fast-moving water and bounce up and off the cliffs of Maryland Heights where the AT climbs sharply out of the gorge. The reverberations seem to go on forever, fading north up the valley, downstream past the village, and beyond to where the Potomac marries the storied Shenandoah. With a newfound vigor born in the merging of waters from mountains in both the north and the south, the river rolls and rambles on, gliding past the marbled monuments of Washington, D.C., and the gleaming glass buildings of Alexandria on the far shore.

There she slows and widens, a river of a certain age, procrastinating on her run to the Chesapeake and the salty dissolution that awaits every great river in the reunion of its waters with a vast and eternal sea.

COMING HOME

WHEN YOU PADDLE ON THE MOOSE RIVER, YOU'RE NEVER ALONE.
You never know what you're going to see when the bow of your
canoe noses around one of the many serpentine bends in the
twenty-five-mile stretch below Holeb Pond all the way down
through to Attean Lake.

After a while, the terrain seems to blur together. It's a repeti-
tious yet varied combination of gravel sandbars, muddy alder banks,
and the occasional boulder. Atop the banks, in upland areas, a towering wall of spruce and fir line the edge with the random tall white
pine standing guard. Here and there are dead-still backwaters that
tempt the adventurous with the hollow lure that one day a jaunt
up one of these unnamed meandering marshes might at long last
lead to something more interesting than just another red-winged
blackbird and a difficult place to turn around.

Signs of civilization are few and far between. Just a seldom-used
cabin or two along the way. In the distance, sitting high on Number
Five Mountain is an abandoned fire lookout tower. It's a distinct
landmark but, due to the meandering nature of the Moose, one
that is worthless for keeping your bearings. On some stretches of
river, when you're trending to the southeast, the tower rises dead
ahead in the distance. After a while, it's well off to river right. Later

in the day, it sits dead ahead again, although a check of the compass reveals on this stretch the water runs due southwest.

Fortunately, there's really only one way to go on the river— downstream. Going with the current always gets you where you're going eventually.

The highlight of any trip on the Moose, naturally, is when you swing around a bend and spot a moose. Despite the river's name, there's no guarantee they'll appear on cue. You can paddle the Moose one year and stop counting after seeing thirty or more. Go back another time (particularly during hunting season) and you'll see nary a one.

Most often, when you see a moose on a lake, it's just a spot in the distance—barely distinguishable from all the boulders and other detritus that clog the shores. When you see one on the Moose, however, it's right there, front and center, usually backside too, often barely ten yards away.

Moose don't have particularly good eyesight. Their ears and noses take up the slack. On any river or stream, there's always a subtle draft of air just above it moving along with the current. By facing downstream, moose can see any danger in that direction and detect the scent of any predators approaching from behind.

The moose, for the most part, are much more nonplussed about these chance encounters. The natural human reaction upon seeing one, particularly for the first time, is to yell "Moose!" as if the folks in the canoe right behind you somehow fail to see twelve hundred pounds of wet hair and antlers standing knee-deep in the stream, pissing right in front of them.

Providing you don't get too close, or yell too loud, the moose will just give you a sideways glance and go back about its business. When it does amble off, it's usually at a reserved pace akin to antique collectors at yard sales making a beeline to a prized find they just spotted yet careful not to transmit any depth of interest through the intensity and pace of their movement.

Moose aren't the only year-round residents along the river. There are otters and raccoons, beavers and woodchucks, waterbirds of every description, and even the occasional black bear. Yet there are other inhabitants too, ones seldom glimpsed, their presence more often sensed rather than seen.

You see, the Moose River also is home to ghosts.

No, they aren't the cinematic specters that cause blood to ooze from the walls of old houses or lurk beneath beds to frighten small children at bedtime. These are the echoes of the Native Americans, woodsmen, river drivers, blacksmiths, camp cooks, trappers, and farmers who traveled this very same route in centuries past.

And on this, the Moose has no monopoly. These spirits are everywhere in the wilds of Maine. The Great North Woods is among the few places left to experience exactly the same thing others did a hundred or even two hundred years ago. A canoe is much more than a way to get from point A to point B. It is a poor man's time machine.

The wind in the pines, the thrump of a drumming spruce grouse in the distance, the cry of a pileated woodpecker, and the scolding call of a kingfisher playing leapfrog as you paddle along all transcend time and mortality. Faces sunburned from the glare of sun off flat water, quivering muscles well into their fifteenth mile of paddling, and the smell of wood smoke drifting through the low slanting rays of the sun at supper are not the province of any one era.

For those attuned to them, the spirits of Maine's wilderness aren't difficult to find. They're out there on the windswept shore at twilight. They hover just above the chill mist in the rapids. They tend abandoned fields that long ago surrendered to the verdant tide of forest succession. By night, they linger in the flickering shadows, drawn to the primal warmth of a generous campfire. Eyebrows raised, they take measure of all interlopers, looking to confirm sincere reverence for the land, true love of the water, and abiding respect for the wildlife.

Voyagers who fail to show proper deference to those who came before will never truly know these wild places. They ignore them at their own peril. Those who scoff at the notion betray a deliberate ignorance—affirmation of a life unchallenged, an intellect empty of curiosity, resigned only to see as far as the next wave while adrift on a boundless churning sea.

—◦—

Early in the nascent years of the Moose River Camping Club, it was decided to canoe the Moose River every ten years or so. The changes experienced between that first trip and the second eleven years later were remarkable. Now, another decade on, as we prepared to put in on Holeb Pond once again, the currents of our lives flowed faster and deeper still.

Over the previous twenty years, we approached each year's Moose trip in classic guided fashion. Each paddler brought his or her own river bag with clothing, sleeping bag, and personal items. There was one set of communal cooking and camping gear, group meals with a single cookee, prearranged menu, and little flexibility in itinerary. Woe be it to him who failed to leave enough room in the canoe for his share of the company's gear and food.

Sure, over the years we honed our system, embracing new gear and techniques when warranted and discarding others as experience and disposable income allowed.

This trip, however, was different—less heavy artillery and more light and fast infantry. Each team of paddlers in each canoe would be self-contained, planning and cooking their own meals; packing their own tents; bringing their own lanterns, water filters, and coolers; carrying whatever they wanted.

Part of the inspiration was the rigorous portage at Holeb Falls that requires everything, the canoe included, be carried a quarter mile through the woods on a slippery, root-choked trail.

Decentralization gives everyone greater flexibility for deciding what and how much to bring, freedom for when and what to eat. Redundancy in gear provides an extra layer of safety should key items be lost in any mishap among the rapids.

Less, we finally learned, is more.

—◆—

Shoving off from the landing on the north side of Holeb Pond, we paddle out into a light southwest breeze. That puts us straight into a gentle chop as we scan for the outlet stream, the opening well disguised in the tall, shrubby vegetation. The water is low this year; there was little rain through August. I anticipate having to drag the boats in some spots as we enter Holeb Stream, and I'm right. Still, it's a warm early autumn day, and the mood, like that at the beginning of any journey, is light. Most groundings result from failing to guess the right channel through gravel sandbars. The beginnings of a beaver dam are conquered with ramming speed and push-offs from the bottom with paddles. When we get to the river just a mile ahead, the water should be higher.

Despite bringing less dunnage, I still have the sense that my canoe, Sneak Route, is riding lower in the water than usual. Perhaps it's because of the extra burden carried in spirit by all who are making this trip. You see, among the sleeping bags and tents, freeze-dried meals, bottles of Canadian Club and Crown Royal, next to the collapsible chairs and stacks of tarps is a nondescript container holding the most precious cargo of all—the ashes of my twin brother, Carl, who died the previous spring while on a Moose River Camping Club adventure on the Potomac River in Maryland.

———

Left, a quick right, then take your second left. That's the order of turns one must take to find the portage trail at Holeb Falls and avoid plummeting over a waterfall. More than any other directions on the Moose, they are the ones I first committed to memory some twenty-one years ago. Follow them precisely, and you'll find the trail. Make a mistake, and you could end up having a very bad day indeed.

Packing lots of creature comforts into your canoe seems like a great idea at the start—not so much when you have to detour overland. Fortunately, the portage trail is mostly downhill, although wet roots and moss-covered rocks make footing tricky in many sections.

River bags are shouldered, and paddles and small gear are carried in hands. Despite our efforts to travel light, several trips are required. The canoes are left till last. While putting a canoe on a vehicle is easier with two people, trying to carry it down an uneven forest trail is not. Solo is the way to go.

Even with extra padding on the carry yoke, balancing seventy-five pounds of canoe across the back of your neck is taxing. On the steep downhill sections, we decide to cheat and slide the canoes along the roots. The plastic hulls will forgive the insult of the small scratches that result long before the sensibilities of purists who would never counsel such a thing settle down.

We arrive to find no one else set up at the best flat, sandy spots right at the base of the falls. The main area has a large fire ring, which, like the many layers of Troy, has risen into a prominent mound, a silty, near-black amalgam of ash, dirt, rocks, charred ends of logs, and bits of foil granola bar wrappers previous campers foolishly thought would burn up in the embers.

The main tarp is stretched over the picnic table. The camp kitchen, stove, and coolers ride shotgun at one end. As soon as the table is protected from any possibility of precipitation, a deck of cards, cribbage board, bottle of whiskey, and block of cheddar are set out for all to enjoy. The MRCC flag with its white skull and crossed paddles on a field of black is ceremoniously hung where all traversing the river will be sure to see it.

Several solo tents rise on flat areas around this hub while others are pitched closer to the eddy pool on the cool sandy ground renewed each year by the spring freshet. Companions with a penchant for loud snoring are good-naturedly cajoled to pitch their tents somewhat farther downstream.

Nearby is an empty log cabin. A bit farther back in the woods is the remains of another, the roof long ago caved in. Years before, a friend related a trip he took on the Moose in the high heat of summer and how he found an attractive blonde woman from New York City wearing only a bra and panties standing on the porch of the cabin now in ruin. "She had been up there for a week while her husband was off fishing the river and nearby ponds," my friend said. "She was bored to tears and couldn't wait to get out of there. She took one look at us and said, 'I will do anything for a drink or a smoke!'"

Like many tales of adventures past, there's no way to confirm if that story is true or not. It seemed plausible, however, and continues to live on in infamy around countless campfires.

After dinner, I walk down near the edge of the eddy pool. Reaching into my pocket, my fingers search for the cool round disk of an MRCC coin.

The coins, custom forged of solid brass, are left to be discovered by others. It signals that someone from the Moose River Camping Club has passed that way and shares in the journey. The coins are left as a way for scores of people who haven't even met to share a love of the out-of-doors. We all tread the footsteps of those who come before us, both on the trail and in every realm of this life. The coins, then, are a symbolic tip of the hat, or salute, to those who follow.

Finders have two options. They can keep this newfound "treasure" as a memento of their own trip and acknowledgment that they are kindred spirits and have walked the same paths or paddled the same river as members of the MRCC. Or, they can leave it at another beautiful spot for someone else to discover.

Possession of a coin or reporting its location on the Internet makes the discoverer a de facto MRCC member. Those who pay it forward can check the website to see if the coin they left was rediscovered and see the life they touched.

A starburst on the coin symbolizes Carl's fifteen-year-old son Blake, who took his own life. The number 42 comes from a story in Douglas Adams's *Hitchhiker's Guide to the Galaxy*. That number is supposedly the answer to "the meaning of life, the universe, and everything." Carl loved that story. He also lived at 42 Sandy Lane.

The coins honor their memories and all the friendships forged over many years spending time in the wilderness.

So far, the coins have found their way to the most incredible natural and man-made wonders on the planets. They have been placed on every continent, including Antarctica. They have been to the Grand Canyon, Mauna Loa, Uluru (Ayer's Rock) in Australia, the tip of the Bermuda Triangle in Puerto Rico, all over the Caribbean, Machu Picchu in Peru, Stonehenge in England, Omaha Beach in Normandy, Devil's Tower in Wyoming, the Acropolis, Guam, Fiji, Giza, Acadia in Maine, national parks all over the

United States, and on the tops of most major peaks in the northeast, including Katahdin in Maine, Mount Washington in New Hampshire, and Camel's Hump in Vermont.

The idea is to keep circulating them until one appears, full circle, in a box lot of items to be sold at Nest Egg Auctions in Connecticut, the company Carl founded and which his wife, son, and daughter still operate.

As the first stars of evening appear in the growing darkness overhead, I place the coin on a rock well above high water, orienting it, like always, right side up, top facing north. It's not an obvious location. I prize a spirit of curiosity in those who will discover the coin. It's the same rock where I photographed Carl helping his son Ryan, then nine, brush his teeth on the first Moose trip more than twenty years ago.

—~—

The third day on the Moose is uneventful. More flat water. More moose.

The day's only excitement comes at Spencer Rips, a quick Class II rapid at the site of an old bridge. A well-maintained camp sits on river right where a long forest road reaches back into the woods from Route 201, some fourteen miles away.

Water level is key to whether the rips are runnable. There are plenty of ancient logs wedged among the rocks—many have vestiges of the old iron spikes that once held them together. It's one thing to scratch or dent a canoe. It's another to puncture a hole clean through the hull.

If the water is high enough, you can just barely bounce your way down through. When in doubt, line the boats from shore.

In no hurry to choose, we decide to have lunch first. In an attempt to toss the ketchup to shore from the cooler in the last canoe, Pauley bobbles the catch. The airborne Heinz hits the gunwale and bursts open, covering the gear, canoe, and Pauley's leg in crimson goo. Cleanup in aisle Discovery 174.

A roll of paper towels is produced and makes quick work of the mess. The resulting debris looks like someone just cleaned up from poaching a moose.

Fortunately, we believe in carrying out everything we pack in. Watertight buckets that hold only food the first day are gradually converted to trash duty as the larder shrinks.

After lunch, the lining begins. Using ropes on the bow and stern, the voyagers rock hop along the shore, pulling and releasing the lines as needed while the canoe, sans paddlers, slides down the rapid on its own. Providing it doesn't get sideways, things usually go pretty smoothly. The greatest risk isn't to the canoe but rather to those moving along the slippery rocks on shore. No one wants to spend the rest of the afternoon paddling in wet pants.

Shortly after getting back on the river, we overtake another party stopped for lunch. As always, our casual inquiries about where they intend to camp that night have an ulterior motive. When two parties appear to be headed to the same spot, an unacknowledged race of sorts can occur. Those who have done a particular river before often know where the best sites are, based on size, accessibility, access to potential firewood, and proximity to amenities such as a picnic table, ridgepole, or outhouse.

Most falls and rapids have a variety of sites, but there's definitely a hierarchy. There's a big difference between a broad, flat site with high pines and plenty of places to put up tents, and a windless, muddy cedar grove with ten thousand hungry mosquitoes for your closest neighbors.

Because we're seldom in a rush, it's not uncommon for us to be passed and to lose out.

The other paddlers reply that they, too, are headed for Attean Falls. As soon as we round the next bend, we raft up the boats and hold a quick powwow. On our first trip on the Moose, we camped at the point at the bottom of Attean Falls. We want to stay there again to re-create the original group photo.

The spirits are especially strong at Attean, a place where the rush of the river ends in the backwater stillness of the deep, slow channel to Attean Lake. Rusty sections of rail and old logging equipment half buried in the duff of the forest betray the industriousness of earlier inhabitants.

A century ago, Attean Falls was a way station for visitors traveling to the renowned Spencer Lake Camps far to the south. Sports would get off the train in Jackman and take a boat to the base of the falls. Above would be another boat and guide to take them upriver to Spencer Rips. From there, it was a long, dusty buckboard ride to the camps.

A plan is hatched. Our two fastest paddlers, Bob and Keith, will push as hard as they can to get downriver and claim the prize. The rest of us won't dawdle. But if the other party comes on strong, we'll still have a shot at the backcountry equivalent of a high-roller suite.

Generally on a trip, I believe in always keeping members of the group in sight of one another. Rescue and retrieval gear is prepositioned in both the first and last boats, as are the most experienced river runners. In the rare event that the call of "Boat over!" is heard, help should be only moments away.

But in this case, Bob and Keith are paddling veterans and know how to handle themselves and a boat in white water. The upper rapids at Attean Falls are not especially difficult and are close to campsites if self-rescue is required. "Don't screw around," I tell them as they release from the flotilla. Obviously showing off, they speed away with perfectly synchronized strokes.

Just as the rest of our party reaches the trail to scout the upper falls, the other group catches up to us. Without stopping, they paddle down the first pitch waving at us. We're the ones smiling, however. Ahead on the point, I can see Bob's canoe pulled up on shore. A thin, gray swirl of smoke telegraphs to us and everyone else that they've already got a campfire going.

After dinner, we pose for the photo, although the giant fallen spruce in the original, taken almost as an afterthought twenty-one years ago, is now long gone. At sunset, I can hear the loons on the lake. Our take-out point is just a few miles farther.

We've taken Carl on his final run on the Moose. Tomorrow, we'll rendezvous with the rest of the family who are converging on Jackman. Right after Carl died, there was the big funeral in Connecticut, the overflowing church, the memorial fund for the paddle sports program at a children's camp, the news story in the *Hartford Courant* that a major figure in the community had died. But this would be a more private affair for those who desire to honor not just his public persona but his private passion as well.

Like every night since he passed, I go to sleep hoping, praying to have Carl appear in a dream. Just a cameo, I ask, wondering aloud why I have yet to see him even once.

He's sent me signs of course.

Not long after Carl died, I hiked to the top of a mountain called the Triad in Acadia National Park a few miles from my home. It had rained earlier in the day. But now the sky was a mix of broken clouds illuminated by perpendicular yellow light as the sun began to disappear behind Penobscot Mountain to the west.

The entire time I walked, I was thinking about Carl, missing him, fingering the ring he got to commemorate the passing of his son Blake that I now wear every day. I wondered where he was and why he hadn't tried to let me know he was okay. If anyone could communicate from beyond, it would be him, I said to myself.

As I headed down a slight downhill section of granite ledge, I noticed the light had changed from the harsh glare and shadows of the sunset to a smooth, even orange-pink afterglow. As I passed a long-dead spruce, its gnarled branches now silver from exposure to years of wind and rain and sun, I was startled by the shrill call of a bird. I stopped dead in my tracks and strained to see the source. I spotted a small gray and white junco sitting alone near the top of the spruce.

After a moment, it burst into song again, this time a long, nonstop trill. It went on and on. I marveled at the volume and how such a tiny creature could keep it up. It showed no fear even though I was just a few feet away. It took a moment for it to sink in, but it dawned on me it was not a coincidence. I said softly, "Okay, Carl. Message received."

The song stopped.

The bird and I faced each other in silence. "I love you, my brother," I said. It flapped its wings once and darted off through the darkening forest.

Since then, there have been other signs as well. There was the white-throated sparrow atop Katahdin that alighted on a nearby boulder and began to sing just after I left an MRCC coin there. One of our favorite things about camping at Chimney Pond at Katahdin was listening to the white-throated sparrows sing all night long. Since that day, while hiking in summer, I never leave a summit until I've heard one sing.

I never have to wait for long.

And then there were the pair of bald eagles that appeared while we were paddling the St. Croix just after I announced how much Carl and Blake loved that stretch of rapids. They came up from behind, in perfect formation, passing us at eye level only a few yards off to the side.

Still, the lack of seeing him in dreams saddens me. I miss the man hugs—hands to back, whiskery cheek to whiskery cheek. Selfishly, I long to see Carl's swagger, to seek his counsel, to confirm he's okay, to ask if by extension that I will be too when it is my time. But dreams desired do not appear on demand. I wonder if the absence is of his design or mine. Why, I ask each night before closing my eyes, can't my subconscious grant a wounded heart this one simple favor?

I awake in the morning to the arrival of an old friend—a freshening nor'west breeze. The sky is clearing to westard. Having a headwind will make the last stretch across Attean Lake a slog. Nothing, it seems, comes easy on the Moose. And I don't know anyone who would have it any other way.

After Attean Pond, the waters of the Moose River pass through a narrow stream, under the rusting steel trusses of the Canadian Pacific Railroad bridge, and into Wood Pond. The village of Jackman, closer to the Canadian border than it is to any large town in Maine, sits on the eastern shore. Far from the boutiques of Kennebunkport and the lobster bars of Bar Harbor, Jackman is the quintessential North Woods outpost. When you gas up your vehicle (always advisable before heading out for a sixty-mile round-trip on dirt logging roads), you can also buy a fishing license, homemade beef jerky, bread, milk, pizza, beer, scratch lottery tickets, a blaze orange nub hat, and a new pair of mud boots in the same store.

Summer is always busy with folks enjoying the lakes, but things really get into swing in fall during hunting season. December is quiet, and then things perk up again when the lakes freeze, the snow flies, and snowmobiling season starts.

There is really just one main street, State Route 201, which rumbles day and night with the sound of large logging trucks hauling the bounty of the surrounding woods to mills down state and in Quebec.

Near the north end of what passes for downtown, the Moose River passes under a nondescript concrete highway bridge as it heads for Brassau Dam and eventually Moosehead Lake in Rockwood, where Mount Kineo stands guard over the far northern reaches. From there, it's into the Kennebec, down through the Forks where it meets the Dead River, and on to the sea.

About a mile downstream from Highway 201, the local snowmobile club has constructed a suspension bridge used by snow sleds in winter and ATVs in summer. Of slender yet stalwart construction, it stands twenty feet above the river where the water pushes over a Class I riffle directly below. It was here we gathered to share our formal goodbyes to Carl, to release his earthly remains to mingle and merge with the waters that had so captivated his soul. It had been decided some time ago that his ashes would be left in several places he loved, including his favorite mountain, where we released his essence to the wind. The lion's share, however, was saved for the Moose.

Carl's wife, Mary Ellen, his children, his brothers and sisters, assorted spouses, friends considered to be family, and others, more than two dozen in all, line up along the downstream edge of the bridge. All stand in silence, alone in thought, transfixed at the water rushing below.

Gently opening the container, Mary Ellen and I begin to pour the silvery dust into the river. Some, carried by the river's draft, drifts off and up past the reds, yellows, and vivid orange leaves of the autumn trees. The contents make an almost sizzling sound as they hit the dark, tea-stained water. There is a splash and flicker as MRCC coins disappear beneath the ripples. We pass the container along. Each who desires takes a turn pouring some out.

"We are here today to honor the memory of a man whose heart was big enough to love each and every one of us," I say. "We don't just share our grief in his death, but rather a bond in the joy of having known him in life," I continue.

"There are some who will wonder why we stand witness here, so far from where he lived, so far from where so many of us live. But in the end, it's here that his spirit really belongs, where he felt most alive. We're not leaving Carl in the middle of nowhere. We've brought him home."

As the words depart on the wind, the ashes swirl and dance in the water and disappear downstream.

In moments of doubt, I question the wisdom of leaving him there. Some see wilderness as a place of loneliness. For those who find diversion only in the artificial and contrived, that just may be true. But those who seek not just natural beauty but also the essence and spirits of the wild will never walk or paddle alone.

There is no grave, no stone to mark Carl's existence on earth. There is no place for those who love him to gather or make a pilgrimage to, no fixed place to mourn. The coins will help keep his memory alive, but it is the epitome of hubris to think that those, too, ultimately will be anything other than a finite and ephemeral effort.

As hundreds of abandoned cemeteries in New England prove, even a well-appointed plot and stalwart granite marker are no ticket to eternity.

There is nothing sadder than an untended grave. Forlorn stones stand as silent witnesses to an innate desire to eke out some sliver of immortality. Once the spirit has fled and the body gone to dust, all that really remains are echoes in the hearts and spirits of those we touched, those we loved, those who loved us. Our contribution to the contents of their characters, and that which they then pass on, is the only true monument to our existence. Physically, we live again for a time in sons and daughters with their father's eyes and their mother's dispositions, but that, too, fades.

Obituaries are published, funerals held, stone carved. But in the end, only the fleeting essence of fragile memory remains, destined to evaporate upon the dilution and dispersal of generations.

Nothing, too, about a river remains fixed and unyielding. Permanence alone resides in the ceaseless flow—always there, always moving, the rhythm of April flood and August drought—an ageless and unbroken cycle. Channels shift, banks erode, landmarks disappear. Ghosts of Indians, explorers, loggers, farmers, campers, paddlers, the very water itself, call to anxious spirits not yet ready to move on, "Follow me."

I still look for signs from Carl everywhere I go. He has yet to appear in a dream. But when again I return to Moose River, I'll know just where to find him. He'll be a whisper in the pines on the windswept shore at twilight. He'll be watching from the mist as we run familiar rapids. He will scold us in the call of the kingfisher perpetually dispossessed of his perch. And his spirit will linger in the flickering shadows, sharing the warmth of our campfire, keeper of the ancient mysteries of deep and dark and timeless waters.

ACKNOWLEDGMENTS

IT IS IMPOSSIBLE TO PUT TOGETHER A COLLECTION SUCH AS THIS without the assistance of many, many people. There are those who served as sounding boards, helping the final form materialize out of the ether of long and philosophical conversations. Others were de facto cheerleaders, egging me on to just get the damned thing done. Many others, some of whom I have yet to meet face-to-face, volunteered as amateur sleuths to help nail down an elusive fact or two that for some reason or another I just felt I had to have.

But first and foremost are the people who inspired me to tell their stories, many of whom you've met in these essays and innumerable others whose stories, no less poignant or interesting, I have yet to share. They, like all members of the Moose River Camping Club, are too numerous to mention here. You all know who you are.

And then there are the legions of friends and family members who continually humored me as I went on and on about "the book," when it was still more concept than reality. That includes White Cat and Black Cat, who kept a close eye on me from the back of the couch in the study whenever I was working.

Well more than a decade ago, independent bookstore owner and literary organization founder Jan Coates urged me to write more essays about Maine's Great North Woods. Well, Jan, I finally did it. Thanks, too, go to Beth Ineson, a wonderful writer and blithe

ACKNOWLEDGMENTS

spirit who nudged me in the right direction with encouraging praise and firm yet gentle and insightful criticism and an incredible knack for marketing.

So many other writers and artists I've met and consider friends have also served as inspiration and as advisors. They include Jennifer Skiff, Susan Rockefeller, Christina Baker Kline, Martha Todd Dudman, Tom Ryan, Roxanna Robinson, Jim Sterba, Dan Burt, Lorie Costigan, the late John Gould, and Laura van Wormer.

Thanks, too, to Laura's dear friend and agent, the late Loretta Barrett, whose response to my nascent attempt to cram many of these stories into a great American novel was "I'm not feeling it." That, ultimately, helped point me in the right direction.

Among the aforementioned sleuths are Bill Green, host and chronicler of all things Maine on his show *Bill Green's Maine*; Jensen Bissell, superintendent of Baxter State Park; authors John Neff, Clayton Hall, Jane Thomas, and Elizabeth Hall Harmon; as well as Karen Alley, reference librarian at the Bangor Public Library, Dave Wilson of Katahdin Forest Products, and Howard Weymouth, who worked on the Golden Road.

Thanks to man-of-the-world and ace copy editor Mark Messer for turning it all into English and Barbara Tedesco for lending her talent and eye to design.

And a special thanks to Michael Steere and the good folks at Down East Books and Rowman & Littlefield.

Enormous appreciation and affection, too, for the wisdom and sagacity contributed by my nephew Ryan Brechlin. A witness to many of these events, he acted as the perfect sounding board, particularly when it came to matters of flow, cadence, and timing. Although still very young, his son Wyatt will soon enough be welcomed into our brotherhood of the paddle.

ACKNOWLEDGMENTS

Finally, I have to thank my lovely wife, Roxie, for her patience. She understood my need to be undisturbed during those precious predawn hours I managed to carve out of my busy newspaper editor schedule to work on my own writing. For some, a reply of "That's nice, dear" to my frequent exaltations over some aspect of the book might have seemed lukewarm. From her, however, it was merely a matter-of-fact acknowledgment of her unwavering belief that there was no doubt *Return to Moose River* would become a reality. Well, dear, here it is. I hope I've done you, the spirits of the Great North Woods, the cats, and Carl proud.

DISCOVER MORE

To find out more about the Great North Woods of Maine contact the organizations below.

Appalachian Trail Conservancy
799 Washington St., PO Box 807
Harpers Ferry, WV 25425-0807
(304) 535-6331
www.appalachiantrail.org

Baxter State Park
64 Balsam Dr.
Millinocket, ME 04462
(207) 723-5140
www.baxterstatepark.org

Katahdin Woods and Waters National Monument
PO Box 446
Patten, ME 04765
(207) 456-6001
www.nps.gov/kaww

North Maine Woods, Inc.
PO Box 421
Ashland, ME 04732
(207) 435-6213
www.northmainewoods.org

Maine Appalachian Trail Club
PO Box 283
Augusta, ME 04332-0283
(207) 778-0700
www.matc.org

Maine Bureau of Public Lands
22 State House Station
Augusta, ME 04333-0022
(207) 287-3821
www.maine.gov/dacf/parks

Maine Huts and Trails
496C Main St.
Kingfield, ME 04947
(207) 265-2400
www.mainehuts.org

Maine Snowmobiling Association
PO Box 80
Augusta, ME 04332
(207) 622-6983
www.mesnow.com